HIGH PRAISE FOR
TREASURE HUNT

"Fascinating . . . in this book, the chase is the thing, and Honan gives us a very good read, full of suspense . . . we can relive the whole story in this exciting and often rather touching book, written in an easygoing style. Take it to the beach—and hope for the movie."

—*The New York Times Book Review*

"*Treasure Hunt* crackles with the intensity of Honan's passion for investigative journalism and his gift for spinning a lean, mean yarn. . . . Honan hooks the reader in the first few pages. . . . With its byzantine convolutions and colorful characters made more vivid still by Honan's energetic prose, this true account reads like a first-rate detective novel."

—*St. Louis Post-Dispatch*

"There is no thriller like a real thriller, and this real thriller, *Treasure Hunt* by William H. Honan, is a throat grabber and a mind bender. The facts are extraordinary, the tracing work the best of journalism and the writing style keeps you on the edge of your seat. Don't miss it!"

—Schuyler Chapin, commissioner,
New York City Department of Cultural Affairs

"In *Treasure Hunt*, Bill Honan demonstrates what a wonderful thing journalism can be when practiced at this level. A treasure recovered, a mystery solved: all the elements of a great thriller. Altogether, a brilliant job of reporting."

—Morley Safer,
co-editor of CBS' *60 Minutes*

"Honan's account has all the excitement of a first-class thriller."
—*Publishers Weekly*, starred review

Please turn the page for more extraordinary acclaim. . . .

TREASURE
HUNT

A New York *Times* Reporter
Tracks the Quedlinburg Hoard

WILLIAM H. HONAN

Delta
Trade Paperbacks

A Delta Book
Published by
Dell Publishing
a division of
Bantam Doubleday Dell Publishing Group, Inc.
1540 Broadway
New York, New York 10036

ISBN: 0-385-33282-3

Reprinted by arrangement with Fromm International Publishing Corporation

Manufactured in the United States of America
Published simultaneously in Canada

June 1998

10 9 8 7 6 5 4 3 2 1

BVG

For Nancy, Bradley,
Daniel, Edith, and Bird

Acknowledgments

THIS BOOK TELLS THE STORY BEHIND THE STORIES of the Quedlin-burg art theft case, which I first broke in the New York *Times* in May 1990, and which remained front-page news for the next seven years.

My first debt is to my distinguished editor, Fred Jordan, whose enthusiasm, sharp eye, and consummate professional skill helped so much to give this book its present shape.

Next, a hug and a kiss for my longtime agent, Ros Targ.

Then comes Samuel Bartos, who painstakingly copyedited this manuscript.

Special thanks go to Park Honan, who had faith in an early draft of the manuscript and made wise suggestions. Nancy Burton and Edith Honan added fine touches to the manuscript.

I'm indebted as well to a number of senior editors of the *Times* who dispatched me at various intervals to try to find the thief, then to locate the treasures, and finally to cover the twists and turns of the plot. Marv Siegel was the most deeply involved of them, but the list also includes a number of good friends and colleagues: Dean Baquet, Soma Golden Behr, Robert Berkvist, John Darnton, Max Frankel, Paul Goldberger, Warren Hoge, Joseph Lelyveld, Dan Lewis, Linda Mathews, Pam Noel, Bill Schmidt, Nancy Sharkey, and Alex Ward.

At the newspaper's various copy desks, where the stories were handled, are many other friends and colleagues I wish to thank, including Gladys Bourdain, Wade Burkhart, Don Caswell, Olive Evans, Wilborn Hampton, Andrea Higbie, Diane Nottle, Suzanne Spector, John Storm, Ronald Wertheimer, and Martha Wilson.

And there were others at the *Times* who were especially helpful, including Adam Liptak, Kathy Mather, Karl Meyer, Rita Reif, Lonnie Schlein, and Ruth Strauss.

Outside the newspaper, my thanks for special assistance go to Robert M. Coon Jr., John Davidson, Colin Eisler, Constance Lowenthal, Ernie Martinez, Matthew McGowan, Lynn H. Nicholas, William Voelkle, and Ingeborg von Zitzewitz.

Finally, my great thanks to Mitch Hoffman of Dell, who made this edition possible.

BOOK ONE

Chapter 1

THE MAN WITH THE GERMAN ACCENT was on the phone again. Third time today. He wants me to help him find some long-lost treasure. Fat chance.

I was about to put him off for good when he said he knew my New York *Times* colleague Karl Meyer. Then I figured I had to listen for at least a minute. I mean, that goes with being a reporter.

He said his name was Willi Korte. Pronounced KOR-tay.

"What can I do for you today?" I asked.

"I was told you can help me crack the biggest and longest unsolved art theft of the twentieth century."

I laughed. "Who told you that?"

"Klaus Goldmann."

"Never heard of him."

"You were given some U.S. Army documents that Goldmann discovered in a German archive," he said. "Did you read them?"

"I can't swear that I did. But they may be under something here on my nice, clean, well-polished desk."

It was beginning to come back to me. That would be the winter of 1989, and a week or two earlier Karl Meyer, a member of the editorial board of the *Times*, had returned from a trip to West Germany. He presented me with a handful of documents which he said had been given to him by a West Berlin museum official. This German—yes, I guess his name *was* Klaus Goldmann—said he had found the papers in an archive dating back to the American occupation of Germany after World War II. Goldmann said the documents might shed light on the long-missing Quedlinburg treasures.

I had only scanned the papers before they melted into the heap of press releases, old telephone messages, notebooks, and sandwich wrappers cluttering my desk. If I remembered rightly, the Quedlinburg treasures—a collection of supposedly priceless medieval artworks—disappeared from Germany in the final days of World War II in Europe. It was assumed that they had been stolen by an American soldier or soldiers, since U.S. troops were then occupying Quedlinburg, a small city in central Germany. It was also thought possible that in the chaos of the war's end they had been taken by Russian soldiers—or maybe by the Germans themselves.

I asked Willi why they were referred to as treasures. "Isn't that a little melodramatic?" I said. "Like pirate's treasure or something?"

"It's no exaggeration," he replied. "We're not just talking museum-quality. We're talking some of the world's most valuable objects. Several of them are worth more than a van Gogh painting—and those go for $80 million today."

"What the heck *are* they?"

"Royal gifts," said Willi. "The earliest German kings—Heinrich I and his son Otto—presented them to the cathedral of Quedlinburg as patronage to help cement the loyalty of the local churchmen. Quedlinburg was a very important spot on the map of medieval Europe."

"Two of the treasures are manuscripts—one of them written in gold ink—and both are encased in bindings decorated with gold, silver, and precious stones."

"Most of the other pieces are reliquaries," he went on, "that is, containers for ancient Christian relics like splinters of wood from Noah's Ark and drops of milk from the Virgin Mary."

"You gotta be kidding."

"Look, it sounds ridiculous, but in medieval times nobody questioned it. The reliquaries are fantastically shaped bottles and caskets made by the greatest artists of their time. They used the most precious stuff they could get their hands on. They are—what else can you call them?—*treasures!*"

As he talked, the name Willi Korte began to sound familiar. I recalled that Goldmann had passed along Korte's name and telephone number, explaining that he was a young German researcher who lived in Washington, D.C., and worked for something called the Foundation for Prussian Cultural Heritage, an organization trying to recover artworks the Germans had lost in the war. That was a new twist. Most of the missing art in Europe was stolen by the Nazis. But I guess the Germans lost some, too.

Goldmann had given Willi copies of the same army documents he'd given Karl Meyer to pass along to me. And he suggested we work together.

"If the treasures haven't surfaced since the end of World War II," I said, "how do you know they haven't been lost or destroyed? How do you know somebody didn't melt them down for the gold and silver?"

Willi groaned. The thought appalled him. "It's true," he said. "Nobody has seen these things for half a century. The last one who saw them—not counting the thief—may have been Heinrich Himmler."

"The head of the Gestapo?"

"Yes," said Willi. "*Reichsführer SS*, he was called. In the old photographs of the Nazi bigwigs, Himmler was always the one wearing black. He had a thing about black leather—big shiny boots, a long black leather coat. If you met him today, you'd say he'd stepped right out of Bloomingdale's!"

I laughed. Willi was growing on me.

"Himmler also had a thing about Quedlinburg," he continued. "He believed he was a reincarnation of Heinrich I, the early German unifier who was buried in Quedlinburg a thousand years ago. Himmler used the treasures to decorate the cathedral and held weird, mystical ceremonies for SS officers there. Quedlinburg was Heinrich Himmler's Camelot."

"Great!" I said laughing. Himmler's *Camelot!*

"You really should read Goldmann's documents," he said. "Then we can work as partners."

"I'm not the partnering type," I said, "—but look at this! I just found Goldmann's documents on my desk. I'll give them a quick read and get back to you."

I knew I never would.

Willi was amusing, but I sensed that his story wasn't for me. How could *I* help solve a mystery that nobody else had been able to crack for half a century? Furthermore, considering the way the Nazis behaved in World War II, I wasn't exactly leaping with desire to help their descendants recover their losses. And finally—this was the main reason—I didn't have a whole lot of time on my hands. After nearly two decades as an editor at the *Times*, I was attempting to return to my first love in the newspaper business and make it as a reporter. The switch from editor to writer is not the usual thing. In this business, it's a truism that aging editors can't write. Once they've served a few years judging the work of others, they seem to lose their dash and swagger. I was determined to prove an exception.

During the first few months in my new job in the cultural news department my stuff appeared on the front page only occasionally. One story concerned the trial of an Indianapolis art dealer with a weakness for stolen antiquities. Another couple of page-one yarns dealt with the perils of the National

Endowment for the Arts, the Federal agency that had come under attack for sponsoring the exhibition of several raunchy photographs by Robert Mapplethorpe and the eye-poking picture of a crucifix submerged in urine by Andres Serrano. But much of the rest of what I wrote, let's face it, had been editorial landfill. If I wanted to make it as a writer, I didn't need more base hits, I needed a home run.

The best story for me to pursue, I figured, was the campaign against the arts endowment. With international communism a dead issue, the right wing had adopted as part of its mission the protection of the American people from the contamination of art, and it was an open question as to how far they could go with it. The previous summer, Senator Jesse Helms had seized the occasion of a sparsely attended evening session of the Senate to pass an amendment that would prevent the arts endowment from sponsoring anything that people like himself did not find soothing.

And now, I had just learned that an upstart congressman from southern California named Dana Rohrabacher—with serious money from the far right in back of him—was organizing a campaign to stampede the House of Representatives into adopting a similar resolution. A vote in the next day or two was likely. And if both houses of Congress adopted these restrictions, it would be the end of the arts endowment. No self-respecting artist would accept a grant from a Federal agency that could permit his or her work to be judged by a bunch of vote-hungry congressmen with the outlook of a vice squad.

I sent a memo to my editor, Marv Siegel, asking permission to spend a day or two in Washington covering the story.

Soon after my talk with Willi Korte, I was seated at my desk reading one of Rohrabacher's rambling orations in the *Congressional Record*. Well, the fellow is no Demosthenes, and my mind wandered. I imagined an ancient, metal-strapped chest in a dingy attic. A man, bent with age, clumps up a flight of stairs. He makes for the chest and opens it. Inside is a collection of gleaming, fantastically shaped artworks, and tucked among them, neatly folded, is a black leather armband emblazoned with a Nazi swastika. Ugh!

My ringing telephone brought me back to reality. It was Marv, approving the Washington trip.

"I'll be on the next shuttle," I said, and began stuffing notes and documents relating to the arts endowment into my briefcase. I checked my watch. If I caught a cab in Times Square immediately, I could make the noon flight. No time to call home—I'd call my wife from the airport.

I made a beeline for the elevator, but just as the door began to slide open, I froze. Slowly, the elevator door closed in front of me. I raced back to my desk, scooped up the copies of Klaus Goldmann's U.S. Army documents and scampered down three flights of stairs and out into Times Square.

On the plane, I dug the Goldmann documents out of my briefcase. There were five of them: single-spaced, typewritten reports dated from 1945 to 1948. In blunt military jargon, they told how the Germans, fearful of Allied bombing raids, had hidden a collection of medieval treasures in a cave on the outskirts of Quedlinburg. When American forces arrived in the city on April 18, 1945, according to one document, the Bürgermeister surrendered Quedlinburg and told the American commander about the cave and what was in it.

A joint delegation of Americans and Germans then inspected the cave and found all the valuables "intact and present." A guard post was established at the entrance to the cave, and with that the Americans continued about their business of rounding up German soldiers trying to avoid capture by dressing in civilian clothes. A few days later, a second team of inspectors entered the cave. They were horrified by what they saw. Several of the crates containing the Quedlinburg treasures had been ripped open and at least a dozen of the most important objects were gone.

One document provided an inventory of the missing items. They included an "extremely valuable" casket decorated with gold, silver, ivory, and precious stones; two medieval bound manuscripts, in gold and silver covers studded with gems; and several crystal reliquaries carved in the shapes of birds, turrets, a heart, and other exotic forms.

Another one of the documents recommended that the theft be reported to the FBI. Still another named the unit that guarded the cave as "Detachment Thirty-five, DMGO, Military Government," and proposed that all members of that unit be interrogated. If any such investigation took place, the documents did not record it. The last of them indicated that American troops soon withdrew from Quedlinburg and the area was then occupied by the Red Army. Eventually, the city would become part of East Germany.

I stared at the ceiling of the jetliner. The vision of the old man in the attic returned. Then I saw newspaper headlines swimming through the air. . . . GREATEST WORLD WAR II ART THEFT SOLVED AT LAST . . . BRILLIANT DETECTIVE WORK BY *TIMES* REPORTER . . . I closed my eyes and enjoyed the fantasy.

In Washington, I interviewed Rohrabacher at his office on Capitol Hill, then raced to the *Times* Washington bureau in the old Army-Navy Club at 16th and I Streets and bashed out a story about how Rohrabacher planned to tack the language of the Helms amendment onto a House appropriations bill scheduled to be voted on the next day. Marv gave it three columns with a big picture of Rohrabacher under the headline HELMS AMENDMENT IS FACING A MAJOR TEST IN CONGRESS.

Next morning I was up early. "The Capitol," I said to my cab driver. My mind was totally focused on the battle shaping up in the House of Representatives, but after proceeding for a block or two, I suddenly got an itch. "Have you ever been to the National Archives branch in Suitland, Maryland?" I asked the driver.

"Why, sure," he said. "It's just a couple miles outside of the District."

The tires squealed as we made an illegal U-turn and sped off to Suitland.

I'd been there once before, so I recognized the squat red brick storehouse that contains—among other things—U.S. Army unit records going back to World War I. I wanted to see if I could find the records of Detachment Thirty-five, the military government unit named in the Goldmann documents as having occupied Quedlinburg at the time the treasures disappeared. If I could find the detachment's personnel roster, I'd have a list of suspects!

With the help of an intense, bearded archivist who told me his name was Richard Boylan, I dug into the files. Reading these musty documents tugged at my memory. Years before, I'd served most of a two-year hitch in the army as the editor of a weekly newspaper called the Fort Devens *Dispatch*. That experience had given me command of army jargon, and I was amused to see that I hadn't lost my fluency. I knew, for example, the difference between NATOUSA, MTOUSA, and ETOUSA (U.S. Army commands in North Africa, the Mediterranean, and Europe, respectively), and I remembered that OMGUS is not a Hindu chant but the acronym for Office of Military Government, United States.

Unfortunately, neither Boylan nor I got anywhere with Detachment Thirty-five. There simply wasn't any record of a military government unit filed under that name. In order to locate any surviving records of Detachment Thirty-five, I realized I would need more information than the Goldmann documents provided.

I hightailed it to Capitol Hill and was able to squeeze into one of the narrow wooden pews in the press gallery of the House of Representatives, just in time to watch Rohrabacher's amendment go down to defeat by a vote of 264 to 153. The enemies of artistic freedom had taken a whipping, though this would hardly be the end of the matter.

I hurried back to the *Times* Washington Bureau, filed my story on the outcome of the battle and was delighted to hear Marv tell me that it would appear on the front page *above the fold* the next morning. Not a homer, perhaps, but a solid double, maybe even a three-bagger. In an expansive mood, I caught a cab for the National Airport, only to miss my flight home by about one minute. Crestfallen, I watched the big silver bird fling itself into the hazy afternoon sky.

I sat down in a cramped phone booth and toyed with the idea of calling Willi Korte. I asked myself: since Willi lives in Washington, couldn't *he* continue to search the National Archives for any record of Detachment Thirty-five?

No way, I protested silently. With everything *I* know about military record-keeping, if *I* can't find any trace of Detachment Thirty-five in the Archives what help can I expect from a foreigner?

On the other hand, I thought, I've got time to kill.

I fished in my briefcase for the envelope on which I'd written Willi's telephone number. My fingers pecked it into the instrument's touch-tone pad. Willi answered at once, as if he'd been waiting for my call.

"I'm in Washington," I said cautiously, "and I thought I'd touch base with you before I catch the shuttle back to New York. How's your investigation going?"

Willi was exuberant. He said he had just located a World War II veteran named Dean Dillard in North Carolina. Dillard recalled having driven through Quedlinburg during the last days of the fighting. As his unit was leaving the town, Dillard had said, he heard a rumor about some stolen treasure, although he could no longer remember the details.

"I'm getting close," Willi said. "Real close!"

Then he asked how my investigation was going.

"What do you mean *my* investigation?" I sputtered. "I never agreed to work on the case."

"I thought by now you would have solved it," he teased.

I acknowledged I'd read the Goldmann documents and had noticed the mention of Detachment Thirty-five. Since I was in Washington, I said, I dropped by the National Archives, but came away frustrated because I couldn't find a single reference to the unit.

Willi laughed. "You'll never find it," he said. "Most of those military government units weren't in existence long enough to keep records. What you can find is that on 23 April 1945 a command post was set up in Quedlinburg by the Fourth Cav."

"You mean the Fourth Cavalry *Division?*" I asked, showing off my military learning.

"Nah," he said, "the only cavalry *divisions* were First and Second. First was in the Pacific, and Second was in North Africa. Fourth Cav is the Fourth Cavalry *Group*, Mechanized, an element of the Seventh Corps."

"So you checked the Group records?"

"Sure," Willi rattled on, leaving me open-mouthed, "but they don't mention Quedlinburg. However; if you assume the Fourth Cav reported about the theft to a higher headquarters you go to the records of Seventh Corps, which is what I did two weeks ago. No luck there either. So now I figure the investigation was handled at a lower level, and there you find that several smaller units were attached to Fourth Cav Group in the vicinity of Quedlinburg—the Fourth Cav Reconnaissance Squadron, Mechanized; the Third Battalion of the Thirty-ninth Infantry Regiment; the Eighty-seventh Armored Field Artillery Battalion; the 759th Light Tank Battalion and the 474th Anti-Aircraft Artillery Battalion. All of these units kept records which may contain information about the theft."

"Hey, when did you graduate from West Point?"

"Don't worry," he snapped. "They don't accept the foreign-born."

Willi continued. "I found a report in the S-3 Journal saying that at ten minutes before midnight on 20 April 45 the Fourth

Cav Recon Squad reported the discovery of a cave at 339590—those are geographical coordinates—which they describe as a large room containing statues and crates of oil paintings and other works of art."

"So you found the unit stationed in Quedlinburg!" I said.

"I found *one* of them," he replied. "The theft could have been investigated by any of these small units—there's no way of telling without reading all of their records. For now I'm checking the names of the officers of the Fourth Cav Recon Squad, and I'm trying to find out where those guys are today."

"The Vets' Administration here in Washington should be able to help you," I said earnestly.

"They won't give you the time of day!" Willi snorted. "They say everything you want is protected by the Privacy Act. However, by a considerable amount of lying"—he chuckled naughtily—"I figured out how to get what I need. I call the Vets Administration offices in small states like Maryland and New Hampshire and tell them I'm trying to find these World War II vets because they inherited some money. When I say that, they're as nice as they can be!

"The problem is," he continued, "all the veterans I've tracked down are either dead or couldn't, or wouldn't, tell me much." He laughed. "It's a little crazy—trying to find witnesses among a group of suspects!"

"Willi," I said, scratching my head with wonder, "how the hell did you learn so much about the U.S. Army? I mean, you're a German!"

"Maybe I'm overeducated," he said with a laugh.

I began to wonder if I'd fallen in with a guy who worked for a West German intelligence agency, maybe the German equivalent of the CIA? I liked Willi, but he scared me a little.

"Suppose you actually get the thief on the telephone," I said. "If he's kept his secret all these years, what makes you think he'd open up now?"

"The thief may not be the one who opens up," he said. "It may be someone who saw the thief. It may be someone who thinks he was cheated by the thief. People talk for a lot of reasons.

"This is what I believe," he went on. "If I squeeze the documents, I can get the names of the soldiers who were stationed in Quedlinburg. If I get the names, I can find the people. And if I find the people, one of them will open up."

"Willi," I said. "You just got yourself a partner."

"The bride is blushing."

"Frankly, I don't know whether you're a German agent or what the hell you are," I said, "but, dammit, you know more about the U.S. Army than even I do and I'm a native son. Stick with what you're doing. Squeeze the documents, like you say. Meantime, I'll work through the art world. Then we'll compare notes."

"That's what I was hoping you'd say!" Willi chirped.

"I'm going to start with a New York City dealer in rare books and manuscripts named Roland Folter," I said. "Goldmann passed along his name with the explanation that he'd heard Folter had been asked once to appraise a couple of medieval manuscripts that could have been from Quedlinburg."

"Yeah," said Willi. "Goldmann's inventory of missing treasures includes two manuscripts."

"I'm willing to share information," I said, "but remember this. I work for a newspaper. And *I'm* the one who says when I publish whatever I want to publish. *Verstehen?*"

That stung. Willi didn't like being talked down to, and he especially didn't like being spoken to in German as if he couldn't understand English.

He registered his annoyance by rattling off a hail of German that was incomprehensible to me.

"What is that supposed to mean?"

A long pause. Then he chuckled. "Let's boogie!" said Willi.

Chapter 2

IT TOOK SEVERAL WEEKS OF CONSTANT CALLING to get Folter to come to the phone. Maybe he was traveling in Europe like his office said, or maybe he doesn't like talking to newspaper reporters—take your pick. Then one day when I called, he answered.

Like Willi, Folter was originally German.

I explained who I was and said I'd been told that several years ago he was asked to appraise a couple of very unusual manuscripts encrusted with gold, silver, and jewels.

"Who told you that?"

I said my source was confidential.

"Then I can't help you."

I replied that the manuscripts he saw were stolen property. Didn't he realize that?

"I don't know what you're talking about."

I had one gambit left. I said I was working with an international team of investigators, and that we were compiling a list of suspects.

"*Suspects?*" Folter said, suddenly curious. "Suspects in the theft?"

I had him.

I said our objective was to bring the thief to justice, and return the treasures to Quedlinburg.

Folter hesitated. Then he said he was beginning to remember a few details about the case, but that he thought it would be prudent to continue our conversation face-to-face. "Telephones, you know . . ." he said, with a world-weary sigh. "I could receive you on, ah, Thursday," he said.

"Say when."

"Ten in the morning."

"See you then."

Wow! I thought, after banging down the phone. This guy *knows!*

It was raining the morning I tramped from Grand Central Station, where I usually arrive in the city, to East 46th Street and found the five-story brick-and-stucco townhouse occupied by H. P. Kraus and Company, the firm then jointly owned by Folter and Kraus's widow. Before entering, I took a quick look in the gallery's display window. Three or four illuminated manuscripts were mounted on easels and dramatically spotlighted. The mellow leather bindings, the creamy parchment, and the infinitely painstaking handwriting made them seem like messengers from another planet.

Inside, I was greeted warmly by Folter. He was a nattily dressed man in his late forties with a round, owlish face, pink cheeks, rimless spectacles, and beady, suspiciously darting eyes. He had the courtly manner of a man accustomed to serving a wealthy clientele, and clearly he had decided to turn on the charm for me.

"Please," he said, ushering me past several assistants and up a flight of stairs. On the parlor floor, we entered a spacious, elegantly appointed room with four gleaming brass chandeliers and large windows overlooking East 46th Street. The walls were lined with shelves packed with books and manuscripts, many of them in richly colored leather bindings. Before this moment I had never seen so many beautiful old books in one place, and as we sat down together at an antique table in the center of the room I asked Folter to describe the collection.

"On the far wall," he said, gesturing over his shoulder to a hundred or more manuscripts in ivory-colored vellum bindings, "is the last of the collection of Sir Thomas Phillipps, a nineteenth-century figure who was the foremost manuscript collector of all time. We acquired what was left of his collection in 1978, and have been slowly selling it ever since."

"What you see here," he continued, rising and striding to the opposite wall, "are books from the first fifty years of printing. We call them incunabula—infants—because printing was invented in 1450 and these were all printed before 1501."

He took a few steps and heaved off the shelf a large, weighty tome in a brown leather cover. "The binding here is original," he said. "It has brass clasps to keep it shut, and spikes so you can stand it upright like this." With an effort, he stood the book up on its metal legs.

"It's a religious treatise printed by John Mentelin in Strasbourg in 1471," he said, laying down the book and opening it to a page where the text was illustrated with a brilliantly colored floral design. He ran the tips of his fingers over the printed surface. "You can feel the indentation of every letter. Try it."

Cautiously, I touched the page. It felt like fine engraved stationery as my fingers traveled the minute hills and valleys. But there was more to it than a tactile sensation. It was like touching the past. I was, perhaps, shaking hands with the fifteenth century.

I asked him how he became interested in old books and manuscripts.

"I've been collecting ever since I was a teenager in Frankfurt," he said. "You can cradle an old book or manuscript in your hands, take it to bed, touch it, smell it, love it. With a painting you have a more distant relationship."

"Tell me about the Quedlinburg manuscripts," I said.

Although we were alone, Folter lowered his voice. "They are very, very extraordinary," he said, almost whispering. "Not like the books and manuscripts you see here, but even older. Five centuries earlier than the Gutenberg Bibles . . ." His voice trailed off for a moment, and his eyes narrowed as if he were visualizing the treasures.

"The covers are spectacular," he went on. "Jewels, gold, ivory. Every precious substance that was available to them. The older of the two—it's called the Samuhel Gospel after the artist who created it, who was named Samuhel—dates to the ninth century! It was presented to the cloister at Quedlinburg by Heinrich I, the first of the great unifiers of the German-speaking states, so it has enormous historical importance as well as great beauty.

"If we had been able to sell it," he said, gazing dreamily out the window, "it could have been the *greatest* manuscript sale of the century, and the Samuhel Gospel might now be the world's most expensive book. There's no telling what the price would have been.

"In 1983," he continued, "a sumptuously illustrated manuscript from the twelfth century—it was called the Gospels of Henry the Lion—was sold by Sotheby's in London for $12 million. But nobody had any idea of what it would go for. Sotheby's announced that they expected it to bring $3.5 million, then it went for nearly four times that amount. The West German Government, which was the buyer, sent a private plane to fetch it.

"One reason these manuscripts command such prices is that they are better preserved than most paintings of equal age. Books are kept closed. The air, the dust, can't get at them. The result is that the lettering, the illumination, and so forth commonly look like they were executed yesterday."

I said I understood that after he saw the Quedlinburg manuscripts, he made inquiries about the possibility of selling them.

He looked at me cagily. "You must understand," Folter said, "it's most unusual for a newspaper reporter to be looking into what are essentially private matters."

I didn't want to start an argument about that. Theft is not a private matter. But, I thought, Folter probably did not mean to be taken literally. He was fencing with me, and meant to convey only that he would not eagerly provide information without getting some in return.

"Let me tell you about my investigation," I said, leaning back in my chair.

"Proceed."

"One of my informants in West Berlin recently discovered an inventory of the missing Quedlinburg treasures made in April 1945," I began. "Another researcher with whom I'm working is compiling a list of the names of every American soldier stationed in Quedlinburg at the time the treasures disappeared. He's attempting to locate and interview all those who are still living. It's very difficult work, and we're hampered by the fact that some of the army units we *know* were present went out of business almost as quickly as they came into being, and left no records at all."

"The Germans would not have been so careless," Folter muttered under his breath.

"Even when we find the thief," I continued, "I don't expect him to be the present owner of the treasures."

"Why is that?"

"Because it doesn't make sense to me that the thief would keep the treasures for more than forty years and then suddenly pack them off to you to be disposed of. I think the thief loved those things—very much the way you say you love your old books and manuscripts. These objects became his children and he kept them throughout his life."

"You think he's dead?"

"Assume the thief was a young soldier of twenty-six in 1945," I said. "That would make him seventy today, or sixty-seven at the time you were approached. That's a normal life-span. I think you were dealing with the heirs of the thief."

"Very interesting," said Folter, clucking his tongue.

"At some point," I said, "I think they got cold feet or maybe didn't like what you told them. But now they're more experienced, and they'll try again."

Folter laughed. "I wish you good luck in your investigation," he said, glancing over his shoulder to be certain that no one had joined us unannounced. "Now I will tell you what I know."

I leaned forward in my chair.

Four years ago, Folter said, while H. P. Kraus, the founder of the firm, was still alive, they had been approached by someone wishing to sell the Quedlinburg manuscripts.

"Who was that?" I asked.

Folter said the man was a banker living in Texas.

Texas? That pricked up my ears. Willi and I had assumed—for no good reason, I realized—that the manuscripts were in the possession of someone living on the Eastern seaboard.

The banker, Folter continued, had sent him about twenty slides showing the jeweled bindings and several inside leaves from each of two medieval manuscripts. However, when Folter told him he needed to see the actual books in order to make a correct appraisal, the banker broke off contact. Folter said he subsequently wrote to the man, but never received a reply.

I asked for the banker's name.

Folter shook his head. "My lawyer has advised me that I could be sued if I divulged it," he said. "I was approached by the man from Texas in strict confidence and I have to honor that. Anyway, he wouldn't be of help to you, since I doubt he was representing himself, and he never told me the name of his client."

"What I *can* show you are these," he said, opening an envelope on the table that I hadn't noticed before. He spread out almost two dozen five-by-seven-inch color photographs. "I had these prints made from the slides because they are easier to handle," he said. "I returned the slides but not the prints."

Feeling a rush of excitement, I studied the photographs intently. If holding one of Folter's incunabula was like shaking hands with the fifteenth century, this was like, well, stroking an even more distant past. The photographs included several views of the two lavish bindings, and a number of inside pages from each book. Some of the writing was gold-colored and appeared to be in Latin. The illustrations were full-page, multicolored portraits of the four Gospel writers of the New Testament. The Evangelist Luke, for example, was finely depicted against a green background. He was shown dipping his pen into an ink pot while writing his testament. I was also fascinated to see that in one photograph, the manuscript was being held by a white-gloved hand. It looked as though the would-be seller was properly respectful of what he was handling.

I pressed Folter for the name of the Texas banker. He refused. I tried again. He weakened. I sensed that he wanted to give me the name but that something was holding him back. I kept nagging him, and finally, as much to get me out of his office as anything else, he made a pronouncement.

"I will reveal the banker's name," he said, "if I am asked to do so by someone in a position of high authority in the West German government."

"Great!" I exclaimed, and said I'd pass that along to my sources. Very shortly, I said, he would be hearing from just such a person.

As soon as I reached my office at the *Times*, I called Willi and told him about the interview. "Folter said that the only way he'll reveal the name of the banker," I said, "is if he's asked by a high official of the Federal Republic of Germany."

"Willi," I said, "I always suspected you were a German agent. Now you're going to prove me right!"

Chapter 3

I THINK WILLI APPRECIATED THE OPPORTUNITY to take a break from his work with old military records, as it had lately proved unexpectedly frustrating. While I'd been trying to get an interview with Folter, Willi had flown to St. Louis, Missouri, and visited the National Personnel Records Center there, which maintains U.S. Army records about individuals. He had found home addresses for about 150 officers on his list of suspects, but he was having difficulty tracking them down. Many of these men had listed incomplete addresses in their service records. Others had moved one or more times since their last listed home address. Still others turned out to be dead. Before the end of the week, Willi's appointment with Folter was duly arranged.

When he showed up at the townhouse on East 46th Street, however, everything went wrong. Willi's tweed jacket and pants weren't pressed, as I observed when he later came to visit me at the *Times*. He presented Folter with a business card identifying himself as a representative of the Foundation for Prussian Cultural Heritage—which Folter had never heard of.

Furthermore, his card was dog-eared and his former address had been scratched out and a new one scrawled below it. Folter must have regarded Willi as a very low-level and poorly paid government functionary indeed, if he didn't take him for a complete fraud. Consequently, he repeated to Willi what he had said to me about his lawyer cautioning him against *ever* revealing the name of the Texas banker.

Willi trudged across town to the *Times* to make his report.

It was our first face-to-face meeting. Willi is slightly built, with bushy reddish-brown hair, piercing brown eyes, a scruffy beard and prominent front teeth which, he later told me, are not the originals but forgeries created in a dental lab after a childhood collision with a hockey puck. He said he was thirty-six—which made me old enough to be his father.

I took him to the cafeteria, where he told me about his encounter with Folter. Prior to this, I had done a background check on Willi, and what he had told me about himself seemed to match the facts. Still, I wanted to know more.

He said he was born in Augsburg, about forty miles northwest of Munich, and had studied in Berlin, Augsburg, and finally Munich, where he received a law degree from Ludwig-Maximilians University in 1981. Instead of practicing law, though, he told me he'd returned to the university to study modern German history, and that he was especially fascinated with the Nazi regime and the postwar period of American occupation.

"Since I was born a decade after the end of World War II," he said, "the Nazi period was both intriguing and incomprehensible to me. It was this enormous thing that happened and screwed up so much that it will take generations for the world to recover. It wiped out the liveliest part of German culture, it started a monster of a war, it gave us the Holocaust, the looting of Europe, the devastation of cities and all kinds of cultural property. It did breathtakingly negative things. I wanted to understand it, so I became a historian."

In 1982 Willi began work as a visiting researcher at Georgetown University, and he had been shuttling back and forth between Washington and his home in Munich ever since.

"I used to spend a lot of time at the Suitland branch of the National Archives," he said. "That's where you asked Rich Boylan to help you find the records of Detachment Thirty-five, remember?"

"You got it, Willi," I said. "I called Boylan the other day when I was checking you out."

"Oh, Jesus!" Willi said with a laugh. "I can just imagine what sort of a recommendation he gave me."

"He called you a real troublemaker."

Willi giggled naughtily. "Boylan was the one who taught me how to read U.S. Army documents. At first the jargon drove me crazy. I asked so many questions he and the other archivists wanted to throw me out a window, but gradually I learned and now I read that stuff like nursery rhymes."

I asked Willi about his family.

"They didn't do too well in the war," he said. He explained that he had lost all his grandparents in the fighting. "My mother was in labor camps and other fine institutions. And after the war she didn't want to talk about it—which only aroused my curiosity."

He said his father had died when he was a child. He'd been a metallurgist and a licensed dealer in precious metals who bought decorative objects containing gold, silver, platinum, and so forth, and then removed the precious metal and sold it to the Nazi government. This was an important business during the war years, Willi explained, because the nation needed gold and silver bullion to finance the war effort. Citizens of the Third Reich were constantly being harangued to turn in their gold wedding rings and silver candlesticks as a matter of patriotic duty. Willi said his father profited from such donations.

"There is also . . ." He hesitated. "I really don't like to talk about this."

I assured him that I would listen sympathetically.

"I don't know a great deal about my father," he said, "but there is a family story that he accumulated several hundred pounds of gold and silver which he did not sell to the Nazi government. I don't know if there's any truth to that, but at the war's end he was living not far from the concentration camp at Buchenwald. Look, if there are hidden, dark parts of my family history I want to find out about them! I want to know everything. Maybe that's why I like to study history, and why I have this interest—you may call it an obsession—with the Quedlinburg stuff. Strange and terrible things went on back then. I want to unmask it all."

We left the *Times* and strolled to Grand Central Station in a somber mood. There was something of Indiana Jones about Willi—the young professor with a crooked smile and a wild gleam in the eye. But he wasn't just an avaricious treasure hunter, fixated on glitter. He carried a burden. Willi may have been born years after the end of World War II, but he was one of its casualties just as surely as if he had been slashed by a shell fragment. Now he was trying to heal himself, in the best way he knew how. I had to respect that.

I also realized that he was doing a pretty fair job as an ambassador for his country, at least as far as I was concerned. He was the first German I had come to know reasonably well, and his passion for the Quedlinburg treasures had driven home to me the point that—despite Heinrich Himmler's infatuation with them—the treasures were not owned by the Nazis but were the patrimony of the German people, indeed heirlooms of all humankind. Despite my initial misgivings, I felt there was no question but that I was on the right side of this struggle.

A day or two later, we were jolted into action. The date was March 19. That morning, I picked up my copy of the *Times* and was horrified to read that the Isabella Gardner Museum, a Venetian-style villa on the outskirts of Boston crammed with Old Master paintings, had suffered what was described as the biggest museum theft in history. Two men posing as police officers responding to an alarm had entered the building at 1:15 A.M., bound and gagged the guards, and made off with twelve masterworks valued at $200 million.

Gone were two Rembrandts—a brooding self-portrait and the dramatic *Storm on the Sea at Galilee,* which is the artist's only seascape. Also taken was a Vermeer masterpiece, *The Concert,* which scholars interpret as the Flemish master's celebration of the power of music to soothe the human psyche— what an ironic choice for a pair of strong-arm thugs! The losses also included five paintings by Degas, one by Manet, and, oddly, a Chinese bronze beaker from the eleventh century B.C.

When I arrived at the office, Marv suggested that to help give readers a sense of perspective on the tragedy I might write an article about some of the great unsolved art thefts of modern times. I could compare and contrast these cases with what had taken place at the Gardner. Naturally, I'd be able to make reference to the Quedlinburg treasures, a theft certainly in the major league of art crimes—and mention of it might prompt someone to call or write to me with a useful tip.

I liked the idea and got to work. I called Willi, explained what I was doing, and asked for his help. My editor, I said, was giving me only two days for the research and writing, and wanted me to include only cases for which we could display a photograph of one of the still-missing artworks. Our photo editor, Kathy Mather, would be able to find most of the pertinent pictures, but she would have difficulty digging up something from Quedlinburg. Could Willi help? He would have only forty-eight hours. As usual with newspaper work, time was of the essence.

"Well, sure," Willi said. "You've got to include the Quedlinburg stuff in your story. That might help us a lot."

For the next couple of days, I worked at a frenzied pace, talking to art experts and doing research at our office library and the library of the Metropolitan Museum of Art. Then I began to write. There are enough stolen masterpieces out there, I began, to fill a museum. The previous year, the International Foundation for Art Research, which compiles data on stolen art, had reported some 5,000 thefts. Masterpieces are not the usual target, as they tend to be so well known that anyone attempting to sell one would have a lot of explaining to do and would probably wind up getting arrested. Aware of this danger, art thieves usually go for relatively obscure works that can be sold without raising questions.

Nevertheless, as in the case of the Gardner, masterpieces are also sometimes stolen. But due to its special status about the only way a thief can convert this booty into cash is to return it to its rightful owner in exchange for ransom. That prospect, law-enforcement authorities told me, is chiefly responsible for some of the most sensational art thefts of modern times. The catch, of course, is that it is almost impossible to receive ransom without being exposed to capture—a belated realization that has driven some thieves to returning the stolen artworks in exasperation. Still others, overwhelmed by the unforeseen complexities of making a deal, have hidden their prizes and then died with the secret.

Probably the greatest unsolved art theft, I wrote, remains the case of one of the panels of the Ghent altarpiece called *Adoration of the Lamb*, by the Flemish masters Hubert and Jan van Eyck. Painted in 1420, this opulently colored work is one of the earliest oil paintings in existence. Its twelve panels depict Christ on the judgment seat, surrounded by a group of angels, apostles, prophets, martyrs, and knights. Colin Eisler, a Renaissance art specialist at New York University's Institute of Fine Arts, told me that it was "among the very greatest works of art in Northern Europe from the fifteenth century."

In 1817 the King of Prussia legitimately purchased six of

the twelve panels. But after World War I, the Allies, outraged by German atrocities in Belgium, stipulated in the Treaty of Versailles that as part of German reparations, the six panels would be returned to the Cathedral of St. Bavon in Ghent, the church for which they were originally created.

In April 1934, in what was regarded as the most shocking art theft since the disappearance of the Mona Lisa in 1911, one of the Ghent panels was stolen. According to Belgian police, the thief hid in the cathedral until it was locked at night, then wrenched loose the fifty-four-by-twenty-two-inch panel and fled. Suspects included German nationalists who had disavowed the Treaty of Versailles, eccentric art lovers, and even members of the clergy.

There was no break in the case until June of that year, when half the missing panel was left in a railway checkroom with a letter asking for one million Belgian francs for the other half. The authorities thought the thief then became frightened—perhaps realizing the difficulty of receiving a ransom without exposing himself to arrest—because communication stopped. A year later, the Belgian police announced that the thief was dead but had been identified as a Belgian citizen. He had taken the knowledge of where he had hidden the half-panel to the grave.

"I don't think they'll get it back now," Professor Eisler told me. "It's been missing too long."

That made me wonder about the Quedlinburg treasures—missing for forty-five years. Had time run its course with them, too?

The remaining panels of the Ghent altarpiece continued to be a matter of international contention. After Nazi Germany conquered most of Europe in 1940, Hitler, seeking to wipe out the last vestiges of the Treaty of Versailles, expressly ordered the altarpiece brought to Berlin. At the war's end, Allied soldiers discovered it hidden in a tunnel at Neuschwanstein and returned it to the Cathedral of St. Bavon.

For my story seeking perspective on the Gardner losses, I mentioned several other big-time thefts. The most unusual of these, the Russborough case, involved two thefts twelve years apart. In April 1974 an armed gang led by a young woman burst into Russborough, the elegant eighteenth-century stone mansion in Blessington, Ireland, of Sir Alfred Beit, a gold-mining millionaire. Sir Alfred and his family and servants were tied up, and the gang stole nineteen masterworks by Vermeer, Goya, Rubens, Gainsborough, Velazquez, Frans Hals, and others. The prize of the collection was Vermeer's *Lady Writing a Letter with Her Maid*, a famous experiment with centrifugal composition, in which the Flemish master created an unusual tension by shifting the focus away from the center of the painting. Aside from a Vermeer owned by Queen Elizabeth of England, this painting was the only one of the approximately thirty-five extant paintings by Vermeer that was known to be in private hands. Another masterpiece taken from Rossborough was Claude Monet's *Impression, Sunrise*, which gave its name to the Impressionist movement.

The thieves demanded a ransom of $1.2 million (a fraction of the true value of what they had seized) and the transfer of four Irish Republican Army members serving life sentences in London to jails in Northern Ireland. Eight days after the theft, the Irish police found the works undamaged in a vacation cottage near Glandore, a resort. They arrested Bridget Rose Dugdale, the thirty-three-year-old daughter of an English millionaire who had rented the cottage. After pleading "proudly and incorruptibly guilty," she was sentenced to nine years in prison. She was released in 1980.

With his collection restored, Sir Alfred installed an alarm system connected to the local police station. At 2 A.M. on May 21, 1986, the alarm went off. The police arrived but found nothing amiss and concluded it was a false alarm. After day-break, it was discovered that eighteen of Sir Alfred's paintings—most of them the ones stolen in 1974—were gone. The police speculated that the thieves deliberately set off the alarm, then hid until after the search. In recent years, Sir Alfred's stolen paintings have been recovered two or three at a time.

Dr. Constance Lowenthal, executive director of IFAR, told me that the lesson of the Rossborough case is that "when art becomes vulnerable, it's *really* vulnerable." The 1974 theft, she said, probably put an idea into the heads of those responsible for the 1986 theft. To cite another example, she said, a small Rembrandt self-portrait in the Dulwich College Picture Gallery at a British prep school outside London had been stolen four times in the previous fifteen years.

I didn't know it then, but the Quedlinburg treasures had also been stolen more than once. Months later I would discover that their history was more bizarre than that of the Ghent altarpiece and the Rossborough collection put together. Meanwhile, as I continued to write about the world's greatest art crimes, I realized that there was another category of theft that far outstripped the Gardner tragedy, yet had much in common with the Quedlinburg case: namely, wartime looting.

Although the theft of art from a defeated foe has been practiced since time immemorial, it was Napoleon Bonaparte who raised it to an art form. Earlier conquerors had spirited off artworks and cultural monuments from a prostrate enemy only to see these prizes retrieved after a subsequent conflict. Napoleon, however, took no chances on such reversals of fortune. He forced those he conquered to sign peace treaties that officially ceded artworks and monuments to the French Empire as tribute. This practice was followed on such a scale as to inflict severe growing pains on the French national museum, the Louvre. In the era of nineteenth-century colonialism, the British Museum and the Imperial German Museum underwent similar expansions.

In more recent times, the Nazi regime specialized in the confiscation of private Jewish art collections and wound up stripping conquered nations and people in a lawless rampage. After the war, Allied investigators recovered literally thousands of artworks and precious objects from Germany and returned them to their countries of origin. Items stolen by the Nazis included everything from paintings by Rembrandt, Vermeer, Utrillo, Matisse, Picasso, and van Gogh to Chopin's piano (found in a German officer's club) and the Hungarian royal Crown of St. Stephen (kept at Fort Knox until 1978).

When the Soviet Union struck back against Germany and came to dominate eastern Europe, the Soviets were, if anything, even more rapacious than the Nazis. According to German accounts, the Red Army seized more than 200,000 artworks, books, and documents. These prizes included Old Master and Impressionist paintings and archeological discoveries such as the Treasures of Priam that Heinrich Schliemann brought to Berlin from Greece and Turkey in the 1870s.

Today, the Russians regard these treasures—recently displayed in Moscow and St. Petersburg—as partial compensation for the destruction of life and property wreaked by Hitler's forces. The Germans, on the other hand, consider the stolen valuables war loot and want them returned. It could take a century to straighten the matter out.

Apart from what I was writing about the Gardner Museum, I could see that the Quedlinburg theft was a mixture of things. Like the Gardner theft, it was carried out by one or more outlaws. Surely no American official had sanctioned the looting of the cave. On the other hand, because the Quedlinburg theft took place amid the chaos of war and because the lost objects are of enormous value and historical importance, the theft was indeed Napoleonic in scope and daring.

I called Willi.

"Did you find a picture of the Quedlinburg stuff?"

"Yeah, but it's going to take ten days."

"What d'ya mean?"

"I found an archive in Germany that has the pictures, but they have to make prints and then mail them."

"Willi, I told you forty-eight *hours!* Now I'll have to leave Quedlinburg out of my story."

"*Don't* leave it out!"

"Willi, I warned you!"

My story ran on March 22—without a single mention of Quedlinburg. Willi blamed me, and I blamed him. We had lost an opportunity to advertise our search and get help.

When we spoke on the phone the next day, I realized that the irrepressible optimist, the master of persistence, was now demoralized. Quite obviously, he was upset that I had not mentioned Quedlinburg, but also Willi was physically exhausted. He said he had been getting up at 4 A.M. every morning for the past month to call West Berlin to report on his progress, trying to keep his superiors interested in what he was doing. It seems that Willi, too, needed to hit a home run. After rising early, he said, he worked every day in Suitland until closing time at 5 P.M., and then labored at home until midnight over the documents he had copied that day. He was now exhausted. He said he thought the only way to pry the Texas banker's name out of Folter would be to file a lawsuit, subpoena Folter, and threaten to have him held in contempt of court unless he revealed the name. Did I know a good lawyer, he asked.

I said I did, and immediately recommended Tom Kline, the young attorney I'd met in Indianapolis the year before when he successfully represented the Autocephalous Greek Orthodox Church and the Republic of Cyprus in their claim to recover a collection of ancient Byzantine mosaics. Here was another treasure-lode that was also the casualty of a war, having been stolen during the fighting between the Greeks and Turks in Cyprus in the 1970s. An Indianapolis art dealer had brazenly offered them for sale, but Tom Kline had put a stop to the sale and saw to it that the mosaics were returned to Cyprus.

Both Willi and Tom worked in Washington, and they hit it off as soon as they met. Together they flew to New York and visited Folter, broadly hinting that they were ready to take legal steps to compel his cooperation. Folter was unimpressed by the tough talk and revealed nothing.

Just before they flew back to Washington the three of us met for a drink at Sardi's, the theatrical restaurant and bar just behind the *Times* building. Tom had lost nothing of his beetle-browed intensity. Then forty-three, he was slightly built and boyish-looking, with a thick clump of dark hair and lively dark eyebrows. Originally a New Yorker, Tom is a graduate of Columbia College and Columbia Law School. Several years before this he had found a job with a Washington law firm, so he settled there. Since I had last seen him, Tom had moved to a new job with Andrews & Kurth—a law firm that just happened to be exceedingly well connected in Texas. More of which later.

The question before us at Sardi's was: how to loosen Folter's tongue? Willi, now disgusted with Folter, wanted Tom to file a lawsuit against him and subpoena his correspondence with the Texas bank.

"We can't do that," said Tom. "We don't have an owner of the treasures who wants us to represent him. We can't just institute an action on our own."

I said I had a hunch about why Folter insisted on seeing a high-ranking West German official. "Look," I said, "he wants to deal. That's his business. He told me it would have been the biggest manuscript sale of the century if he had been able to handle it. Maybe he still thinks he can.

"His problem," I went on, "is that even if he got the Samuhel Gospel he couldn't sell it because it's stolen property, and you can't convey legal title to something you don't own, right?"

"Right," said Tom. "But there's an exception. You can sell stolen property to its rightful owner. *That* purchaser has already got legal title to it."

"There you go!" I said. "That's Folter's game. He wants to let us flush out the owner, and then come forward and offer to sell the stuff for him back to the Germans. That's why he wants us to put him together with a high German official. He wants to make a connection with the eventual customer."

This assessment of Folter, I believe, was essentially correct; however, we never did figure out how to make him talk. Not then, anyway. We didn't have to. Events took over.

A day or two after our meeting at Sardi's, I received an excited call from Willi. The West German government, he said, had just purchased one of the Quedlinburg manuscripts. "Maybe somebody got scared and struck a quick deal because we were asking too many questions," he said.

I made a series of transatlantic telephone calls and produced a front-page exclusive for the *Times* the next morning. Hey, this was the sort of home run I'd been looking for!

My story told how a West German governmental agency, the Cultural Foundation of the States, had acquired the Samuhel Gospel, the older of the two manuscripts and the most valuable object among the Quedlinburg treasures, by agreeing to pay a "finder's fee" of $3 million to a lawyer representing an American client. The bulk of the missing treasures—eleven of them—were still unaccounted for, but this recovery was certainly promising.

Klaus C. Maurice, the head of the West German agency, had told me over the phone that the manuscript was "absolutely a national treasure." I quoted him and also Folter, who had called it "one of the foremost among the manuscripts of the German patrimony."

I asked Maurice if the "finder's fee" weren't a euphemism for paying ransom.

He avoided a direct answer but said that the agents who

offered to sell the manuscript had taken it to Switzerland, and once it was under the protection of Swiss law there was no alternative for him but to purchase it. Swiss law is notorious for favoring property claimants with only the shadiest title to what they say they own. Maurice said that if the manuscript had instead been in the United States when offered for sale, his government surely would have used legal procedures to recover it.

I urged him to tell me the name of the American lawyer who had sold the manuscript to him. He would say only that the transaction involved a number of people, and that he had paid the $3 million to a West German rare-book and manuscript dealer named Heribert Tenschert. I called Tenschert and he too refused to divulge the name of the American lawyer. Part of the agreement that both he and Maurice had signed, Tenschert told me, was that the identity of the seller would never be made public.

I called Maurice again, badgering him for the name. "Wasn't the seller from Texas?" I asked slyly.

Maurice acknowledged having been told that the manuscript was stolen in 1945 and had been taken to Texas by a returning American soldier. He said the soldier's name was never mentioned in the course of the negotiations. Maurice also said that Tenschert told him he was representing "an American client from Houston who had taken the manuscript to Switzerland in order to sell it."

I included all of this in my story. When I read it in the paper the next morning, I noticed that I'd mentioned Texas no fewer than three times.

Chapter 4

News begets news. There is no more important ally an investigative reporter can have than an editor with nerve enough to publish his story in installments as it unfolds. If the investigation is a good one, readers get caught up by the drama and some of them ply the reporter with offers of assistance. Most of these offers are not helpful, but now and then something comes along that's pure gold.

As a result of the page-one display the *Times* gave the Quedlinburg story on May 1—illustrated with the portrait of the Evangelist Luke from the Samuhel Gospel—telephone messages ran off the tape in my answering machine. Some messages were congratulations from friends, acquaintances, and the usual crowd of press agents. A few were from cranks, like one that denounced me as a "neo-Nazi" for having drawn attention to art stolen from Nazi Germany as opposed to art the Nazis stole from others. Several callers were well-meaning but not helpful. One was priceless.

That call was from Henry Forsythe, a Midwestern art collector and an extremely savvy lawyer besides. Actually,

Forsythe is not his real name. He insists on my using his pseudonym. He said he followed the international art market closely, and had been of assistance to my New York *Times* colleague Rita Reif several years back when she was working on a story that ultimately prevented a London auction house from selling a stolen Goya masterpiece. (Rita later spoke highly of Forsythe to me.)

Forsythe said the mysterious Texas lawyer who sold the Samuhel Gospel to the Germans was doubtless John S. Torigian, an attorney who practices in Houston. He said Torigian had tried to sell the same manuscript to him.

"He was completely unsophisticated about the art market," Forsythe continued. "I looked him up in Martindale-Hubbell, the lawyers directory, and could see that he's in his mid-thirties and a graduate of the University of Texas and the South Texas College of Law in Houston. He's strictly provincial, not the type you'd expect to find active in the international art market."

Forsythe gave me another tip as well. He said he had learned that Torigian originally arranged to sell the Samuhel Gospel for $9 million to a Paris rare-book dealer by the name of Paul-Louis Couailhac. The understanding was that Couailhac would resell the manuscript to the West German Cultural Foundation of the States. But at the last minute, Forsythe said, Torigian welshed on the deal and sold the manuscript for only $3 million to a Swiss dealer, who in turn sold it to Heribert Tenschert, the German dealer who then sold it to the West German Cultural Foundation. Forsythe speculated that Torigian took the lower offer from the Swiss dealer because he realized that Swiss law would afford much greater protection than French law in a shady transaction of this sort.

Couailhac was so angry about Torigian's double dealing, Forsythe said, that he was considering suing him for breach of contract. He might be angry enough to tell his story to a reporter.

What luck! About the only thing Forsythe hadn't been able to tell me was the name of the client for whom these front men had been working. I thanked him heartily. Over the succeeding months, Forsythe became a valued counselor upon whom I would rely for advice. He never asked for anything in return.

I wrote Torigian's name on a scrap of paper and pinned it to the cork partition facing my desk. This was not the time for me to approach him directly. He would simply deny everything. I would have to arm myself with a lot more information about the peregrinations of the Quedlinburg treasures before confronting him. Consequently, I called Couailhac in Paris. Did he know a Texas lawyer named John S. Torigian, I asked.

Couailhac laughed. "C'est possible."

After some good-humored fencing, he confirmed everything Forsythe had told me.

During the next week, I made a number of calls in an effort to learn more about Torigian's efforts to sell the Samuhel Gospel. I figured that if he had played Couailhac off against a Swiss dealer he might have approached other dealers, too. And if I could track them down, I might be able to learn a great deal—including, maybe, the identity of the Quedlinburg thief.

My first few calls drew blanks, but I began to get lucky when I phoned Christopher de Hamel, the manuscript specialist at Sotheby's in London. De Hamel, who is one of the rare auction-house salesmen to have earned a doctorate in his field, turned out to be both well informed and articulate.

"I first heard that the Samuhel Gospel was on the market in 1983," he told me. "I've never actually seen it, but over the years stories have made the rounds. It's our business to know about these things, you understand. As time went on, the stories became more and more frequent. In the last six months, there was a new rumor about it at least once a week. I wouldn't be surprised if every major manuscript dealer in the world didn't have a nibble at it."

"The trouble, of course," he went on to say, "is that it was stolen, and so no reputable dealer would have anything to do with it once he realized that. It's simply nursery-school morality that you can't sell something that isn't yours."

"But, believe me," he continued, "we would have stopped at nothing to get it if there had been an opportunity to handle the manuscript legally—if, for example, the church of Quedlinburg had renounced ownership. The fact is, it's one of *the* great manuscripts. If it had come on the market legally it would have been the greatest manuscript sale of this century."

I asked why.

"Most surviving medieval manuscripts," de Hamel said, "belong to the *end* of the Middle Ages, which is roughly the late fourteenth or early fifteenth century. Consequently, a ninth-century manuscript, and one that is illustrated like this, and has even part of its original binding, is supremely rare. The full-page paintings in it are among the earliest examples of Western portrait painting. The texts of the manuscripts tell of the spread of literacy and the gradual advance of civilization in the Middle Ages. And it has an astonishing treasure binding that's phenomenally important. It sheds light on the aesthetic principles, sculptural techniques, and precious-metal work of the period. It's hard to conceive of anything of greater importance in this field."

I next called Thomas Kren, curator of manuscripts at the J. Paul Getty Museum in Malibu, California, one of the richest museums in the world. If anyone were trying to sell a medieval manuscript for seven or eight figures, I guessed, sooner or later he would have found his way to Kren. I asked him if he had been offered the Samuhel Gospel.

"Is this off the record?" he said warily.

No reporter likes to talk to people off the record. It limits the use you can make of what you learn, and it can be an especially bad bargain if you're told something you already know your subject knows and in that way become trapped

into concluding the interview with less publishable information than you started with. Still, I could tell from Kren's
abrupt tone of voice that (1) he knew something worth my
hearing, and (2) I'd never hear it if I didn't promptly accept
his terms. I said O.K. (A few months later, Kren agreed to put
this and a subsequent conversation on the record.)

He said that earlier in the year he had been shown the
Samuhel Gospel, but even speaking off the record he could
not say by whom.

Brashly, I said, "Oh, you must mean John Torigian, the
Houston lawyer, right?"

A pause. Then he said, "So you know."

"Oh, sure."

That seemed to relax Kren a bit. I think he figured that
other people, too, had spoken to me in confidence and that I
could be trusted.

He continued. "When Torigian brought the manuscript to
me, it was pretty clear he had no experience in the art market, and it was easy enough to get the impression that the
manuscript had come into his hands by questionable means.
He was incredibly careful about protecting the owner's identity."

"We did the sort of research we do when anything is
offered to us," Kren went on. "We found the Samuhel Gospel
in the literature. It had been at Quedlinburg up to a certain
time, and then it was gone. Consequently, there was a problem with ownership. Our museum requires that before we
buy anything the seller has to sign a warranty attesting to
legal ownership. That way we make sure there aren't any
legal problems. It was clear in this case that the seller would
not be able to sign the warranty. When we realized that, we
broke off the discussion."

(After the case had come to trial several months later, it
turned out that Kren had come a great deal closer to buying
the manuscript than he let on in our first conversation.)

*   *   *

Now it was Willi's turn to advance the investigation. He acted so boldly, in fact, that it stretched our fledgling partnership to the breaking point.

I called Willi and gave him a quick briefing on what I'd learned to date, and asked him to keep up the pressure on Folter.

"I'm finished with that guy," said Willi. "I'm working on my army documents. You're the one who's supposed to be talking to the art people."

"Folter is an exception," I said. "He's afraid to talk to me because he thinks if he makes a slip of the tongue I'll broadcast it in the *Times*, and then whoever patronized him before will be sure not to do so again. But you don't pose that kind of a threat. Also, you speak his language. Come to New York again and this time speak with him very privately—in German."

Although wary of another rebuff, Willi flew to New York to see Folter a day or two later. This time he was better dressed than before, and when he spoke to Folter in German, he later told me, it seemed to put both of them at ease. Furthermore, Willi reported, it warmed Folter's thoroughly German heart when Willi let drop the fact that he has a degree in law. Folter himself holds a Ph.D. in comparative literature from the University of Illinois, and he, like many of his countrymen, is wowed by anyone who has earned the right to call himself *Doktor*.

Things went so well, in fact, that Willi didn't even have to remind Folter of what he was trying to find out. Folter brought it up himself. But in a strange way. At one point during their conversation, Folter said that although he still could not reveal the name of the Texas banker he would be willing to make Willi a photocopy of the letter the banker had sent to him four years earlier requesting an appraisal. However, said Folter, when he copied the banker's letter he would be obliged to mask out both the letterhead and the signature block at the bottom.

At first, Willi later told me, he thought this was ridiculous. What use could he possibly have for the text of the letter without the name of the sender or even the name of the bank? Nevertheless, said Willi, he watched with growing curiosity as Folter opened a large atlas on his desk and, without uttering a word of explanation, turned to a map of Texas. Then, very carefully, Folter placed a ruler on the map before getting up to take the banker's letter to a copying machine. When Folter left, Willi said, it suddenly dawned on him that Folter's fussing with the ruler and the map—and then departing—was an unspoken invitation for him to take a look at the map and where he had placed the ruler on it. It might allow Willi to learn the name of the town where the bank is located without being able to say that Folter had told it to him. Willi is not one who needs to be asked twice under such circumstances. He sprang up from his chair, peered intently at the map, and saw that the end of the ruler had been placed precisely under the name *Whitewright*, a small town in northeastern Texas. He made a mental note of the name and sat down.

When Folter returned, Willi said nothing about what he had just learned. He departed with a handshake, and rushed across town to the *Times*, where he arrived visibly excited.

"Folter left me sitting there next to his desk after he'd very elaborately placed a ruler on the map," Willi told me, almost shouting with excitement. "He never *told* me the name of the town. He protected himself. If anybody were to question him about giving away confidential information, you see, he can always say that he never divulged his client's name or whereabouts, and that I only discovered it by snooping in his office. What he wanted all this time was a cover story to hide behind!"

We headed for the cafeteria again. There was much information to share and strategy to discuss. An hour later, we left the cafeteria barely on speaking terms.

After we seated ourselves, I began by explaining in detail everything I'd learned since we last met. I said I'd decided not to confront Torigian right away since he'd only tell me to get lost, and would perhaps throw up obstacles to make our investigation even more difficult than it already was.

"Better to sneak up on him," I said.

Willi agreed.

I asked Willi for the name of the Texas town he'd spied on Folter's map.

He stared at me. "Tell you later," he said.

"Wait a minute!" I shot back. "I gave you Torigian's name. Now it's your turn to give me something."

He looked at me sheepishly. Then he said carefully, as if having difficulty pronouncing the word. "Vightvright."

"Whatright?"

"No. *Vightvright,*" he said a little louder.

I pushed a paper napkin and a ball-point pen across the table to him. "Spell it out."

He wrote the name "Whitewright" on the napkin and slid it back to me.

"I'll be damned," I said, looking at what he had written.

"It doesn't look like much on the map," Willi said. "I'll tell you more about it after I've been there."

"*Been* there!" I stammered. "Are you kidding?"

"Not at all."

"Come on, Willi. What are you talking about?"

"I gotta go there."

"You could blow the whole investigation!"

"Not if I'm careful."

"Careful? How can you be *careful* if you don't even know who you're looking for?"

"I have some ideas."

"You can't be serious, Willi. If you go down there, you'll alert them—assuming the thieves are still in Texas. They'll hustle the stuff on the next jet to Geneva beyond the reach of U.S. law. You'll blow our only chance to catch the bastards and recover the stuff!"

Willi was adamant. "They've already had plenty of opportunity to take the stuff out of the country," he said.

"Exactly," I interrupted. "By now, *all* of the treasures may be in a Swiss bank vault waiting to be sold. I realize that. In which case we're screwed. But there's still a fighting chance that the stuff is in this country. If that's the case, then the *last* thing we want to do is to alert the thief to the fact that we're on his trail. We have to find him before he realizes we're looking for him—then, if we have enough evidence, maybe we can get the stuff impounded by a court order until a judge decides who it belongs to."

"No, no, no," said Willi. "We can't wait until we have a perfect case against the thief. We've got a good lead now and we have to move."

"Look, Willi," I said trying hard to sound conciliatory, "we've done fabulously well up to now. You did a *great* job of opening up Folter, and now the name of the guy who's been running around the world trying to peddle the stuff has fallen into our lap. We're on the verge of cracking the case! I know it's been frustrating, but—Jesus—be patient. Hang in there until we get the thief's name. Then we'll make our move."

Willi shook his head. "I need something now to show to my people in Berlin," he said.

"Fine, but not at the sacrifice of the investigation."

Willi listened to what I was saying, but I could tell he'd made up his mind.

"When was the last time you were in Texas?" I asked.

"Oh, it's been years."

"Be serious, Willi. You've *never* been in Texas. Am I right?"

"Right."

"With your accent, you'll stand out down there as if you'd dyed your hair purple."

"I'm not planning to announce my arrival from the rooftops."

"Do you know they call Dallas the murder capital of the world?"

"Yeah, I've seen that on television, but it's mostly husbands shooting wives."

"Willi, you know the cash value of what we're looking for. Don't you realize they'll shoot you like a dog to protect that?"

"If you're so worried about my health why don't you come with me?"

"Because my editor wouldn't send me to *Newark* on the strength of what you've got! Look, Willi, I'm not just concerned about your blowing the investigation. I'm concerned about your getting yourself blown away. I don't want to get a call in the middle of the night to come to Texas and identify what's left of you."

"Who said I was using you as a reference?"

I was losing my cool. Nothing I said seemed to get through. Then Willi really burned me up.

"I guess the problem is that you're playing Sean Connery to my Harrison Ford," he said.

"What the hell do you mean by that?"

"You think I'm an impetuous young jerk while you have the wisdom of the ages."

"Goddammit, Willi," I said, "I'm trying to reason with you, and you turn this into personalities. Screw that! Why can't you deal with what I'm saying?"

"I thought I was, and that was what annoyed you."

"Do you know how much goddamned time I've put into this investigation?"

"Not as much as me."

"That's bullshit, Willi, *bullshit!*"

People seated nearby were looking at us with annoyance.

"Let's get out of here," I said, and quickly left my seat.

We walked to Grand Central Station without exchanging a word. Willi found a cab that would take him to the airport.

"I'll send you a postcard," he said.

I stared after him. Then I called: "Take care of yourself!" And muttered under my breath, "stupid son of a bitch."

Chapter 5

No POSTCARD, NATURALLY, but Willi did call as soon as he returned to Washington.

"Where are you?"

"Home."

"You O.K.?"

"Saddlesore."

"Why the hell didn't you call? I was more worried about you than the goddammed stuff!"

"Hey, you never told me."

"Shut up and tell me how you made out. Have you got a suitcase full of treasures?"

"If I did, I'd be in Zurich opening an account."

"Shut up. Did you find the banker?"

"Yeah. And the banker's lawyer."

"Holy cow! Do you think they still have the stuff?"

"Let's just say they know more than they were willing to admit. I'll tell you the whole story as soon as we get together. I don't like talking about this over the telephone."

"You're beginning to sound like Folter."

"Sure. My role model."

About a week later, I had to rush to Washington because John Frohnmayer, the goodhearted but ineffectual chairman of the National Endowment for the Arts was giving—of all things—a song recital at the New Zealand embassy. Frohnmayer had a mellow baritone voice but lacked the sense to see that with his agency fighting for its life his musical performance would be ridiculed in the press as fiddling while the arts endowment burned. I called Willi from the air and asked him to meet me at the New Zealand embassy at around nine, by which time I figured Frohnmayer would have sung himself hoarse.

Willi was there waiting. After the recital, he drove me in his beat-up Chevy to the Jefferson Hotel, where we had a late dinner. I was still provoked by the thought that Willi might have sacrificed the best chance we had to recover the treasures, but I was also relieved that he'd made it back safely from what I imagined as a kind of gun-toting Dodge City. If the treasures were now gone as a result of Willi's impetuousness, then they were gone, and there was nothing either of us could do about it. I just had to hope that there were some parts of it still out there and worth our looking for.

Despite Willi's customary ebullience, I could tell he'd been through an ordeal. We had a couple of drinks before we got down to business, and before long we were jabbering and laughing like old times.

"Did you actually go to Whitewright?" I asked.

"Yeah. It's a fun town. About sixty miles north of Dallas, up near the Oklahoma border."

"Jesus!"

"That's what I said when I got there: *Jesus!* It's like the ghost towns you see in old western movies. You look around and you see nobody. *Nobody!* The main street is one block long, and it's got tin roofs shading the sidewalks, but the tin is rusted and busted and banging in the wind. Everywhere you look you see caved-in roofs and burned-out buildings and cracked sidewalks. At one place on the sidewalk you see broken blue tiles spelling the name of a bank—the Planters Bank or something like that—but no bank! Instead, there's a florist's shop there with about two flowers in the window for sale, and inside, a woman who seems to be asleep. Maybe she's dead! Maybe she *been* dead for years. Then you come to the movie theater. It's boarded up and if you look in the window of the box office right where you expect to see a human face there's a sun-bleached cow's skull nailed to the wall."

"What about the bank?" I asked.

"It's called the First National Bank of Whitewright—a new building with a vault full of big, stainless steel drawers roomy enough for all the treasures. I went inside and asked to see the president."

"What?"

"Sure," said Willi, beginning to giggle. "They said he wasn't there."

"Then what?"

"Then they told me that the main branch of the bank is in the next town, called Denison, and that's where the president usually hangs out."

"So?"

"So I drove to Denison. Bigger town, lots of people on the street. And the bank is like an old western saloon, with brass rails and varnished wood all over the place."

Willi went on to describe how John R. Farley, the peppery president of the First National Bank of Whitewright, invited him into his office, motioning for an assistant to join them, not knowing whether to expect a stick-up or a practical joke.

"I told them I represented the Federal Republic of Germany, and that I'd come to collect the Quedlinburg treasures," Willi said with a peal of laughter.

I broke up, too. It wasn't that we didn't take the investigation seriously, but this was our first chance to unwind after a pretty intense week or two.

"I gave the president my business card," Willi continued. "It was the dirty one with the scratched-out address that so impressed Folter. I also had some photographs of the Quedlinburg stuff, and your article. Naturally, I pointed out where you quoted me by name. Being quoted in the New York *Times* was more impressive than any business card I might have had. I could tell they hadn't seen the article before. They read it with a lot of interest."

"And what did they say?"

"They gave me the line about all of the bank's business dealings with its customers being private, and then showed me the door."

"Then what?"

"Then nothing for a couple of days until I got a call from a guy in a fancy Dallas law firm who said he was representing the bank. He wanted to see me."

"And did you see him?"

"Damn right! At his office in Dallas. He told me that all of the bank's business dealings with its customers were private, and then showed me the door."

"And that's all?"

"Sure that's all, but that's plenty! I knew I *had* them!"

"Willi, what are you talking about?"

"They were *scared* of me! I could tell. They didn't just throw me out on my ass! They *knew* about the treasures!"

"Well, sure they knew about the treasures," I said. "They tried to get them appraised four years ago. But that doesn't mean they have anything to do with them now, or even know where they are."

"I think they know," said Willi. "They know where the stuff is. They may not have it themselves, but they know where it is."

That was only a hunch, of course. It was nothing we could

act upon, and consequently we decided to continue our work as before. Willi would try to make contact with the 150 or so American army officers on his list of suspects, and I'd press ahead with my sources in the art world.

We would now continue to be partners—but with a difference. Willi's bolting to Whitewright over my heated objection made it clear to both of us that we were not teammates, but rather distinct individuals in pursuit of a common goal. It would not be the last time during the investigation that we would decide to go our separate ways.

I admired his guts for having traveled to a remote town on the Texas prairie where the residents might have made things uncomfortable for a stranger with a foreign accent who asked disturbing questions. Furthermore, if Willi had blundered into the thief or the present owners without realizing it, there's no telling what might have happened to him. Considering how high the stakes were, Willi had taken his life in his hands.

But I think that he risked more than his own skin on that trip. I believe he took a chance on losing the treasures for all time. As it happened, the real reason they were not spirited off to Switzerland immediately after his appearance in Texas was something we never could have dreamed the night we dined at the Jefferson Hotel.

And the biggest irony is that in a few weeks' time I would repeat Willi's mistake. In fact, although I'm not superstitious, when I look back on how close we both came to losing the treasures, I start to imagine that either Heinrich I or his son Otto, who patronized Quedlinburg in the Middle Ages, may have intervened on our behalf with his ghostly presence.

Chapter 6

A MAJOR BREAK IN THE CASE finally came to us one drowsy afternoon in late May. I was slouched behind my desk at the *Times* talking on the telephone to Thomas Taylor, proprietor of the W. Thomas Taylor Rare Book Company in Austin, Texas. For the past three weeks, while Willi had continued to look up and interview U.S. Army veterans who had been stationed in or near Quedlinburg in April 1945, I'd been calling book dealers and art and estate appraisers throughout the Southwest. Over and over again I'd repeated the question: "Have you ever been asked to appraise or buy two lavishly bound medieval manuscripts?" Some dealers laughed at the idea. One dealer in San Antonio joked: "Well, suh, we's fresh out of ancient manuscripts!"

Taylor's response made me sit upright. "Hold on a minute," he said with just a trace of tension in his liquid, Southern-accented voice. "I want to take your call in my back office."

There was a long silence. Had Taylor been shown the Samuhel Gospel? Or was it only that he liked to gab and wanted to settle down in a comfortable chair?

"Who told you to call me?" he said when he came back on the phone.

"Maureen, the woman who runs the Jenkins Book Store in Austin," I said. "She told me she'd never seen or heard of any such manuscripts in Texas but thought that conceivably you might have."

"I never saw them personally," he said slowly. "But I know someone who has."

"Really? *Who?*"

"Unfortunately, I can't tell you," Taylor said. "This gentleman is a very private person who uses an unlisted telephone number. He'll never talk to you."

"My God, you *know* him?" I said, "You've *got* to help me. As someone who appreciates rare books, you of all people should want to see them put back where they belong!"

"I'd like to help," said Taylor, "but I can't betray a confidence. This gentleman would never forgive me if I gave you his name."

The more he resisted, the more determined I became not to allow this lead to slip through my fingers. We talked for several minutes while I dredged up every conceivable reason I could think of as to why Taylor should tell me the name of his friend. He wouldn't budge.

Finally, I said, "How about this? Let me send you a letter addressed to 'To Whom It May Concern.' I'll ask in the letter if the person who saw the manuscripts will come forward and speak to me. When you receive my letter, all you have to do is forward it to your friend. If he decides to respond, fine. If not, you haven't betrayed a confidence."

There was a pause. Then Taylor said: "You'll never hear from him, but O.K., send me your letter."

"It's a deal! Thanks very, *very* much."

I agonized over the letter, revising it three or four times throughout the day. The very first sentence, I realized, would have to reflect well on Taylor for having protected his friend's privacy. If that weren't established immediately, I figured, Taylor would wad up my letter and chuck it. Also, my letter had to appeal to the person for whom it was intended, but, of course, I knew almost nothing about that individual. I did recall that Taylor had twice referred to him as a gentleman. That led me to guess that he may be elderly, professionally accomplished, and certainly someone who shared Taylor's enthusiasm for rare books and manuscripts. Such a person would wish to see the Quedlinburg manuscripts preserved and returned to their rightful owner, I surmised. Consequently, I decided to try to appeal to the gentleman as a scholar.

Here's the letter I mailed to Taylor on the evening of May 25:

To Whom It May Concern:

Out of a sense of respect for your privacy, Thomas Taylor would not tell me your name but kindly agreed to forward this letter to you.

You may not wish to reply, but I hope you will at least consider my proposal.

I wrote the first news story about the return to Germany of the so-called Samuhel Gospel. The story appeared on the front page of the New York *Times* on May 1 (photocopy enclosed).

Since then, I have learned the identity of a certain person who offered it for sale. I understand that you know additional facts about the case. Consequently, I am writing to ask you to call me collect [I included my phone number] to discuss the matter. You need not tell me your name, or if you wish I will promise you confidentiality.

I ask you to assist me in bringing to light the whole story for two reasons. First, where national treasures of this importance are concerned, I think the public has a right to know what happened. Second, in revealing as much of the story as can be learned, I hope it will be possible to restore to the rightful owner the other parts of the Quedlinburg treasures that are still missing.

I do hope to hear from you.

Sincerely,

I figured there was about a ten-percent chance of my receiving a reply. A week later, my telephone rang.

"I decided to call you," a mature man said, "because I read what you wrote about the Byzantine mosaics case in Indianapolis last year. I liked the way you handled that."

"Are you calling about . . . ," I stammered, ". . . about the letter I sent to Thomas Taylor in Austin?"

"That's right. My name is Turner. Decherd Turner."

The voice was straightforward yet cultivated. Turner explained that he had recently retired as director of the Humanities Research Center, a research library at the University of Texas at Austin. For thirty years before that he had been director of the Bridwell Library, the rare-book and theological library of Southern Methodist University in Dallas.

"So I know a little about old manuscripts," he said. "I've lost sleep over the Samuhel Gospel. It's clearly a wrong that has to be righted, and I've long felt that if they could be returned to where they belong, I could go to heaven more peacefully."

I told Turner how delighted I was that he'd responded to my letter, and asked how he first learned about the manuscripts.

Four years ago, he said, he received a call from a young man who said his name was Meador, and that his father wished to have "a couple of old books appraised." Turner said he tried to discourage the young man because almost every day someone would call him trying to sell a collection of old books, and just *two* books did not seem like a collection that would be worth his time. But the young man was persistent, and Turner finally agreed to see him.

The young man and his father arrived at the appointed time but without the books, Turner went on to say. "When I asked the older man for his name," he recalled, "he repeated the name Meador. He was a man of a certain age—lower-middle-class and completely unsophisticated. He explained he hadn't brought the books with him because they were too fragile, but had brought some slides."

"When I looked at his slides," said Turner, "I thought I might faint! I immediately told him: 'These are probably the most valuable books ever to have entered the state of Texas.' When I asked where he got them, the older man said his brother found them in the gutter at the end of World War II in Germany, and had 'liberated' them. He said his brother had died, and he was now the owner.

"I was flummoxed," Turner said. "The older of the two manuscripts might be even more valuable than the great Henry the Lion manuscript that sold for $12 million in 1983.

"When I told them the older manuscript was extremely valuable," Turner continued, "the man said he knew it was because H. P. Kraus, the New York manuscript dealer, had offered to buy it for a lot of money."

"Offered to *buy* it?" I asked, recalling Folter's insistence that he and Kraus had been interested only in identifying and appraising the manuscripts.

"Oh, yes," said Turner. "He said Kraus wanted to buy it."

Turner went on to say that he told the Meadors he could not make a precise appraisal without being permitted to examine the actual manuscripts.

The elder Meador replied that he would be glad to show them to him but that Turner would have to fly to Dallas because he did not wish to transport such fragile manuscripts a great distance. He would pay for Turner's flight. A date was set about ten days ahead.

"But that was the last I saw of them," Turner explained. "The day I was supposed to fly to Dallas, the younger Meador called to cancel the trip. He gave no explanation."

Turner said he was profoundly disturbed by the experience. "I knew these were very important manuscripts," he said.

In an effort to reestablish contact with the owners, Turner said, he looked up the name Meador in the Dallas telephone directory, and to his dismay found the name to be quite common. He called a few of the numbers listed but could find no one named Meador who had the slightest familiarity with medieval manuscripts. It seemed to Turner as though Meador and his son had vanished into the murky unknown from which they had suddenly materialized.

I asked Turner how he could be sure that the manuscripts shown in Meador's slides were from Quedlinburg. He told me there was no doubt about it, because when he happened to be visited a few months later by Christopher de Hamel, the Sotheby's of London manuscript expert, and told him about the slides, de Hamel immediately said that they must be the same Quedlinburg manuscripts he had just identified from photographs given to him by Roland Folter.

I chuckled when I heard that. I was beginning to learn that the world of people who deal in medieval manuscripts is small indeed. I had talked to de Hamel only a few weeks previously, and Folter, of course, was now well known to both Willi and myself.

"De Hamel is a very old friend," Turner explained. "When he dropped by I naturally told him about the slides I'd been shown and I described the manuscripts to him as carefully as I could. Instantly, he knew what they were. De Hamel said that just before he left London Folter had come to him with color photographs of two manuscripts he had been asked to appraise. Folter, said de Hamel, had not yet been able to identify them."

I said I'd seen Folter's photographs myself.

De Hamel told Turner he immediately compared Folter's photographs with pictures of the Samuhel Gospel of Quedlinburg in Adolph Goldschmidt's *German Illumination*, a basic reference work on central European medieval manuscripts. Folter, de Hamel said, was astounded.

"Oh boy," de Hamel recalled having said to Folter, "you've got trouble with these. They're stolen."

Folter, according to de Hamel, had replied gravely: "I guess so."

After de Hamel's visit, Turner said, he was even more upset about the manuscripts than before. Now that he knew exactly what they were, he said he felt an obligation to do something to try to have them returned to Germany. Yet all of his efforts to contact the Meadors proved fruitless.

"One day in 1989," Turner said, "I received a call from a man I presumed to be the younger of the two Meadors. He said his family no longer owned the manuscripts but that if I was still interested in them I should get in touch with John S. Torigian, a lawyer who lives in Houston. I immediately called Torigian and he came to see me in a day or two. We had lunch at the Metropolitan Club.

"He said he represented the owner of the manuscripts, but refused to say who it was. I told him I would privately undertake to raise $1 million as compensation for anyone who would return the manuscripts to where they belonged. He scoffed at my proposal and said he had received much better offers from all over Europe, including from the Vatican Museum in Rome.

"And that," said Turner, "was my last contact with the situation. It's the greatest peripatetic art story of our generation."

Excited by what I'd learned, I thanked Turner for being so open with me, and asked if I might call back with additional questions as I reviewed my notes. He gave me his unlisted telephone number. I called him three or four times that afternoon and evening to be sure I had his story exactly right.

In one of these later conversations Turner gave me another extremely important tip. He said that several years before he had spent a few days in the company of a Dallas man—a professional art and estate appraiser—while they worked together to determine the value of an estate that had been bequeathed to the Humanities Research Center. They got to talking, Turner said, and the Dallas man told him about once having been asked to appraise two medieval manuscripts under peculiar circumstances. It was not long afterward that Turner had his encounter with the Meadors. "I always meant to ask the Dallas man if the manuscripts he was asked to appraise could have been the same ones that I'd seen slides of, but I never got around to it," Turner said. "If you want to pursue that, you can call him. His name is John Carroll Collins."

I found Collins listed in the Dallas telephone directory and called him at once. The man who answered spoke with a lilting Southern accent and an earnest tone of voice.

It didn't take long to explain what I was after. Collins said he recalled the case distinctly, even though his first meeting with the people who showed him the manuscripts had taken place seven years before. He also remembered mentioning his experience to Turner. Although he considered his business strictly private, he was willing to make an exception in this instance because it was—and remained—so distressing to him.

Collins said that most of the work he does involves appraising estates, and that in this part of the country they never include rare manuscripts. It happens, however, that he is trained in the study of medieval art, and while working toward a doctorate in art history at North Texas State University in Denton devoted two full years to the study of the paintings in medieval manuscripts.

He therefore vividly recalled an experience that began in January 1983, when he received a call from R. L. McSpedden, a Dallas lawyer who occasionally had referred clients to him. McSpedden asked him to appraise "two old books" that were unlike anything he had ever seen before. Collins said he was too busy. McSpedden replied that he had nowhere else to turn and that the books were so extraordinary Collins could charge whatever he pleased if he would accept the job. Reluctantly, Collins said, he set "a stiff fee" of a hundred dollars an hour, and agreed to visit the lawyer's office to examine the books.

At this point in our talk, Collins consulted his diary. He said that according to what he wrote at the time, he visited McSpedden's law office in downtown Dallas on January 6, 1983. He was ushered into a conference room, where McSpedden was waiting with two grim-faced men. McSpedden greeted Collins but pointedly did not introduce the men. After several minutes of awkward silence, the group was joined by two women, one of whom was carrying a large cardboard box.

"I could quickly see that the box contained two very fine and rare medieval manuscripts in jeweled bindings," Collins recalled. "I was furious at the way they were being treated, with the heavier one dumped on top of the other with not so much as a piece of tissue paper between them. I could see that the nose of a Christ figure in a relief sculpture on the cover of one manuscript had been flattened by being bashed around in this way. I scolded them for treating such objects as if they were last year's telephone directories.

"When I examined the manuscripts carefully, I went into orbit!" he said. "According to notes I made at the time, I thought the old one was perhaps ninth- or tenth-century. There was elaborate filigree on the front cover and jewels. Inside were the four Gospels. The lettering was gold, and there were beautiful, full-page portraits of each of the four Gospel scribes. I could tell it was the Saint Jerome translation from Greek into Latin.

"The pages looked as if they had never been touched," Collins rhapsodized. "They seemed just as fresh as the day they were written. For me, handling such things was one of the fantasies of a lifetime come true!"

"The second manuscript," he continued, "was not as old as the first although it was beautifully bound. It had a silver and gilt cover with sculpture in high relief—which included the figure of Christ with the flattened nose."

The women in the conference room, Collins recalled, kept referring to the manuscripts as "Bibles" even after he explained that they were only the first four books of the New Testament and not the entire Scripture. The people also behaved very secretively, he said. "They asked me for an appraisal but wouldn't allow me to take photographs or measure the manuscripts. I told them that was like asking a doctor for a diagnosis but not allowing him to use a thermometer. They just said, 'Well, do the best you can.'

"I asked where the manuscripts came from," Collins said, "and they would only say that they had been inherited. I had a strong feeling that something was not right. I told them that in all probability they had been stolen from somewhere in Europe during World War II. They shrugged and asked how much they were worth.

"I said that although the manuscripts might be worth $2 million they were worth almost nothing to them because they couldn't sell them legitimately. 'If you do the correct thing,' I said, 'you'll give them back to where they belong.' I spoke to them quite sternly and they just looked at me. Then one of the women said with a simpering whine, 'But what if we don't *want* to give them back?' I said, 'Then it will be on your conscience.' "

I asked Collins if he remembered or had made note of the names of the people who showed him the manuscripts. He said that he had written in his diary, "Cook Estate."

Well! McSpedden hadn't been quite so scrupulous as Torigian in concealing the name of his client. Cook, indeed!

Collins said he thought he had made himself so unpleasant by expressing disapproval of their mercenary attitude that he would never again hear from McSpedden's clients. In fact, he did hear from them again, but not for three years.

In March 1986, Collins said, he received a second call from

McSpedden telling him that the people with the manuscripts would like to see him again. As before, they would pay his hundred-dollar-an-hour fee. Consumed by curiosity, Collins agreed to meet them. This time when he arrived at McSpedden's office, said Collins, there were about five or six people present and they had with them the same manuscripts. They didn't give their names but only identified themselves as members of the family that had inherited the "Bibles."

"They were not cultivated or educated people," Collins said. "Right off the bat, I told them I thought the manuscripts had been acquired under very dubious circumstances. It was not likely that a legitimate collector had purchased them because there were only two of them, while a genuine collection usually consists of at least several such items. They again asked me what I thought the manuscripts were worth, and I said: 'At least $2 million.' I then read them the law about stolen property and told them again what I had said before— that the manuscripts were so valuable and important that if put on the market they would be immediately recognized as stolen property and no one would be fool enough to buy them. Consequently, I said, they should be returned to their rightful owner. I added that if they wanted my help in finding out where they had come from I would have to have them photographed by a professional. Then I left."

Later, Collins said, he was called by one of the women who had been at the meeting and told to proceed with photographing the manuscripts. On the day of the appointment, however, the woman called again and said they had decided against having the manuscripts photographed. Collins never heard from the owners of the manuscripts again.

"I couldn't sleep," Collins said. "I asked my lawyer about it and he told me I'd better keep out of it or I'd get myself in trouble. But, you know, I never stop thinking about it. It's haunted me all these years. I'm still upset about it."

I told Collins it sounded to me as though the manuscripts

he had examined might be the long-lost Quedlinburg treasures that Turner had seen slides of in 1986. We then began
to compare notes on what we knew about the manuscripts.

Collins mentioned that, according to his diary, one of them
had a date on the cover written in Roman numerals—
MLCXIII—which he took to mean 1513.

That rang a bell. I jumped up from my seat and said: "Hey,
I think that's the date on one of the manuscripts *I'm* looking
for!" I quickly scanned the inventory of missing treasures in
one of the U.S. Army documents provided by Klaus Goldmann. I thought I had seen some such date there. "That's it!"
I exclaimed. "That's the date—1513—given in the description
of the second Quedlinburg manuscript!"

What a day this had been! In just a few hours, I'd managed
to interview two different people who had come into direct
contact with the Quedlinburg treasures. To be sure, hearing
about the treasures wasn't the same as finding them, but I
sensed that I was on the verge of a discovery.

I called Willi. He wasn't home. Bursting with excitement, I
left a message on his telephone answering machine. "Call
me," I said. "I've just cracked the case!" The next morning, I
told my editor, Marv Siegel, that I'd scored a breakthrough.

My words to both Willi and Marv were premature. In fact,
as I began to mull over what I'd learned, I realized that I'd collected a bewildering tangle of details rather than a neat solution to the case. In an effort to figure out what to do next, I
drew up a rough chronology of the case so far. My object was
to summarize on a single sheet of paper all of the basic facts
I'd learned about clandestine efforts to sell the manuscripts.

When it was finished, my chronology read like this:

January 1983—McSpedden, lawyer for Cook estate, asks
Collins to appraise manuscripts.

March 1986—Cook estate again seeks appraisal by Collins.

10 days later—Cook estate breaks off relationship with
Collins.

Spring 1986—Whitewright bank president sends slides of manuscripts to Folter.

Spring 1986—Meador and son visit Turner in Austin seeking appraisal.

Spring 1986—Folter shows manuscript photos to de Hamel in London.

1989—The younger Meador refers Turner to Torigian.

Late 1989—Torigian scoffs at Turner's repatriation offer.

Early 1990—Torigian tries to sell manuscript to Kren of the Getty Museum.

Early 1990—Couailhac, Tenschert, and other European dealers try to acquire the manuscripts.

April 1990—The West German Government buys the Samuhel Gospel from Tenschert for $3 million.

As I studied the list of dates, the events of 1986 caught my eye. This was the time at which Meador and his son seemed to replace the Cook estate as the people who were trying to sell the manuscripts. Furthermore, it seemed that the Cook estate people vanished suddenly when they canceled the photography session at the last minute. That could have been the result of jumpy nerves, but I also wondered if perhaps the Cook people sold the treasures to Meador in 1986 and no longer needed photographs, since by then they had a buyer. Or did Cook die in 1986, after bequeathing the treasures to Meador? Collins's note about the "Cook *estate*" suggested an inheritance.

Or suppose, I asked myself, that Cook was an alias used by Meador until March 1986, when he dropped the disguise and used his real name after becoming convinced the law would never catch up with him. Or suppose Cook was a real person who had tried to help his friend Meador get the treasures appraised. Meador, after all, had been described by Turner as uneducated, and maybe Cook was Meador's somewhat more sophisticated neighbor, lawyer, or doctor, or old army buddy or in-law, and Meador had somehow prevailed upon him to help find out what the treasures might be worth.

These were all intriguing possibilities, but I gradually realized that several practical difficulties stood in the way of my pursuing them. For one thing, if Meador is a fairly common name in northeastern Texas, as Turner had assured me it is, Cook is even more so. That suggested that pursuing Cook would amount to looking for the proverbial needle in a haystack—not an inviting prospect. Furthermore, my speculations about Cook struck me as being a little too fancy, what I sometimes call police-inspector theories. One lesson I've learned from my years as a journalist is that investigators must resist the temptation to get carried away with "brilliant" or overingenious suppositions while overlooking the obvious. Edgar Allen Poe captured this failing in "The Purloined Letter," which describes a police inspector vainly searching an apartment top to bottom for a missing letter that is in plain view the whole time. Poe explained how easy it is to ignore "the hyperobtrusive."

What seemed hyperobtrusive now in the evidence before me in this case was that Meador may have told Turner the truth, that he had indeed inherited the treasures from his brother who found them—or stole them—while in Germany near the end of World War II.

There were a number of reasons for believing Meador's story. Turner had painted him as a crude, uneducated man, which suggested he may have stuck to the truth simply because he was not imaginative enough to spin a convincing lie. Then, too, Meador's use of the word *liberated* had the right ring. I knew that expression became a common euphemism for theft in World War II—American soldiers used to say jocularly that they *liberated* a camera, a carton of cigarettes, or a case of champagne whenever they picked up such plunder during a lull in the fighting.

Even more important, Meador's story fit the theory I had discussed with both Willi and Folter and had come to favor the longer I worked on the case; namely, that the reason the

Quedlinburg treasures were beginning to surface after having disappeared for more than forty years was that they had been inherited by someone who, unlike the original thief, was only interested in their cash value.

Accordingly, I hatched a plan. Given the scant information I had about Meador and Cook, it seemed unlikely that I would be able to track them down right away, though of course their names would be vitally important as the investigation progressed. But some record of Meador's recently deceased brother, if in fact such a person had ever existed, should be relatively easy to find. I could check courthouse records for a notice of his death; and assuming that, like his brother, he had lived in or near Dallas, that's where I'd start looking.

Recognizing the Quedlinburg thief when I came across him should pose no problem, I thought. I quickly drew up a profile. He would have died in the early 1980s—before January 1983, when the earliest attempt that I knew about was made to have the treasures appraised. My thief would be a World War II veteran stationed in Germany in April 1945, when the treasures disappeared. He was probably assigned to the Fourth Cavalry Group, or one of the smaller units Willi had traced to Quedlinburg. Also, he was not survived by a wife or children, but left his property to his brother. Finally, my thief will have had some relationship with someone named Cook.

There was, of course, a great deal of guesswork in that profile—too much to allow me a sound night's sleep for the next few days. How, for example, could I be sure that my thief had lived and died in or near Dallas? This was the shakiest of my assumptions. Who was to say he hadn't settled and died in Minnesota? Or New Jersey? Or Oregon? But I had to start somewhere, and I sensed that the only place I could even begin to answer these questions would be in Texas.

I told Marv Siegel I was ready to travel. He took me at my word and asked me to submit a prospective budget. I had it on his desk the next morning. In essence, I asked him to gamble roughly $5,000 on the chance that I could solve the case in about a week. It was a tough decision for Marv. If I blew it, the blame for the wasted effort and expense would fall on him as much as on me, that being the culture of a large bureaucracy like the *Times*. Mindful of this risk, I proposed to save a few dollars by combining my Texas trip with an already-planned overnighter to Washington to cover the growing miseries of the National Endowment for the Arts. Several committees of Congress were then debating whether to extend its life or let it slide into the oblivion of well-intended but insufficiently appreciated federal programs.

Marv checked with Warren Hoge, then the assistant managing editor who supervised the culture report, and together they approved my plan. Even so, Marv looked at me a shade suspiciously. "Remember," he grumbled in his characteristic manner, "this isn't a fishing expedition."

I flew to Washington the next morning and dashed around Capitol Hill, catching several hearings concerned with the fate of the arts endowment. Senator Jesse Helms was again throwing his weight around, and while I did my level best to cover all sides fairly, my personal favorite among the quotes of the day came from Rep. Pat Williams of Montana, who chaired the House of Representatives subcommittee that oversees the arts endowment. Williams, a longtime champion of the endowment, remarked: "The American people are speaking overwhelmingly against Big Brother censorship by right-wing evangelical cuckoos!" Way to go, Pat!

After I'd filed my story and retired to my regular Washington hangout, the Jefferson Hotel, I called Willi. He answered drowsily, evidently having been up late the night before poring over old Army records.

"Yes . . . ?"

"Hey, it's me. I'm in Washington."

"Oh, I was asleep. . . . What's this about your cracking the case?"

"It's fantastic, Willi! I've got the names of a couple of people who tried to have the treasures appraised."

"You mean Torigian?"

"No, no, I think these are the people who *hired* Torigian. These people are either the original thieves or damn close to them."

"What are their names?"

"I'll tell you later. I'm going to have to go to Dallas first."

"You could blow the whole investigation."

I laughed. Sleepy as he was, Willi was tarring me with the same brush I'd used on him just before he took off for Whitewright.

"I'm not going to visit any bank presidents," I said. "I'm gonna sneak up on 'em, remember?"

"Dallas, you know . . . they call it the murder capital."

"Not to worry."

"I don't want to get a call in the middle of the night . . ."

"So long, Willi. I'll send you a postcard."

Chapter 7

THE 102-DEGREE HEAT hit me like an open furnace when I stepped out of the air-conditioned Fairmont Hotel. I'd arrived in Dallas close to midnight the night before, when it had been much cooler, so until this moment I hadn't felt the full wrath of three-digit Texas heat.

I hopped a cab and asked for the Dallas County Records Building, where deed records and vital statistics are stored.

We had driven a block or two when the driver addressed me in an expressionless monotone: "You are near the spot where President John F. Kennedy was assassinated on November 22, 1963."

"I know. I know," I said. "But I don't have time for a tour. Please take me directly to the County Records Building."

He continued: "On your right is the grassy knoll where some investigators believe a second marksman fired at the president. . . ."

"Excuse me," I said, "I'm trying to concentrate on my work."

I might as well have been talking to a cactus.

He went on about the conspiracy theories—that the president may have been slain by hitmen in the pay of the Soviet Union, Castro's Cuba, organized crime, or even the CIA.

"I asked you to cut it out," I said angrily. "Now, *please!*"

He glowered at me in the rearview mirror. It was as though my lack of interest in the Kennedy assassination was unpatriotic, like refusing to recite the Pledge of Allegiance.

When the driver finally stopped the cab, he continued his recitation in the same expressionless patter. "On your left is Philip Johnson's white marble cenotaph in memory of the late president. A cenotaph is a monument erected in honor of a person whose body is elsewhere."

"I'm getting out of this cab," I said. "I told you I didn't want a tour of the city. I asked for the County Records Building."

"It's right there," he said.

He was pointing to a squat, Gothic Revival stack of pale limestone directly across the street from the cenotaph.

"That's it?" I said with a gulp. "Right *here?*"

"I can't get you any closer."

I realized that I hadn't been kidnapped after all. Somewhat chagrined, I paid him, stepped out into the suffocating heat, and plodded into the Records Building.

Then it occurred to me that the cabbie might not have been amiss in talking about conspiracies after all. I don't buy the idea that President Kennedy was gunned down by anyone other than Oswald, but that doesn't mean every conspiracy theory about everything else has to be a paranoid fantasy. Come to think of it, who's to say there weren't more people than just Somebody Meador and Somebody Cook involved in the Quedlinburg theft? Considering the value of this stuff, it could have attracted the interest of organized crime, drug barons, or a group of international thugs.

I don't think I'm easily spooked, but I reminded myself that I was a stranger in this part of the country and that while I was here I had better conduct myself as if . . . well, behind enemy lines. I certainly didn't know whom I could trust. If there were in fact a sizable number of people at present in control of the treasures, I had no way of knowing how far their tentacles reached and how quickly they might detect my presence in Texas. As I entered the County Records Building, I glanced furtively over my shoulder—and not for the last time while in Texas.

I took the elevator to the rather seedy county clerk's office on the second floor. There I was directed to stand in line in front of a counter with a sign over it saying "Birth Certificates."

"We don't have a Death Certificates sign yet," a clerk told me apologetically.

When my turn came, I asked if I could see the death certificate of someone named Meador who died in the early 1980s.

The clerk, a cheerful black girl who had a case of the hiccups, punched up the name on her computer. "Well, let's see," she said. "Oops! Excuse me. I've got thoo-ree by that name."

"What can you tell me about them?"

"The first," she said, "is Carl—Oops!—Meador. He lived in Farmer's Branch, Texas. Died in 1982, age fifty-one, carcinoma of lung. . . ."

"Too young for World War II. Who's next?"

"Alvin L. Meador. Lived in—Oops!—Excuse me. Garland, Texas. Died September 10, 1988. Respiratory failure. . . ."

"Too recent. Who comes after that?"

"Charlie E. Meador. Carrollton, Texas. He was sixty-four. Emphy . . . sema . . . How we doin'? Oops!"

"How are *you* doing?"

"I can't help it, mister."

"That's O.K. Just tell me: When did Charlie Meador die?"

"Hmmm," she said, squinting at the screen in front of her. "He died on December 10, 1982."

That would have made him twenty-seven in 1945. "Perfect!" I said as I scribbled the details in a steno notebook. "What else can you tell me about him?"

"He lived at 1021 Noble Street in Carrollton. That's all I can tell you."

"What's on the screen that you can't tell me?"

She giggled. "Oops! I can't tell you that. The Privacy Act, you know."

"Thanks!" I said, and danced around the corner to the Probate Department. There I learned that Charlie Meador's last will and testament, if he left one, was never probated, that is, it was never substantiated by a court. Too bad, because a probate record would have provided me with a lot of information, such as whether he had bequeathed any medieval treasures to his brother or to someone named Cook.

Still, Charlie E. Meador fit my profile snugly. He was the right age and, as I thought about it, it made sense that his death occurred one month before January 1983, when John Carroll Collins was first approached about the manuscripts. It might have taken just about a month after his death for his heirs to get around to having his war booty appraised. I could imagine Charlie's family discovering the treasures in his attic and carting them right off to McSpedden's law office to find out what they were worth.

On the ground floor of the Records Building, I found a bank of public telephones and a narrow marble shelf I could use as a desk while I looked into Charlie's background.

First, I called the Municipal Court in Carrollton since it, too, should maintain records on the births and deaths of local residents. Surprisingly, the clerk I spoke to couldn't find anything under Charlie Meador's name, but she gave me a sterling piece of advice.

"Call the local funeral parlors," she said. She recommended in particular a mortician by the name of Stan Null. "He knows more'n anybody about this town."

When I got Null on the phone, I discovered one of America's best-kept secrets: namely, that in rural areas of this country the local funeral directors know more about the populace than the county clerk, maybe even than the tax collector. I also learned that morticians, if Stan Null is any guide, are not the stereotypical sunken-eyed dispensers of prepackaged comfort one sees on television sitcoms and in the movies, but are natural politicians who enjoy shooting the breeze.

Null, like my early-morning taxi driver and a number of other Texans I was soon to meet, had to get one or two things off his chest before he would cater to my needs.

"Mister, you came to the right place," he vowed when I told him I was looking for information about a man who had died in 1982. "I know everybody in Carrollton, living or dead. I know *them,* I know their children. I know the names of their fathers and mothers. I know how they all died, where they're buried, and where they're *gonna* be buried. I love people. That's how I got in this business."

His records about the townspeople of Carrollton, he went on to say, go far back. He said he remembered the name Meador quite well, and obligingly called up Charlie Meador's name on his computer.

"There he is," said Null, swelling with pride. "He was buried in Lot P-23 of the Hilltop Cemetery in Carrollton. His wife, named Johnie Mae Meador, was born in 1920, and she's deceased, too. The survivors are three sons and a daughter, thirteen grandchildren and four great-grandchildren."

Uh-oh. My thief was supposed to have had no offspring and therefore bequeathed the treasures to his brother. With Charlie Meador having so many descendants it seemed unlikely that he would have left things of great value to anyone other than his immediate family. Well, I thought, maybe he did bequeath the treasures to his wife, and his brother got involved only when he tried to help her cash in on them. That was a fair assumption. I decided I shouldn't be too rigid when applying my profile to a likely suspect. The profile, after all, was based merely on guesswork.

I thanked Null for his help and called the competition, Rhoton's Funeral Home. A young woman answered and she, too, graciously looked up Charlie in her computerized records. She confirmed the large number of Charlie's offspring, and added a few facts besides, the most interesting of which was that Charlie had worked as a stock clerk at the Ford Motor Company. Now *that* was the sort of information I could never find in a courthouse.

I called Ford. A company spokesman said they had an assembly plant right there in Carrollton, but that if I wanted information about a former employee I'd have to write to company headquarters in Detroit. What might be more helpful, I was told, would be to visit the United Automobile Workers union hall in Dallas. The hall had scheduled a retirees' meeting next Monday. If I cared to drop by, more than likely there would be someone present who would remember the man I was interested in.

I made note of all this, and then called the Carrollton *Chronicle*, the weekly newspaper that serves the town, asking if I could see any obituary notice they might have published concerning Charlie's passing.

"Sure thing," said the perky young woman who answered the phone. She said she would be happy to show me back issues, and if I knew the person's date of death I could probably find an obituary article.

I took a taxi to Avis, rented a blue Pontiac Grand Am and sped off to Carrollton on Route I-35—a drive of about sixteen miles to the north. I flicked on the car radio and learned that there was an excessive-heat advisory in effect. This can be dangerous, the newscaster cautioned. A thirty-eight-year-old Fort Worth garbage collector named Milton Smith had just died from heat stroke. It was the first confirmed heat-related death in Texas this season. I'd better take it easy, I told myself. I recalled having read somewhere that John Wayne's swagger was not so much an expression of belligerence as the gait adopted in the Southwest to reduce the strain of locomotion during the summer months. Eastern dude that I am, I was going to have to practice that. In Dallas, I'd seen people hopscotching down the street from one shady spot to the next even if it increased the overall distance they walked. I'd have to master that, too, if I planned on being here long.

I spun off of I-35 at Beltline Road, looped around a seven- or eight-story grain elevator that proclaimed in huge block letters, JESUS IS LORD, and found the office of the Carrollton *Chronicle*. After I had introduced myself, a clerk brought me a package carefully wrapped in brown paper containing all the issues of 1982. The musty odor affected me like perfume. I love old newspapers for their soft pulpy paper, quaint bits of information tucked in unexpected places, the advertisements that tell more sometimes than the articles, and the crazy juxtaposition of things.

There was one story that said a lot about this part of Texas. Carrollton, it was reported, had grown so fast in the late nineteenth century that nobody stopped to write down whether the town was named after Joseph Carroll, George Carroll, or Carrollton, Illinois. Another story in the old newspaper I was scanning made it plain that if the townspeople were a little vague about their history they were sticklers for getting straight what really matters. The biggest catfish ever hauled out of nearby Lake Conroe, a banner headline proclaimed, weighed 86 pounds.

Then I came to Charlie's obituary. It was thirty-three lines long. I read it twice and then a third time in stunned silence. Charlie never served in the armed forces. He had an unspecified physical disability—flat feet, perhaps. There's *no way* he could have been in Quedlinburg. He'd probably spent the war years working at Ford and serving as an air-raid warden scanning the skies over Texas for German bombers.

I'd wasted the whole morning! That was a rude fact I couldn't bring myself to accept immediately, and so I clung to a slim hope that Charlie was my man, after all. The obituary had stated that in addition to his children he was survived by a brother and a sister. The brother was identified as J. L. Meador of Denton, Texas. Could *that* be the man who visited Turner with his son back in 1986? I thanked the clerk at the *Chronicle* and, though I tried to smile, I couldn't hide my disappointment. It was a glum drive back toward the JESUS IS LORD grain elevator.

Suddenly realizing I was both famished and dehydrated, I turned off the road at a restaurant, called Catfish Cabin, that had a phone booth in the parking lot. I climbed out of my car, but had to wait for someone else to finish a call before I could place mine. The metal skin of my Grand Am was hot as a skillet, and the heat was making me pant and perspire copiously. I thought of Milton Smith, the late Fort Worth garbage man. Then I started hearing in my head Noel Coward's line about mad dogs and Englishmen going out in the midday sun, and couldn't get it to stop. Over and over. My turn at the telephone came, and I asked for Denton information. "Do you have a number for J. L. Meador?"

"Shore do. Would'ja lah-kit?"

Sure did. I dialed. An elderly woman answered, and she couldn't have been more helpful. But J. L. Meador didn't have a son, she said. He was never married. "Wish I could help you, suh."

I plodded into the Catfish Cabin and slid into a seat. Yes, I'd wasted more than half of my first day in Texas on a goose chase. Had I oversold this story to my editors in New York? I wondered. Had I underestimated the difficulties? Maybe what had seemed hyperobtrusive about Meador's story was a delusion. Or maybe his story was true but he lived in Houston near the lawyer, John Torigian, or maybe . . . maybe . . .

"Are you aw-raht, suh?"

I sat up with a jerk. Groggily, I realized the waitress had been standing over me for nearly a minute. I had buried my head in my arms on the table and konked out.

Chapter 8

WHERE NOW? Back to Dallas? Or should I continue driving north into the next county—whatever that is—to see if I can turn up another dead Meador who fits my profile?

The waitress told me I needed "a little ole plate of broiled catfish." I said no thanks. What I really needed was a Diet Coke. Two of them. She brought me the Cokes and tried again to interest me in some catfish. I asked for another Coke. At some point, I may have agreed to try the little old catfish because it soon arrived, sprinkled with paprika and parsley. I picked at it.

A huge, muscular Hispanic gentleman with a pencil-thin mustache seated nearby was keeping an eye on me. Maybe he'd heard my Yankee accent and was curious. I smiled shyly and said, "Howdy?" (What else do you say in Carrollton, Texas?)

"You're not eatin' your catfish," he rumbled accusingly. "Them's real good."

Suspecting that the oversized gentleman was the proprietor, and being in no shape to pick a fight, I expressed vehement agreement.

"Them's from Mississippi," he blustered. "Real sweet!"

"How do you catch them?" I asked absentmindedly.

"*Catch em!*" he said, exploding with laughter. "You catch 'em with tractors and a net! That's how you catch 'em!"

I took a deep breath, bracing myself for some local hilarity about Texas-sized catfish requiring heavy earth-moving equipment to be dragged out of a lake. "You're kidding me," I said stupidly.

"Hell says I am!" he roared.

Damn, I thought. Now I've gone and provoked the son of a gun.

"I done it myself!" the gentleman continued. "Down yonder in Mississippi them fish farms is ten to twelve acres, each one. When them catfish is the size o' your plate, we'd take a thousand foot seine net and hitch it to two full-size tractors, understand?"

"I think so," I said.

"Them tractors draw that net right down the whole pond," he continued. "The mesh on that net has got to be jus' so. That's how you catch the ones that's ready to eat and let them little suckers wriggle through and grow up. Understand?"

What do you know? This was no joke. The man seemed to be telling the literal truth.

Just then he was summoned to the telephone. While I pondered what he had said, I noticed that my energy was returning. My recovery may have been the result of fluid intake, but I also thought it might have something to do with what the extra-large gentleman had just said about fish farming in Mississippi.

Because it struck me that, except for one error, the profile I had devised for catching the Quedlinburg thief was a net of just the right mesh—last name of Meador, World War II vet, no children, etc. etc. When I had swept this net through Dallas county, I had come up with only one suspect—not thirty or forty of them, which would have indicated the wrong gauge mesh. Consequently, I reasoned, if I stuck to my present course and kept on drawing a net of this particular mesh through county after county around Dallas I stood a good chance of eventually catching my thief.

When the Hispanic gentlemen returned from the telephone, I rose and asked if he knew the name of the next county seat to the north.

"Denton," he said. "That's where I live. Half an hour north on I-35."

The fact that I was so close to a vantage point from which I could explore another county helped make up my mind about where to go next. It was now 2:30. I could reach Denton shortly after three, check the courthouse records and also stop by the local funeral parlor, library, and newspaper office before driving east to still another county seat. I probably wouldn't get to the second courthouse before closing time, but since it was Thursday the local public library might be open late. If so, I could work there until perhaps nine o'clock, and in that way wring the most out of the day before heading back to Dallas.

Buzzing along the interstate again, I looked in the rearview mirror and began to imagine things. Marv, my editor, was sitting in the backseat wearing a look of disapproval. "Remember," he said sternly, "This isn't a fishing expedition!"

"Certainly, not," I replied, and then added with an idiotic cackle, "It's a *catfish* expedition, Marv!"

"What if the guy you're looking for lived in Maine or California?" Marv said.

"O.K.," I replied. "I know I'm gambling on the chance that he lived and died here in Texas near his brother. I think that's likely, but of course I can't be 100-percent sure."

"Or Tennessee or Hawaii?" Marv grumbled.

"Look, I really can't deal with *every* possibility now. It's too damn hot!"

That blew Marv away.

"Well, dammit," I thought to myself. "My net is the right mesh. I just have to keep on dragging it around Dallas."

I flicked on the radio. Nothing but rock and country-western stations. I dislike most pop music. I resent being manipulated by its siren calls. Furthermore, the appearance of Marv reminded me that I couldn't allow myself to be lulled now. I had to be alert *every second*. I punched off the radio and began turning over in my mind the characteristics in the profile I'd worked out. I went over it again and again.

Four or five tall buildings came into view on the horizon. That must be Denton. As I pulled into the city, I saw crowds of young people lounging in the shadow of a massive yellow brick building surmounted by a dome. I realized that Denton, in addition to being the county seat, must be a college town. I stopped near a blond, blue-eyed young woman wearing a short, tight skirt and asked if the building with a dome was the county courthouse. No, she said, it was the administration building of Texas Woman's University. I said thanks and patrolled onward. The other students lounging around all looked just like the first—blond, blue-eyed, and miniskirted—as if they'd been screened by a Hollywood casting agency, not a college admissions office.

The courthouse was in a rambling cluster of one-story municipal buildings, all of them fronted by a spacious lawn and an oasis-like sunken garden. As I parked about a block from the entrance, I could see people moving with a slow, rolling gait, like prowling lions. As time was short, I scrambled across the lawn, and found myself panting when I reached the sunken garden. I sat down to catch my breath on a bench shaded by cedar elms and euonyus shrubs with bright red berries. Then I entered the city clerk's office and was greeted at the counter by a handsome, middle-aged woman.

"You doin' all right so far for today, suh?" she sang out cheerily.

How could I answer that? Not with the truth, certainly. "So far, so good," I replied.

When I explained that I was looking for any record of a man named Meador who had died about ten years ago, the woman drew a long face. "I hate to disappoint you, suh, but death records are closed to the general public for twenty-five years. That's the law."

"What law?" I demanded.

"The Texas Open Records Act of 1973," she said apologetically. Then she confided in a whisper: "It's to stop illegal aliens from using the information on death certificates to assume a false identity."

"But I'm not an alien!" I said. "I'm an American citizen."

"I can only approve your request for a death certificate if you can demonstrate a legitimate interest in having it," she replied.

I asked what's a legitimate interest.

"Well," the woman said, "are you related to the person? Or can you tell me the person's date of death? Or—better yet—do you work for an insurance company?

I threw out my chest. "I work for a newspaper!" I said.

"A *newspaper?*" she said laughing. "That doesn't mean a thing. You have to be able to tell me something about the person—maybe his parents' names?"

This was a nightmare! Insurance companies had greater legitimacy than newspapers? Perhaps this devoted civil servant thought the freedom to investigate insurance claims was in the Bill of Rights—somewhere between free speech and the right to bear arms.

I pondered my next move. I could ask to see the supervisor and demand access to the records under the provisions of the Freedom of Information Act, but that would take days, maybe weeks. I tried the genial approach. I said I just didn't know many particulars about the person whose record I was looking for but that I'd come all the way from New York

City—*you* know, the Big Apple?—and I'd *really* appreciate whatever she could do to help me. She asked about Broadway and Bloomingdale's, the usual "are you really from New York?" patter. Then a conspiratorial smile crept over her face. "Don't go away," she said.

She disappeared for two or three minutes. I could see the top of her head bobbing like a cork over the filing cabinets as she opened and closed one large record book after another. Then she returned to the counter.

"Well, suh," she said, "You should give me at least this individual's first name before I can release any information." She added slyly: "Could his first name be Earl?"

"That's it! Earl Meador!" I said. "That's the name."

She winked. "It'll be eight dollars if you want the certificate."

I shelled out the money as heedlessly as a riverboat gambler.

She disappeared again and in a minute or two returned with a certified copy of a death certificate.

I thanked her, and sat down on a plastic-covered chair across from the counter, quickly scanning the document.

Earl Carrington Meador . . . retired pilot . . . died November 14, 1983 . . . age seventy . . . metastatic cancer of the liver. . . .

Looks promising . . . What's this? . . .

Never served in the Armed Forces.

Damn!

I left the courthouse in a hurry, and made a series of quick visits to the Denton *Record Chronicle*, the public library, the Jack Schmitz Funeral Home, and another court building, which keeps records of deaths throughout the county. But my net failed to bring up even one specimen for examination.

I was working my way clockwise around Dallas. When I asked for directions to the next county seat to the east, the receptionist in the Jack Schmitz Funeral Home explained how to get to Sherman, Texas. It was now almost five o'clock, so I called the Sherman Public Library to see if it would be open late. Yes, I was told, the library would be open until nine, and the local genealogy section maintained a good collection of obituaries.

I bought a sandwich and three Diet Cokes before leaving town, then sped east.

Scratch another county, I thought, humming over the rolling prairie. By rights, I should have been depressed. The day was coming to a close, and I was no nearer to discovering my thief than I'd been when I rolled out of bed ten hours earlier. Yet maybe that's not the way to look at the situation, I thought, ever the optimist. The process of elimination might be drawing me closer to success than I had any way of knowing.

After traveling east about twenty-five miles, I swung north toward Oklahoma on Route 289. A century ago, herds of buffalo grazed out here on the waist-high sagebrush. At this season, the countryside was dotted with splashes of vibrant red, yellow, and white from an abundance of wildflowers, plants with names like Indian blanket, Mexican hat, and white prickly poppy.

The road itself was stained with equally brilliant colors of another sort. Every few miles, it seemed, I came to a crushed box turtle or an armadillo. Some drivers, I'd been told, make a game of hitting these defenseless creatures. There oughtta be a law!

Approaching a crossroads named Gunter, I slammed on the brakes and squealed to a stop. I leaped out of the car, sprinted back a hundred feet, and scooped up a small, yellow-splotched box turtle that had been marching across the highway oblivious to the whizzing angels of death on every side.

I've always had a soft spot for turtles. I think of them as

toy dinosaurs. But I take strong exception to the *Jurassic Park* stereotype. Since turtles can be tamed and taught to take food from your hand, there's no reason to think that their supposedly savage forebears wouldn't be just as amenable to nibbling Chuck Wagon or Kit'N'Kaboodle if treated affectionately. Contrary to all the scare stuff about dinos, I think we could have shared the planet with them quite nicely, training them for service as bulldozers, forklifts, and power shovels. Maybe some day someone will find a frozen egg and hatch it. I hope so.

As I was sharing these thoughts with my passenger, humming down the highway, I made another emergency stop and collected a second turtle, a little smaller than the first but similarly marked with yellow designs. I christened the larger and presumably senior reptile Heinrich and the smaller one Otto in honor of those early monarchs who had bestowed treasures on the cloister of Quedlinburg.

"This has to be a good omen," I said as Heinrich and Otto began burrowing into the upholstery.

Sherman is a town of 30,000 just fifteen miles south of the Oklahoma border. It was seven o'clock and the city was streaked with long shadows as I pulled into the parking lot in front of the public library. Inside, a tall, slim young woman with wide brown eyes ushered me to the Genealogy and Local History section, and directed me to a group of pale blue filing cabinets containing folders of obituaries. The clippings, taken from several local newspapers, had been carefully mounted on sheets of white paper and filed alphabetically. So it was easy to pull out a manila folder labeled MEA–MEJIA, containing sixty or seventy pages.

I sat down at a reading table and opened the folder. The name Meador seemed fairly common hereabouts. Flipping along, I counted a couple of dozen obituaries of people with that last name.

On my previous library visit in Denton, I'd perfected the

technique of scanning an obituary quickly and scrutinizing the last paragraph or two to find the names of the survivors. That was critical information. The first obituary to catch my eye was a five-inch item from the Sherman *Democrat* dated November 1, 1978, and headlined simply "Mrs. Meador." The story reported the death of Mrs. C. J. Meador, an art teacher who succumbed at the age of 86. She lived in . . . *Whitewright!* What do you know? That's the town Folter had directed Willi to visit. Among the survivors listed were a son named Jack M. Meador and a daughter identified as Mrs. Don Cook of Mesquite.

I felt a tingling sensation in my stomach. Was this a misprint? Or had I come upon the Meador-Cook connection?

Hunching forward, I scanned several more obituaries of people with the last name Meador until I came across a clipping from the Sherman *Democrat* headlined "Young Physician Dies." This one told of Dr. John Manning Meador, a thirty-seven-year-old Sherman physician and former president of the Grayson County Medical Society who died of diabetes in 1983. He was the son of Mr. and Mrs. Jack Meador of *Whitewright*. There it is again! Among the survivors was his brother—Jeff Meador of Austin.

I drew a long breath. Could these be the names of the father and son who visited Decherd Turner in Austin in 1986?

The Meador family saga unfolded before me on that library table. I turned the pages in the folder cautiously, fearful that I might overlook something. Then I came to an obituary of Jack Meador's older brother. His name was Joe Tom Meador. He had served during World War II in the Eighty-seventh Armored Division in Europe, was never married, and died in 1980. A *perfect* fit with my profile!

Heart thumping, I studied the next-to-last paragraph of the obit. It read, "Surviving are his brother, Jack Meador of Whitewright, and sister, Mrs. Don Cook of Mesquite."

"Meador and Cook . . . Cook and Meador . . . ," I whispered under my breath, sneaking a glance around the nearly deserted library. No sooner had I unmasked the Quedlinburg thief than I began looking apprehensively over my shoulder for his beneficiaries.

Chapter 9

As I LEFT THE SHERMAN PUBLIC LIBRARY it looked as if there might be another hour or two of sunlight left, and I couldn't resist the chance to take a look at Whitewright. According to a road map I'd picked up earlier in the day, it appeared to be a drive of about ten miles from Sherman, all over backroads but in the general direction of my Dallas hotel.

The main thing I remembered about Willi's description of Whitewright was that it was almost a ghost town, epitomized by the bleached longhorn skull in the movie-theater box office. Had Willi been pulling my leg? Was a cow's skull *really* there? More important, I wondered, what secrets about the thief might the town yield? How had Joe Tom Meador—this back-country bumpkin—pulled off one of the greatest art thefts of the century? And why and where had he kept the loot all these years?

That was only the half of it, of course. Where are the treasures *now?* I wondered. In Jack Meador's attic? Was *he* the old man in my daydream who clumped up the stairs to fondle the stuff?

Skimming over the blacktop, I felt giddy with success. I started singing "Oh, Susannah," punctuating the lyrics with rhapsodic blasts on the horn. *Hey, Joe Tom Meador, I found you out!* I cut loose with a rebel yell, and exuberantly lectured Heinrich and Otto.

"I knew that finding you guys was a good omen! Remember my saying that? And now, by God, we *got* the son of a bitch. *Yahoo!*"

As I approached Whitewright, I was suddenly seized with doubt. Had my mind been playing tricks on me? Had I somehow misread the obituary? I pulled off the road at a windswept Dairy Queen huddled beside an Exxon station, where I'd spied an outdoor telephone stand. Ducking out of the car, I grabbed the telephone and called Willi.

"I'm just a stone's throw from your favorite town in Texas," I said when he answered.

"Yeah? Where's that?"

"It begins with W and it's not Wuppertal."

"Will you be giving my regards to the bank president?"

"Willi, I *found* the son of a bitch!"

"What's his name?"

"Tell you later, but I have to know something right now. This guy served in the Eighty-seventh Armored Division. Is that one of the units you traced to Quedlinburg?"

"Yeah, but you don't have the name exactly right."

"What was it?"

"The Eighty-seventh Armored Field Artillery Battalion, temporarily attached to the Fourth Cav Group. It moved into Quedlinburg in April 45, which is when the stuff disappeared."

"That's it! I've got the son of a bitch, Willi! I've just been reading his obituary."

"That figures. We thought he might be dead."

"His heirs—his brother and sister—are the ones who've been trying to sell the stuff."

"When are you going to introduce me to these fine people?"

"Soon. I gotta run now."

"The suspense is killing."

"I'll call you tomorrow."

The sun had gone down and there was a chill in the air, but I couldn't tear myself away from the telephone—not now. I called information and asked for the number of Jack Meador in Whitewright. *He was listed!* I dialed, the phone trembling in my hand. A man answered. A deep, slow voice filled with the funky music of the Deep South. I tried to sound casual.

"That you, Jack Meador?"

"Yeh."

I couldn't believe it was this easy. I was actually *talking* to the thief's brother—the man probably had the treasures in his attic! I told him who I was and that I was writing a story about the Quedlinburg treasures. Just like that. Just as *plain* as that. I paused. He said nothing, but I could hear him breathing heavily. I said I'd been working on the story for quite a long time, several months in fact, and that I knew his brother Joe Tom had "liberated" (that had been Jack's word to Dechard Turner) the pieces from Germany at the end of the war. I said I'd like to tell him what I knew and hear his reaction. My object, of course, was to get the guy to start talking.

"Ah have no caw-ment," he said.

That accent! He sounded like he had a mouthful of something. Had I caught him in the middle of dinner? Was this the way he usually talked? I babbled on, hoping he would pick up on something and start spilling the beans. I said I'm calling because I want to be fair. That was true enough. I wanted to hear his side of the story.

"I won't ask you any direct questions if you wish," I promised. "I just want to tell you what I already know—

which is a lot—and then give you a chance to correct me if you think I've got it wrong or that I'm doing you or your brother an injustice."

"Yew may speak to mah lawyah if yew weesh," he said, cucumber cool.

"You mean Torigian?"

That was foxy. I gambled that Meador had dealt directly with John Torigian, the Houston attorney who Forsythe told me was the agent who sold the Samuhel Gospel to the Germans. I thought that if I displayed some inside knowledge of the case, Meador would be less likely to lie to me, and just might open up. No such luck.

"Talk to John S. Toree-gin," Meador said. "He leeves in Houston."

Well, he wasn't exactly singing, but at least I was right about the Torigian connection. In fact, Jack Meador's naming Torigian as "mah lawyah"—when combined with the fact that he lived in Whitewright and had the same last name as the man who showed slides of the treasures to Decherd Turner— was virtual proof that he was the owner, at least co-owner, of the Quedlinburg treasures.

I asked again if he would listen to what I knew about the case. I insisted I was trying to give him an even break.

He repeated his "no caw-ment" again, but this time I thought I could detect a slight tremor of fear in his voice. I wondered if he realized that by mentioning Torigian's name he'd given away the show. But he wasn't talking.

"O.K., Jack. Suit yourself," I said and hung up.

I'll be *damned*, I thought. I've just been talking to the son of a bitch who *has* the stuff. Then I stiffened. He's going to call the Cooks and warn them to keep their mouths shut! I'd better try to get to the Cooks before Meador decides to warn them.

I picked up the phone again and asked for information in Mesquite, a suburb of Dallas. Was there a Don Cook listed?

Yes! Two listings, a residence and the office of a doctor or dentist. I dialed the residence.

The man who answered sounded considerably younger than Jack Meador. And he was plainspoken, without that greasy Southern accent.

"Dr. Don Cook?"

"Yes."

I identified myself, told him about my investigation, and asked him if I might pose a few questions.

"I have no interest in your story," he said softly.

I repeated the routine I'd gone through with Meador, and he repeated his lack of interest. Then he hung up.

These telephone conversations left my mind spinning, but they led me to surmise one thing: uncooperative as these men had been, they were both behaving as though they had plenty to hide.

When I drove into Whitewright, I wasn't expecting Disneyland. On the other hand, I wasn't prepared for the desolation I saw as I rolled slowly down the main street. The sidewalks on both sides were cracked and buckled. Overhead, they were covered by sagging and rusted corrugated roofing. Several stores looked as if they had been gutted by fire. More than half a dozen storefronts were boarded up, and everywhere I looked I saw broken windows and scabrous, peeling paint.

The Palace movie theater in the center of the block had been slathered with plywood from which the paint was curling up like dry leaves. Entrances to either side of the box office were nailed and padlocked shut. A loose wire dangled from the roof. And there, in the glass-enclosed box office, just as Willi had reported, I caught sight of a sun-bleached cow's skull nailed to the wall. It cast a spectral presence over the town.

Grand Street, as it was called, was deserted. I pulled into a diagonal parking space in front of Bill's Bargain Shop and switched off the engine. Then I took a deep breath.

Silence.

I became conscious of the sound of my breathing. Just then it hit me that I'd been stupid to let both Meador and Cook know I was on to them. That gave *them* the advantage.

For all I knew, Jack Meador might be lurking nearby in the shadows watching me this very minute. Turner had said that he was "lower-middle-class" and completely unsophisticated. But what did that mean? Was he a redneck? An ex-con? A trigger-happy cotton farmer? I hadn't a clue.

What I did know was that Meador wasn't in this alone. Besides his brother-in-law, Don Cook, and the women described by John Carroll Collins, who I assumed to be their wives, there could be a host of other partners in this business. Willi's suspicion that the bank was still in cahoots seemed increasingly likely, now that I knew Jack Meador lived here in Whitewright. And maybe there were others in town—ranchers, farmers, and all sorts of unpredictable characters—who had been drawn into the conspiracy. In fact, the same thought occurred to me as at the scene of the Kennedy assassination in Dallas—maybe organized crime was involved here, too. I had damned well better watch my step!

Strange, scary thoughts careened through my head. I remembered how on the very day I arrived in Dallas the local newspapers were fairly swelling with civic pride as they reported that the monthly murder rate in Dallas had just leaped nearly three hundred percent and the city was well on its way to breaking the four-hundred-murders-per-year mark. It was explained that one reason for this extraordinary homicide rate, not only in Dallas but throughout the state, is that Texas law on the use of deadly force, originally written as a deterrent to horse-stealing in frontier days, remains much more lenient than the laws of most states. Apparently, shooting someone who gets in your way in Texas is as natural as yodeling in Switzerland.

I guess I'm as brave as the next man, but these thoughts

began to give me the creeps. The exultation I'd felt while driving here gave way to clammy apprehension. From now on, I realized, this was no paper chase. I had told these men—who possessed enough war booty to make a Colombian drug lord whistle with envy—that I was about to expose them, and then rashly delivered myself to their doorstep. What the hell had I done *that* for?

I'd blundered into the very same trap I'd warned Willi against.

Prayerfully, I apologized to Willi for having given him a hard time when he wanted to visit the local bank. I wondered why we both had made the same thoroughly unprofessional mistake. Maybe it was akin to what deep-sea divers call rapture of the depths, which can cause even veteran divers to take foolish risks when they get below a certain depth. After coming to within reach of our prize, maybe neither Willi nor I could resist reaching out and touching the people who possessed it.

As these thoughts came tumbling through my mind, I noticed a mud-spattered red pickup truck drive down the street and park directly across from me. A skinny man with a beaklike nose dressed in farm clothes and dirty clodhoppers stepped out, followed by a boy of about eight or nine. They started working on something in the doorway of one of the stores across the street. Their truck blocked my line of vision, so I couldn't see what they were doing. What I *could* see, however, was a rifle mounted on a gunrack clamped to the rear window of the pickup.

Could this be Jack Meador come to look for me? Had he traced my call to the Exxon station outside of town? Maybe he'd heard highway traffic in the background as I was talking to him on the phone and guessed I was calling from out there! Wait a minute. This is crazy. This guy *couldn't* be Jack Meador. Meador had a grown son, and this guy was too young for that. However—maybe Jack Meador *sent* this guy to look for me.

Whoever the driver of the pickup was, and whatever he was doing here, I felt queasy about that rifle. I'm not accustomed to firearms. I realized, of course, that in Texas it's perfectly legal to carry a rifle or shotgun in your car, and I'd already noted that the conspicuously well armed pickup truck seemed to be the vehicle of choice here in the back country. Consequently, this particular gun should be no cause for alarm. But it was. It frightened me.

Trying to assess the situation calmly, I figured it would be better to make this guy aware of my presence than risk startling him by suddenly driving away. He may have thought my car was unoccupied when he parked across the street from it. I decided to let him know I was here.

I took a deep breath, got out of the car and slammed the door hard, hoping he would hear it. He didn't. Then I shuffled and scraped my feet on the road as I crossed the street toward him.

Still no reaction.

Then I called in a loud voice: "Hey! You know where I can get something to eat around here?"

He spun around in a crouch like a boxer, twisting his face and squinting as he sized me up.

"Naw," he said.

The boy started to say something, but was silenced by a quick motion from the man.

He spoke again, gruffly: "Maybe out on the highway . . ."

I nodded and returned to my car. I backed out, spun the steering wheel hard, and heard the tires squeal as I shot off down Grand Street, leaving town the way I'd entered but now half-expecting a rifle slug to crash through the rear window. I guess I was pretty hopped up by the events of the last hour or two.

When I reached Route 75—one of the main north-south arteries in east Texas—I drove fast toward Dallas. In the shelter of my blue Grand Am, my buoyant spirits returned, and I guess I was concentrating more on singing "Oh, Susannah" than observing the road signs.

I got lost.

It was around one in the morning when I finally pulled into the garage of the Fairmont. I felt like ordering champagne but was achingly tired, so I took a shower instead. Then I put some cool water in the tub for Heinrich and Otto. They stuck their heads down into it and drank deeply. It had been a long day for them, too.

Chapter 10

BEFORE RETURNING TO WHITEWRIGHT, I figured the best place to start educating myself about Joe Tom Meador would be in Sherman, the seat of Grayson County, where I'd found the Meador family obituaries at the local library. This time, I would go to the county courthouse to search the official records for Joe Tom's will, death certificate, probate records, and anything else that might prove illuminating. For example, I'd be eager to learn whether he had bequeathed to his brother and sister certain objects of medieval origin, and if so whether they had paid any inheritance tax upon receipt of such items.

Afterwards, I planned to make my way back to Whitewright. Naturally, I'd want to explore this most unlikely hiding place for a medieval king's treasures, and then I'd try to interview local residents who might remember Joe Tom and be able to tell me what sort of person he was. My toughest challenge would be to find an eyewitness—someone who would acknowledge having seen the treasures in the possession of Joe Tom Meador. The *Times* would never publish the story I wanted to tell about the Meadors unless I could provide that sort of substantiation.

Throughout the day, of course, I would also try to avoid bumping into Jack Meador. It didn't take much imagination to realize that he'd have me tarred and feathered and hustled out of town with a pitchfork if he could. Dodging him all day while trying to find and interview people who knew his brother would be tricky, to say the least. And, just to complicate matters, the *Times* code of ethics requires that I not deceive people as to my profession or employer. No posing as a janitor, that sort of thing. But that didn't mean I had to advertise my presence either, especially in a situation where it might provoke hostility. I would have to walk the line between inconspicuousness and outright deception.

Over a quick breakfast at the Fairmont before checking out, I asked my waiter—a cheerful black S.M.U. student—if he knew the best way to get to Sherman.

"Yes, sir," he said, smiling broadly. "That's my home town!"

I explained that I'd come from that direction the night before and had gotten lost. "I want to find the local courthouse," I said. "What's the best way?"

A shadow fell across his face, and he mumbled something unintelligible.

"There's got to be a courthouse there," I said. "Sherman is the county seat, right?"

The waiter spoke in a choked voice. "You best find somebody else," he said, and backed into the kitchen.

That was odd. What could I have said to upset the guy like that?

Later, the concierge provided me with a map on which he marked the route to Sherman. When I mentioned my waiter's strange behavior, the concierge dismissed it.

"The only thing I know about Sherman," he said, "is that when I was growing up people used to call it Trumpettown.

There were several colleges there, each one with its own symphony orchestra."

When I arrived in Sherman after an hour and a half's drive from Dallas, I got the last available room in the city at the Inn of Sherman, a motel with a swimming pool on Route 75. The town was booked solid, I was told by the room clerk, because of a well-attended air race outside of town. My room was small, but I was grateful that it included a writing desk and that there was a nice, clean bathtub in which Heinrich and Otto could make their ablutions.

After unpacking, I drove directly to the courthouse. It was a sleek, geometric affair sheathed with ivory-colored slabs of limestone. An historical marker on the front lawn proclaims it the site of great revelry in 1905, when Theodore Roosevelt stopped by on his way to a reunion of the troops he had led in the Spanish-American War, the famous Rough Riders. The city, it seems, nearly went crazy welcoming him.

Just before entering the courthouse, I saw an elderly black man with a cane approaching. I waited until he came within speaking distance.

"Excuse me, sir," I said. "This is the county courthouse, isn't it?"

"Yes, sir."

"I wonder if you could help me," I said. "I'm a stranger in town and I've heard that there's something unusual about this courthouse. Do you know what I'm referring to?"

"I don't know what you're talking about, sir."

"I thought you might live around here and would know what people say."

"I said I don't know nothing about it."

I tried a provocation. "Well," I said, "maybe you're not old enough to remember."

He glared at me and stood erect without the aid of his cane. "I'm seventy-two years old," he said, "and I *am* old enough to remember it."

"Yes?"

"All the black folks in Sherman know about it," he said. "The white folks, they don't *want* to know about it."

"*I'd* like to know."

He glared at me again. "I was twelve years old when it happened," he said. "The man's name was George Hughes. My own father knew him well."

"What happened?"

The elderly man spoke slowly. "Hughes was arrested for knowing a white woman. . . . A lynch mob was formed. . . . Hughes was locked in the basement of this courthouse for protective custody, they said. . . ."

"Yes?"

"Then the lynch mob burned down the courthouse. . . . Hughes was burned to death and the fire also destroyed county deeds and other records. . . . They said Hughes was responsible for that, too."

I was reduced to silence. All I could do was grasp the man's hand.

"Now you know," he said with a look of defiance.

"Yes, thank you," I said. "Thanks very much."

As I entered the courthouse, I noticed several more historical markers, but no mention anywhere of George Hughes or the lynch mob. As far as the town of Sherman is concerned, the fire and the murder never happened.

In the county clerk's office, I stood in line behind a couple of ranchers wearing dusty boots, jeans, and sagging ten-gallon hats. They had filled out a mark-and-brand application to register their cattle brand. Another thing to make me realize how far I'd come from the Big Apple.

When it was my turn at the counter, I asked for a copy of Joe Tom Meador's death certificate. The clerk found it and promptly handed me a copy. I decided not to ask why things were more lax here than in Denton. If I was receiving preferential treatment because I'd been mistaken for the friendly

Prudential adjuster come to reward some grief-stricken widow, then so be it.

From the death certificate I collected data that would help unlock various aspects of Joe Tom's life. I now had his date of birth, the names of his parents, his Social Security number, and the fact that he had never married. There was also a statement to the effect that he had died of cancer of the prostate, and that he was buried at Oak Hill Cemetery in Whitewright.

Next, I asked the clerk to see if Meador's will had been probated; that is, substantiated as valid by a court of law. She opened a gate and led me down a narrow flight of metal stairs to the dimly lit basement where, I suppose, the spirit of George Hughes lingers. The walls were lined with shelves filled with heavy record-books, some bound in red with gold lettering and others in green with ivory lettering. A few volumes dated back as far as 1846, when Grayson County was founded. Evidently, these few had survived the fire.

"You can search for yourself down here," said the clerk. "Just turn off the light when you leave."

The room had the clammy feel of a dungeon. All was quiet, except for the creak of an ancient ceiling fan and a neon light that buzzed intermittently like a hive of bees. I figured this must have been the room where George Hughes died. I closed my eyes and could hear the faint but frenzied cries of the mob outside torching the building, but I couldn't bear the thought of it. I shook my head and commenced my search.

In less than a minute, I held in my hands a folder containing Joe Tom Meador's will and other documents relating to the disposition of his estate. I sat down at a table to make notes.

His will, made out a year before his death in 1980, left a few items of silver, china, and crystal to his nieces and nephew, but the bulk of his property was to be equally divided between his brother and sister, Jack Meador and Jane

Meador Cook. He also named Jane as executrix. There was no mention of the Quedlinburg treasures—nor anything like them.

In another document, I found that Jane, in her capacity as executrix, had arranged to have her brother's property inventoried and appraised for tax purposes. The total value came to $105,556.77. Of that sum, $81,225.57 was for stocks and $24,331.00 for a few parcels of local real estate including the house in Whitewright at 507 South Bond Street where he had lived with his mother. Again, there was no reference to any medieval treasures encrusted with gold, silver, and jewels. Jane had even signed a sworn statement that this list of her late brother's property was "a true and complete inventory of all the property, real and personal, belonging to said Estate that has come to my knowledge."

The document trembled in my hand. How could she lie like that? How *could* she! It filled me with disgust. It wasn't just that greedy Jane and greedy Jack had cheated the IRS. We read about that sort of crookedness in the newspaper every day. It was that the Meadors had callously plundered the treasury of humankind, appropriating historic artworks for their private pleasure and profit just as villainously as Heinrich Himmler had Nazified them for his evil purposes. Himmler, of course, was a criminal without parallel, yet the wicked spirit that infested him also guided the Meadors and inspired the mob that lynched Hughes right where I was seated. Ugh! I hated the Meadors, I hated this hell hole, and I *hated* Texas. I hated its buffalo stupidity, its sidewinder viciousness, its cactus treachery. *"Give it back to Mexico!"* I muttered to myself as I thumped up the stairs.

I soon calmed down and proceeded to the Grayson County Appraisal District building two blocks away. I'd discussed with Willi the possibility that the people who sold the Samuhel Gospel last spring had acted precipitously because they were in financial trouble and needed cash. Consequently, I wanted to check any public records I could find that might shed light on Jack Meador's financial condition. For example, had he recently declared bankruptcy? Any tax delinquency? Had he sold any real estate lately?

At the Appraisal District building, I could find no evidence that Jack Meador was in a financial bind (only later would I discover that my suspicions were well founded). Nevertheless, I learned that in addition to his home on West Maple Street in Whitewright Jack Meador owned several other parcels of real estate in town. I thought it might be useful to locate them on a town map so that when I visited Whitewright I could take a look at what he owned and perhaps learn something.

The clerk in the mapping department was a pretty, dark-haired young woman who said her name was Annette. I gave her the account numbers of the five properties I'd found that belonged to Jack Meador, and asked her to help me locate them on the town map.

"Oh, do you know Jack?" she said musically.

"No I don't," I said. "Do you?"

"Shore do. For a long time." Then she added, "Oh, yes—a *real* long time."

I cursed my bad luck as I walked back to where I'd parked my blue Pontiac. I knew that the minute I left the mapping department Annette would call Jack and tell him that somebody with an Eastern accent had been there checking up on his real estate holdings. And Jack would know it's me—the guy from the *Times* who had called him yesterday. I was *stupid* ever to have called him. Stupid. Stupid. *Stupid!*

I stopped at a small shopping plaza across from the courthouse. The heat was suffocating and I couldn't help thinking about that lovely swimming pool at my motel. But I'd have to buy a bathing suit if I wanted to take a dip.

The last men's store in Sherman where I might have bought such an item had closed a year ago, I was told by a sales clerk in a tobacco store. For a swimsuit, I'd have to go to the mall.

I drove north as directed. At the Midway Mall, I learned why Whitewright looked so desolate. The mall had been in operation since 1986, I was told, and like a giant sponge it had soaked up business from Sherman, Whitewright, and a number of other towns in the vicinity.

At the J.C. Penney store, I bought myself a pair of bright blue swimming trunks. Then something else caught my eye.

Under a sign that read "Western Apparel," I saw a rack of white Dacron short-sleeve shirts with fake mother-of-pearl snap buttons. By now I'd seen several Texans wearing these shirts. I stripped off the boldly striped blue shirt I was wearing and tried on the western shirt. It fit, so I plunked down my $14.00 and strolled out of the store, rolling my shoulders and moving just like a native. Annette in the mapping department might already have told Jack I was wearing a boldly striped blue shirt, so changing into an all-white western-style shirt to make me less conspicuous seemed like a good idea.

Arriving in Whitewright a few minutes later, I parked again in front of Bill's Bargain Shop. By this time, it was late morning, the sun was high, and Grand Street was deserted. I wanted to have a look at the bank that Willi had visited, but first I sauntered across the street to Meador, Inc., the hardware store operated by the Meador family. I felt confident enough in my new shirt to think I could take a quick look through the window without arousing suspicion. Nevertheless, my heart was pounding as I peeked in. This was my quarry's lair.

Whatever it used to be, Meador Inc. had fallen on hard times. Dingy was the word for it. Way in the back, I could see a man seated behind a counter reading a newspaper. As nearly as I could make out, the store seemed to be filled with dusty bins half filled with junk like rusty steel hinges and rusty drill bits. It seemed more like a railroad-salvage outlet than a store that carried a full line of hardware.

I best not tarry, so I crossed the street and entered the First National Bank of Whitewright, a low, modern building with a glass front and a drive-by teller's window that seemed incongruous here on crumbling, wind-blown Grand Street. I walked up to a teller—a pretty young girl with a shy smile—and asked for change for a $50 bill. While she was counting out the money, I turned around and sized up the square-sided walk-in vault lined with the gleaming stainless-steel doors of safe-deposit boxes. Most of the boxes were the small standard size, but there was also a row of boxes with doors nearly two feet square. Several of these large boxes, I estimated, would provide plenty of space for all the missing Quedlinburg treasures.

My inspection of the vault attracted the attention of a bank officer, who emerged from his office, folded his arms, and stared at me. He may have thought I was an aspiring John Dillinger casing the joint, but more likely, I thought, Jack had told him to keep an eye out for a *Times* reporter. After receiving my change, I nodded thanks to the officer—which went unrequited—and left.

Now I reversed course and headed up Grand Street. After proceeding a short way, I noticed that half a block ahead of me a man emerged from a storefront. He stood in the middle of the sidewalk with folded arms and glared at me. A moment later, there were two men blocking the sidewalk and staring. And then suddenly there was another. This must be Jack's welcoming committee! My Dacron shirt with the fake mother-of-pearl snaps had obviously been about as effective a disguise as—what had I told Willi?—as if I'd dyed my hair purple. They knew who I was. There was a confrontation in the making.

I trudged ahead, determined not to be intimidated. This *is* a free country, I told myself. And there must be *some* policemen in town who will protect the rights of . . . my stomach began to feel queasy. If the object of these gentlemen had been to intimidate, they were doing meritorious work. Now there was gooseflesh climbing up the back of my spine. I sure could have used a Diet Coke.

I considered the possibility of turning tail and dashing back to the bank as a possible sanctuary, but just then saw something I could hardly believe. The storefront abreast of my path had a sign in the window saying, "The Whitewright *Sun*."

A *newspaper* office!

Feeling like a hunted man taking refuge in a church, I opened the front door and stepped inside. At once, I was in another world.

A man and a woman—in late middle age, wide-bodied and good-natured—looked up from their work. The man smiled warmly and the woman said "Howdy" in a cheerful voice. I introduced myself. In unison, they came to their feet and stepped forward to marvel over their visitor from the East. They told me their names are Jesse and Jo Waldrop and that they are, respectively, the editor and publisher of White-wright's weekly newspaper.

I knew I was among friends. The Waldrops, who could have stepped out of the pages of a Dickens novel, were physically immense yet had a quality of sweetness about them certainly not to be found in Jack Meador's cronies—who I devoutly hoped were frying their brains out on the sweltering sidewalk.

Jesse, who had tattoos running up and down both hairy arms, told me he was a retired pressman from Emory, Texas. Fulfilling every newspaper worker's dream, he said, he and his wife Jo bought the Whitewright *Sun* with his retirement money five years ago. "Business," he said, "could be a whole lot better."

Jo, who was even larger than Jesse and said she had a

heart condition, waited on her husband like a doting bride. When I asked if I could look up an obituary concerning someone who had died in town ten years ago, it was Jo who immediately began heaving weighty bound volumes of the newspaper from one shelf after another until she came to one labeled 1980. Since I knew from the death certificate that Joe Tom had died on February 1, 1980, it took less than a minute for me to find his obituary. Illustrated by a large picture of Meador standing in a greenhouse surrounded by orchid plants, it was a much larger presentation than the clipping from the Sherman *Democrat* that I had seen at the public library the night before.

I was a little awed at coming face-to-face, so to speak, with the man I'd been tracking all of these months. He looked as if he were in his late fifties when the picture was taken. A receding hairline gave him a high-domed forehead and a somewhat professorial presence. But the expensive silk shirt he was wearing seemed completely out of place in a greenhouse. Vanity was written across his face and all over his clothes. He seemed prissy, a poetaster, a dilettante, possibly one of Baudelaire's "pedants who think too highly of themselves."

The obit focused on the fact that Meador had devoted his life to virtually every aspect of orchid cultivation—growing, breeding, showing, judging, and publishing. He seemed to have been a leader of every orchid society in the nation, and the obit writer had earnestly spelled out each and every one of his various positions: president of the Dallas Orchid Society in the early sixties, president of the Southwest Regional Orchid Growers Association for a couple of years after that, then trustee of the American Orchid Society throughout the 1970s, and on and on.

Shortly before his death, the obit stated, Meador was notified that a new variety had been named the Joe Tom Meador orchid.

At the service at the local Earnheart Funeral Home, banks of floral arrangements surrounded his casket. Members of the Greater North Texas Orchid Society had worked until 5 A.M. the night before, it was reported, arranging a huge casket spray of many colors, along with several rings of orchids, a green cross of orchids, and a ring of bronze red orchids.

"His extensive greenhouses here," the obit concluded, "had been in decline since illness had forced him to only limited activity some two years ago. The last of his orchids were lost in last winter's ice storm."

It didn't surprise me that there was no mention of his collection of medieval art. That, surely, had been kept secret. And his secrecy was going to make it difficult for me to find someone to whom he had let his hair down, so to speak. Somehow, I would have to penetrate his inner circle.

I thanked the Waldrops for their help and returned to the sidewalk, hoping that by now Jack's intimates had tired of the game and dispersed. Unfortunately, they were still grimly at their posts. I pretended nonchalance, but could feel their eyes burning holes in the back of my now sweat-soaked Dacron shirt.

After taking a few strides in the direction of my blue Grand Am—the only car parked on Grand Street—I saw a tall man wearing a black hat turn toward me and block the sidewalk. My heart was racing again. I thought it prudent to concede the sidewalk to the gentleman, and proceeded to march a little stiffly down the middle of Grand Street. Getting into my car was like stepping into a furnace, but I cared little about the discomfort of that. My concern was that the motor should start. Will it or won't it? But wait! Even before I tried to start the car, I locked all the doors, as I didn't fancy having the guy wearing the black hat reach in and drag me out of the car. (I was too proud to sneak a look over my shoulder to see if he had followed me to the car.) So—lock doors. Good. Key in ignition. Good. Then . . . Yes, thank God! It was the Detroit

Philharmonic in full roar! I backed into the street and drove away, leaving Jack's committee, I must say, like so many crows sitting on a fence.

After traveling a couple of blocks I could see that I wasn't being tailed, and so I began to drive in a circle around the outskirts of town until I came to Bond Street. I followed that partway out of town to 507 South Bond, the comfortable-looking yellow clapboard house that the Meadors had shared for most of their lives and that I'd learned about in the court-house at Sherman.

I rang the bell of the next-door neighbor. A rawboned, middle-aged man and his wife both came out to greet me. Quite obviously, they were not part of Jack's coterie. I gave them my business card and they introduced themselves as Mr. and Mrs. Everett Chisholm. They had known Joe Tom and his mother well, they said, having been neighbors for a number of years.

"Joe Tom was different, real strange," Chisholm told me. "A little guy, he was always traveling somewhere."

Mrs. Chisholm added: "He'd invite us into his greenhouses, back there behind the house, but he never let us into the house. We thought that was strange."

I asked if they had ever seen or heard of his medieval trea-sures. Quite clearly, they had no idea of what I was talking about, but suggested that I call Mary Lou "Douse" Thrasher, a local woman who had been another neighbor of the Meadors throughout her childhood, and had once worked for Meador, Inc.

"She knew him better'n anyone," Chisholm said.

I drove out to the Exxon station where I'd made my phone calls the night before. Once again, the place looked deserted. I parked in front of the telephone stand so that when I got out of the car and used the phone I'd be less visible from the road. I called Douse Thrasher. She answered, in a husky down-home voice, and agreed to speak on condition that I not mention her name in anything I wrote for the *Times*. I said sure. (After the publication of my first story on the subject, she agreed to talk on the record.) In this conversation, she spoke at length about the Meador family, and then, when I asked if she had ever seen Joe Tom's artworks from Europe, there was a pause.

A *long* pause.

I sensed another turning point in the case. Douse cleared her throat a couple of times and then asked me to repeat my promise to keep her name out of the newspaper. I gave her my word. Then she said, speaking very deliberately, that Joe Tom, whom she remembered fondly, had occasionally brought "ancient old books" written in gold to the store to show to the people who worked there.

"It was all Greek to me," she said, "I never did know what happened to that stuff after he died."

This was what I'd been looking for! Now I had an eyewitness who had seen the Quedlinburg treasures, or something like them, in Joe Tom Meador's hands.

I slung myself buoyantly into my little blue Pontiac, figuring that I'd been pressing my luck with Jack Meador and his buddies and might as well drive back to the Inn of Sherman, where I'd checked in that morning. I took an indirect route, making several U-turns in the middle of deserted blocks just in case I was being followed. When I pulled into the motel and entered my room, I found Heinrich and Otto doing just fine. Here I'd be able to turn on the air conditioner and continue to interview people by telephone in relative comfort. After my reception in Whitewright, I felt much more secure in the motel—a feeling that would soon prove illusory.

I must have made a couple dozen phone calls, many of which served only to direct me to someone else who might remember Joe Tom Meador. It took several calls just to track down the headquarters of the American Orchid Society, which had recently moved from Cambridge, Massachusetts, to West Palm Beach, Florida. There, a staff member gave me a list of names of society members likely to have known Meador. I called several of them. The most interesting was Merritt W. Huntington, a former secretary of the society, who said he had served on a panel of judges with Joe Tom at least two or three times a year between 1964 and the onset of his illness in 1979.

Huntington said he considered Meador a great conversationalist. "Joe used to joke, 'Whitewright is the biggest city in Texas, but it hasn't been developed yet,' " he recalled.

Another revealing interview was with the Reverend Dale Gore, who had been the Meador family pastor and had conducted the funerals of both Joe Tom and his mother, at the First Baptist Church in Whitewright.

"Meador was one of the aristocratic names in town," Reverend Gore began. "Joe's father, C. J. Meador, started the farm equipment business, and, until about 1967, Whitewright was a boom town. I used to have dinner with Joe Tom and his mother at their home. It looked pretty good to a young pastor, I can tell you. Beautiful rugs, antiques, paintings on the walls. There was an oil portrait of Joe Tom in uniform, though by the time I knew him he had gray hair and a paunch and I didn't recognize him in the painting except for his flashing eyes. All of the Meadors had dark eyes like that."

"No," he said in answer to my questions about the treasures. "I never saw any jewel-covered manuscripts. Nothing like that."

"Joe Tom was a mystery to the town," Gore continued. "He was a loner, reclusive. He loved to show you his orchids, but you didn't see a whole lot of him. We never really knew him. He wouldn't let us."

My last call of the day was to a Whitewright man I'd been told was a close friend of the Meadors. When he answered the phone, it seemed as though Jack Meador had told him to expect my call. He was surly and demanded answers to a series of questions about who I was, where I was calling from, and what I was trying to accomplish. I answered his questions forthrightly, but refused to explain the reason for my interest in Joe Tom.

"That man's been dead ten years," he said angrily. "Ain't you got no respect for the dead?"

I said my investigation was in no way disrespectful.

"Then tell me what you're looking for," he said defiantly.

At once, I realized that this man hadn't been cut in on the treasures. If he had been, he never would have asked me what I was looking for.

Mischievously, I decided to sow discord in the Meador camp. "If you're so curious to know why I'm asking questions about Joe Tom Meador, ask Jack," I said. "*He* knows what brought me here. I'm surprised he hasn't told you. I guess he really doesn't trust you."

Naturally, that infuriated him. "Don't let me catch you in town, mister," he snarled. "Don't let me *catch* you!" Then he hung up.

I gave the man no further thought—for the time being. Maybe that was enough reporting for one day, and what I needed now was to figure out what it all added up to. I changed into my bright blue J.C. Penney bathing suit and slid into the pool. The cool water had a gorgeously analgesic effect on my parched hide. I was all alone, as apparently everyone else at the motel—probably everyone in Sherman— had left town to watch the air race. I held my breath and submerged. Then I surfaced, and exhaled very slowly, like a huge leathery sea turtle rising from the ocean depths.

Drifting in the pool, I turned over in my mind what I'd learned about the Quedlinburg thief. To begin with, Joe Tom Meador was a thoroughgoing aesthete who craved things of beauty the way other men seek power or love. In all probability he'd inherited this taste from his mother, who had been an art teacher, according to the obit in the Sherman *Democrat*.

He must have been gay, I figured, never having married and having lived with his mother for most of his life. That, of course, was consistent with his aestheticism, but probably at odds with what must have been the drab existence of a hardware-and-farm-equipment salesman in Whitewright.

Meador probably satisfied his sexual interests, according to what the Reverend Gore had said, by traveling frequently and developing a double life. Yet why hadn't he cleared out of Whitewright altogether? Did his mother demand his presence at home?

I was doing a lazy breast stroke up and down the pool, luxuriating in the feeling of relief from the oppressive heat.

What turned Joe Tom Meador into a thief? I asked myself. Perhaps he discovered that he lacked the talent to create, and therefore devoted himself to orchid cultivation, collecting antiques and, when the opportunity presented itself, art thievery.

I recalled a line from Albert Camus' *Caligula,* something about those who cannot create finding fulfillment in "the rapturous power of a destroyer." I had never fully understood that line, but it came into focus now. To some twisted individuals, stealing art—taking it from others or even destroying it—could be as exciting as the act of creating it. Was that the psychological key to Joe Tom Meador? Was that the explanation for Sen. Jesse Helms? Or for Rep. Dana Rohrabacher? I wondered about that.

My mind drifted back to the belligerent man I had talked to just before entering the pool. I recalled the opening of that conversation, when he asked where I was calling from. I volunteered that I was in Sherman and, in an effort to be as forthcoming as I hoped he would be, volunteered that I'd managed to get one of the last rooms available at the Inn of Sherman out on Route 75. So he knew where to find me. I glanced over to the motel parking lot. It was deserted. I panicked.

I rushed out of the pool and ran to my room. Without taking time to dry myself, I slithered into the sweaty clothes I'd taken off twenty minutes before. I scooped up my possessions and dumped them into the back seat of the Grand Am. Heinrich and Otto, too. Sorry about this, pals!

"I've had a change in plans," I told the woman in the motel office, returning the key and asking for a bill.

"Well, I hope y'all come back."

"What's the best way to get from here to Oklahoma?" I asked breathlessly.

"There's only one way, so I guess that's the best. Right out chere is 75 North. Just get on the highway and go."

"Thanks."

As I was pulling out of the parking lot, a drab colored station wagon drove in carrying three or four grim-faced men, the same gents who had played hopscotch with me on Grand Street an hour or two before. Something convinced me not to jump out of my car and say Howdy. Instead, I slouched down in my seat, looked the other way and prayed they wouldn't recognize my car. I had no intention of going to Oklahoma— that was just my crude attempt to mislead anyone who might ask the clerk where I'd gone. I drove south, frequently hitting ninety. After rocketing about thirty miles, I squealed off the highway at a town called McKinney. I picked a run-down motel—what I considered an unlikely place for an East Coast reporter to bed down—and parked behind the central building out of sight from the road. I went in and asked for a room. The nightly rate was $19—and I soon understood why.

The bathroom smelled so vile I had to keep the door shut. Cockroaches the size of mice had colonized the bureau, so I kept clear of that, too. Heinrich and Otto had to rough it in a paper bag with ventilating holes punched in the top.

I called home and gave my wife a sanitized account of what I'd been through (no need to worry her) and spoke to each of our three kids. I asked them what kind of present they'd like to have me bring back from Texas. The orders included a puppy, a camel ("if they have them in Texas"), and a surprise. I asked if a couple of Texas box turtles could substitute for the camel, as camels are scarce in Texas. They said they'd think it over.

Next, I called Marv at the *Times*. I explained that I had a terrific story, and that I'd moved to a new motel because I'd been unnerved by an unfriendly reception in both Whitewright and Sherman.

Marv wanted all the details. I recited them.

"Sounds like you cleared town just in time," he said. "Take care of yourself. We want you to come home without any extra holes in your shirt."

I told him we were in perfect agreement about that.

Then I called Willi. It was a chance to unwind, as I recounted the day's events and we gabbed for at least an hour about the case and about how each of us had become involved in it.

"I can't thank you enough for getting me mixed up in this business," I told Willi. "I mean, here I am in an evil-smelling hovel somewhere on the Texas prairie with a wild-eyed posse scouring the countryside for me. Willi, you inspire the most stimulating vacations!"

"No charge," he replied dryly. "My package tours always include backup accommodations—just in case of trouble."

Chapter 11

I WAS WORRIED THAT HEINRICH AND OTTO might suffer some hard knocks if I put them in my suitcase before passing through airport security at the Dallas/Fort Worth airport on my way home. So I stuffed Heinrich in one pocket of my seersucker jacket and Otto in the other, and, bulging in odd places like a typical homebound tourist, cleared the gate, and boarded my plane. No one took any particular notice.

The moment the wheels jumped off the runway, I relaxed for the first time in at least a week. But not completely. I might personally be out of harm's way, but I believed the Quedlinburg treasures were at this moment in greater jeopardy than at any time since their disappearance in 1945. I, if not Willi, had alerted the present owners to our interest in their booty. If they hadn't already removed the objects from the reach of United States law, they might very well do so now.

Despite that, the truth is I'd stopped flogging myself for having phoned Jack Meador and Don Cook as soon as I discovered who they were and where they lived. I am, after all, not a detective but a newspaper reporter, and it is second nature for me to give the subject of an investigation a fair chance to explain away any possibly damaging information before I publish it. Sure, it might have been smarter not to show my hand until my story was all set to be published, but sooner or later I would have to confront the Meadors and their lawyer with everything I knew—assuming they were willing to listen. That, of course, would give them a chance to make a quick getaway with the treasures. But—no escaping it—that was a risk an ethical reporter has to take.

I also clung to the hope that if the treasures remained just another few days in Whitewright, or perhaps Mesquite, where the Cooks lived, it would then be virtually impossible for someone to make off with them after my story broke into print. I once expressed this conviction to Willi and Tom Kline when they asked me to hold off publishing the story until after they had made their move in a court of law. I explained that the appearance of an exposé like the one I was preparing would have the same effect as switching on the lights in a darkened room during a children's game I knew. Everyone would have to freeze. After all, the Meadors and their attorney were already in danger of being prosecuted for illegally trafficking in stolen property, and now, if they tried a fast one they could be seen as flouting the law even more openly.

With these thoughts in mind, I pulled a yellow legal pad out of my briefcase, and began to write:

"WHITEWRIGHT, Tex., June 10—A hoard of medieval artworks and illuminated manuscripts missing since they disappeared from an ancient castle town in Germany in the final weeks of World War II, have surfaced in this small farm town in northeast Texas, fifteen miles from the Oklahoma border.

"Evidence from interviews with art experts, lawyers, and rural neighbors," I continued, "marks a former army officer, Joe Tom Meador, a reclusive art lover and orchid fancier who was stationed in Germany at the end of the war and who died here in 1980, as the man who carried off one of the biggest art thefts of the century."

I explained that some of the artworks had been kept for a thousand years in Quedlinburg, but during the war were hidden for safekeeping in a cave southwest of town. Part of this hoard disappeared shortly after the arrival of American troops in April 1945.

I then described the treasures, contrasting the magnificence of these kingly gifts with the desolate appearance of Whitewright, whose most conspicuous features are empty storefronts and caved-in roofs.

Next, I told the story of Joe Tom Meador—how he had studied art with his mother and later served in World War II with the Eighty-seventh Armored Field Artillery Battalion, fighting his way across France and Germany. On April 18, 1945, I wrote, his unit occupied the medieval town of Quedlinburg in what would soon become East Germany.

Following Joe Tom's death in 1980, I explained, his possessions were equally divided between his brother and sister in accordance with his will—which made no mention of the treasures. Probate records also revealed nothing about medieval artworks encrusted with gold, silver, and jewels; nevertheless, it was not long before his brother and sister set about trying to sell the two Gospel books through John Carroll Collins, H. P. Kraus, Roland Folter, Decherd Turner, and others, ignoring repeated warnings that the treasures were stolen property.

I then recounted the reports I'd picked up concerning Torigian's efforts to sell the manuscripts in the United States and Europe, culminating in the sale of the Samuhel Gospel to a middleman who in turn sold it to the West German Cultural Foundation of the States.

Something Klaus Maurice had said to me on the telephone stuck in my mind as a fitting way to end the article. I quoted him as saying, "When all the treasures are finally returned, we [Germans] must view them not only as a sign of our ancient past, but also as a reminder of what happens when a state goes out of control, as we did in the Nazi period, and suffers invasion."

Back home in Connecticut, I hugged my wife and kids and distributed souvenirs from Texas. But the cowhide belts, glitzy silver earrings, and "Texas-size" gimcracks I'd acquired in my travels were quickly upstaged by Heinrich and Otto. These star performers delighted the kids by hungrily devouring bits of grape and pear right from their fingers.

I rushed back to the office to flesh out my story.

After I'd made that call to Willi from the phone booth outside Whitewright, telling him I'd discovered the name of the Quedlinburg thief, he and Tom realized that there was no point in their attempting to duplicate my work. They decided to concentrate on locating the treasures. They began by holding a series of telephone conversations with Timothy Powers, the Dallas lawyer representing the First National Bank of Whitewright with whom Willi had spoken back in May after visiting the president of the bank. Their discussion would soon bring to light one of the greatest surprises of the case.

At first, Powers later told me, he was skeptical about Willi. "It didn't add up that he was from West Germany, while the treasures belonged to a church in Quedlinburg, which is in East Germany," he said.

On the other hand, when Willi told Powers that the Quedlinburg church would be represented in the United States by Tom Kline, who was a member of the law firm of Andrews & Kurth, Powers was impressed. He had never heard of Tom, but, like every other lawyer in Dallas, he was aware that Andrews & Kurth—which has an office in Dallas—is the former law firm of James A. Baker, at that time secretary of state and a confidant of President George Bush.

"I thought that was very clever of Willi Korte," said Powers, who is a specialist in international law. "I thought this meant he was planning to use the 1970 United Nations Treaty on Cultural Property. Under that treaty, which both the United States and East Germany are parties to, a country that believes it has lost cultural property can make a claim to a designated authority in the country that is thought to possess it. In the United States, the designated authority is the secretary of state, i.e., Jim Baker."

"I don't mean to suggest that there was anything improper going on," said Powers, "only that Willi's using Baker's old law firm was a good way to get the ear of the State Department and have them pay some special attention to resolving this problem."

The truth, of course, was that neither Willi nor I had been half so clever as Powers thought. Willi teamed up with Tom on my recommendation because I'd been impressed by the capable way I saw Tom handle the Cyprus mosaics case in Indianapolis the year before. I hadn't the remotest idea of what firm Secretary Baker had practiced with, let alone that the U.S. secretary of state had been designated a functionary of a twenty-year-old United Nations treaty.*

Nevertheless, the upshot was that Willi and Tom gained a large helping of credibility in Texas even before they arrived. They also had going for them the fact that, though one of their adversaries (John Torigian) was hardly likely to be friendly, the other (Timothy Powers) was a man of great integrity. Powers listened carefully to what Willi said, and early on formed the opinion that his claim might well be bona fide.

Accordingly, Powers asked Willi for a list of the missing treasures. Privately, that made Willi whoop with joy. Why would the bank's attorney ask for a *list* if the bank was not holding at least some of the treasures? "By God!" Willi

---

*In fact, Secretary Baker had nothing to do with the eventual decision to prosecute the case. That step was finally taken in 1995, during the Clinton Administration, by Attorney General Janet Reno and the Assistant U.S. Attorney for the Eastern District of Texas, Carol K. Johnson.

exclaimed in one of our telephone conversations after I'd returned to New York, "They've *got* the stuff!"

Willi and Tom immediately gave Powers a list of eleven items (all but the Samuhel Gospel, which had already been returned), based on the inventory of missing treasures that had been prepared on December 17, 1947, by the U.S. Army's Office of Military Government for Bavaria. This was one of the documents Klaus Goldmann had found in a Munich archive.

The list included the manuscript dated 1513 that John Carroll Collins had described to me; a casket-shaped reliquary decorated with gold, silver, precious stones, and carved ivory; an ivory comb trimmed with gold and gems dating to the seventh or eighth century; several reliquaries of cut rock crystal believed to be of Islamic-Egyptian origin, dating from the tenth century; a heart-shaped reliquary from the fifteenth century; and other objects.

Powers's response to the list was startling. He said that the bank appeared to have in its vault about half the items on the list. But the best was yet to come. The bank had possession of the treasures, Powers said, because it had accepted them as collateral for a loan! Powers explained that, after Willi had visited the bank on May 7 and claimed that the treasures had been stolen from Quedlinburg, the bank's customary outside attorney had advised John Farley, the Whitewright bank president, to insist that the borrower immediately pay off his loan or substitute new collateral and then dispose of the treasures as speedily as possible. Farley, however, was skeptical. He knew that under the National Stolen Property Act it is a crime knowingly to accept stolen property as security for a loan. Consequently, he consulted with Powers, and Powers was emphatic. "Don't return the objects to the borrower until the dispute is resolved," Powers said. He explained to Farley that under the circumstances the bank could subject itself to civil and perhaps even criminal penalties if it returned contested property to one claimant when it really belonged to another. Accordingly, the bank should advise its customer that it had impounded the property and would hold it until the claim brought by Willi had been cleared up.

When Willi told me this news, I let go with a whoop of my own. At last we understood the reason why the treasures had not been rushed off to Switzerland the day after Willi visited the Whitewright bank, or the day after I spoke on the telephone to Jack Meador and Don Cook. The treasures were tied up in a loan agreement with the bank, and the bank now believed itself compelled by law not to release them.

"What a bunch of lucky stiffs we are!" I exclaimed to Willi. And lucky was the word—but only for the time being, for in a short while news from Europe would shatter our confidence.

Meanwhile, when I told Willi I wanted to include in my story his discovery that the treasures were being held as collateral, he balked. "We promised Powers we wouldn't talk to the press," he said, "and if you put that in the newspaper he'll know that it had to have come from us."

That was a problem. I was torn between my friendship with Willi and my professional obligation to tell everything pertinent to the case that I knew. It began to dawn on both Willi and myself that although we had been working closely together on the case for nine months our separate interests were now coming into conflict. Luckily, I found a way out of the dilemma, so that I was able to tell the full story in print without embarrassment to Willi. I knew that Willi was giving regular reports about the progress of the investigation to Klaus Maurice at the Cultural Foundation of the States in West Berlin. Furthermore, Maurice had always spoken to me quite openly. I figured Willi probably had told Maurice about the collateral arrangement, and therefore I might be able to worm it out of Maurice and use *him* as my source.

When I got Maurice on the phone, I asked if it was true that the treasures were being held by the bank in White-wright.

"Yes," he responded cheerfully. "They can't release them because they are being used as collateral for a loan."

"You don't *mean* it!" I exclaimed.

"Oh, yes," he said. "It was rather careless of them, wouldn't you say?"

I thanked Maurice profusely for this information and promptly called Willi, declaiming in my best Erich von Stroheim accent: "I have just been informed by a top cultural official in West Berlin that the First National Bank of Whitewright carelessly accepted the Quedlinburg treasures as collateral for a loan!"

We had a good laugh.

I told Willi I planned to attribute this information to "a participant in the purchase of the Samuhel Gospel." That would remove Willi from suspicion and protect Maurice. Willi said that would be fine. No problem, except that, of course, we both knew Powers would be—as they used to say in this part of the country—fit to be tied.

I then turned to a different aspect of the story, one that again brought me into conflict with Willi and Tom; this time, the matter could not be resolved so painlessly.

Near the top of the rough draft of my story, I had indicated my intention to insert a paragraph or two telling the reader how important the Quedlinburg treasures are and roughly what they are worth. It wasn't being crass about these objects of astonishing beauty and historical richness to think that *Times* readers ought to know whether they are valued at, say, two hundred thousand dollars—or two hundred million dollars. Were they merely good-quality medieval artworks or world-class treasures?

I called Frau Professor Doktor Florentina Mütherich in Munich. A former deputy director of the Institute for Art History in Munich, she is widely recognized as the world's leading authority on European medieval manuscripts. Mütherich is along in years, and when I reached her in Munich she told me that she recalled having seen the Samuhel Gospel on a visit to Quedlinburg in 1935, when she was a child. When I asked about the value of the treasures, she whistled. She said that when taken as a whole the treasures were of such artistic and historical importance, their loss could fairly be described as "one of the world's greatest art thefts, surpassed only by the plundering of Egypt in the nineteenth century."

Next, I called Richard Camber, a London specialist in medieval art. He told me the treasures are "rare beyond belief" and said it was impossible to determine their value, as no such objects had ever been offered for sale on the art market. He added, with a poetic touch: "In the Middle Ages, these objects could transport you to another world. They flashed across the night sky like shooting stars."

I also called Dietrich Kötzsche, a leading expert in medieval decorative art at the State Museum in West Berlin. He said that several of the Quedlinburg treasures were each worth individually "perhaps more than a van Gogh painting." The last two van Goghs to be sold at auction had fetched $54 million in one case and $82 million in another. This meant the Quedlinburg treasures could be worth upwards of $200 million!

When I told Willi what I'd learned, he begged me not to specify the value of the treasures in my story. "We're in the middle of negotiations with Torigian, and he's a tough son of a bitch," Willi said. "Let's not let him know the value of what he's got."

I told Willi I couldn't withhold information for the benefit of one party or another. I was obliged to tell the story impartially.

Willi grumbled. I think he asked Tom also to try to persuade me to withhold the value of the treasures because later that day Tom called with the same plea. I told him I regretted that I couldn't oblige. Both Willi and Tom understood. But it stung.

It didn't help our strained relationship that all week long Willi kept pestering me for the name of the thief, and I kept putting him off. I felt uncomfortable being cast in the same role as Roland Folter, the man who knew but wouldn't tell. But it couldn't be helped. Fond as I was of Willi and Tom, it was becoming more clear every day that each of us had different loyalties. If I told them Joe Tom Meador's name, Willi or Tom might find themselves shooting the breeze with another newspaper reporter and let it slip out, or they might put the information in a court document which could become public. No, the *Times* had invested too much time and money in having me discover the name of the Quedlinburg thief for me to risk losing an exclusive.

At one point, Willi read me a long list of names, asking: "Just tell me if I'm getting warm."

There was no Meador on his list. "No luck," I said, feeling like a traitor.

Later, when I asked Willi and Tom questions about the progress of their negotiations in Texas, they excused themselves and said their dealings with Powers and Torigian were confidential. Now it was my turn to feel left out.

On Tuesday, June 12, shortly after submitting my draft to Marv Siegel, I trudged over to the New York Public Library at 42nd Street. I happened to know that the library has an unusually good collection of military unit histories from World War II, and I thought I might learn something of interest about the unit in which Meador served.

I was in luck. I found a marvelously detailed scrapbook-size history of the Eighty-seventh Armored Field Artillery Battalion. Its disintegrating red leatherette cover was emblazoned with a fierce-looking rattlesnake springing forward from a puff of smoke. The book contained a diary of the unit, beginning with its Normandy landing on D-Day Plus One and continuing to the occupation of Quedlinburg shortly before the surrender of Germany. Forty-five battle maps in the back listed the names of the Forward Observers in each action, and I saw Meador's name repeatedly. It was evident that he had seen his share of fighting, and I decided that in fairness I would add something about that to my article, as a finishing touch.

The story, which ran to nearly 3,000 words, rolled on the night of Wednesday, June 13. It appeared on the front page of the *Times*, illustrated with a photograph of Whitewright that captured the town's desolation. The jump of the story occupied most of an inside page and included the picture of Joe Tom Meador in his greenhouse that had appeared in the Whitewright *Sun*, a picture of the reliquary casket, and maps locating both Quedlinburg and Whitewright. I was particularly delighted to hear from Bob Berkvist, a longtime friend at the *Times* who worked on copyediting the story, that when he submitted it to our legal department to assess the danger of libel, the reply came back: "No problem. The writer has nailed the suspect sixteen different ways."

I reached Willi in Tom Kline's office at about 6 P.M. "The story is running in tomorrow's paper," I said, "and I want you to be the first to know the name of the thief."

"Yeah?" said Willi almost apprehensively, as if uncertain that he was ready for this heady moment.

When I pronounced the name Joe Tom Meador, I could hear Willi inhale sharply. He insisted that I spell the name. Then, obsessively, he checked the spelling with me—not once but twice, as if savoring a rare liquor. Later, I faxed Willi and Tom a copy of Meador's death certificate and other documents that might prove useful.

After closing the story, I caught a late train home, kissed my sleeping children, dozed a couple of hours and was back at La Guardia in time to board the 7 A.M. flight to Dallas/Fort Worth. As soon as I landed, I called Marv at the *Times* to discuss what sort of follow-up story I would file from Whitewright. He said: "Hold on. I've got someone here who wants to speak to you."

It was Max Frankel, the executive editor of the *Times*. He had just stopped by Marv's desk to congratulate him on the story. "I want you to know," Max told me mischievously, "that Marv and Bob Berkvist are here taking all the credit for what you've written." Then he congratulated me. I have to admit it felt pretty good.

And then Max, being Max, added a few words of caution: "When you get back to Whitewright," he said, "you're going to find TV crews parading up and down the street and reporters everywhere. Just remember that we report the news; we don't want to become part of it."

He was exactly right. The New York *Times* circulation in north Texas is negligible, but the mass-circulation Dallas *Morning News* is a subscriber to the Times News Service and had fronted my complete story. That alerted the local newspapers and television news shows, so that when I got to Whitewright, Grand Street was thronged as it hadn't been since the last days of the cotton boom. I spotted TV camera crews from CBS, ABC, World News Tonight, the Cable News Network, local channels 4 and 8, and a score of newspaper and magazine reporters including a crew of four from *People* magazine. Then someone discovered who I was, and the cameras all swung my way. I covered my face, like a newly arrested drug dealer.

It was better to be dodging cameras than imaginary shotgun blasts, let me tell you. For the first time, I was in Texas without feeling like a secret agent slinking around behind enemy lines, fearful that at any moment I might get myself zapped. Now that the media at large had picked up the story, now that there were cameras and reporters everywhere, it was Jack Meador, Don Cook, and their accomplices who had to hide. I had the bums on the run.

I recognized a number of townspeople on the street. They had left their homes to watch the reporters who were watching them. Several were indignant about the invasion. A middle-aged man with a fiery red face who refused to give me his name declared that the publicity was bound to attract "unde-sireables" and lead to a spate of burglaries. Several other residents had managed to get a copy of the *Times,* and they expressed their displeasure with the picture of Whitewright carried by the newspaper on our front page. They said it made Whitewright look like a hick town.

"Why couldn't you have taken a picture of the Methodist Church?" one woman asked me with reproach in her voice.

A day or two later, the Denison *Herald,* the daily newspaper published in the town just north of Whitewright, would describe the revelations about Joe Tom Meador as "earth-shattering." The people of Whitewright, the newspaper reported, were "stunned as if they were being pelted with bullets."

Well, maybe so, but at least a few locals took a light-hearted view of the uproar. Jim Bryant, a neighbor of Jack Meador's and a veteran of the war in Europe, remarked with a chuckle: "Gol' darn! Now I'm a-gonna have to send that French girl's garters back!"

Someone pointed out Clarence Tillett, the mayor of Whitewright, who was standing outside the municipal building watching the cars loaded with curiosity-seekers prowling down Grand Street. A heavyweight, bald, cheerful gentleman in his middle sixties, he wore a puckish smile. I introduced myself.

"I never seen so many out-of-state license plates in all my days," he said. "That's the third one today from Colorado."

Tillett invited me into his office.

"The last time we had something like this was the machine-gun deal," he said with a grin. He explained that in 1981 the press discovered that a local judge had sent off to a mail-order gun dealer for four machine guns with silencers. In Texas there is nothing wrong with that, except that the judge placed the order in the name of the town of Whitewright to avoid paying the sales tax.

"He was a friend of mine," Tillett said, "but I had to ask him to step down as judge."

Tillett went on to tell me that he had been an infantryman in World War II, and that after a battle he frequently picked up souvenirs and mailed them home. "I still have four German bayonets and an ornamental German sword," he said. "Of course, I'm not justifying what they say Joe Tom Meador took. That's a little different."

Together, we returned to Grand Street. Police Chief Larry Kenealy, a tall, fleshy-faced man in his thirties, trotted up to us, his six-shooter bobbing on his hip. "I just got another call from a TV network," he said breathlessly. "They want hotel accommodations for eighteen and a satellite hookup. I told 'em, 'Shoot, this town don't even have a *stoplight!*' "

We chuckled over that.

"You know, Mayor," Kenealy went on, "with all of this extra traffic, I'm puttin' in for a raise."

Tillett was not amused.

By calling from the town's one public telephone, I had a brief conversation with Willi back in Washington. He said he and Tom were preparing to fly to Dallas in the morning. He was in a buoyant mood. With the treasures impounded by the Whitewright bank, and international media now focused on the treasures, it seemed as though he and Tom would have all the time they needed to continue negotiating with Powers and Torigian. I made that assumption, too—prematurely, as it turned out.

I next called the *Times* and dictated my second-day story, as a follow-up is known in the trade. I started by explaining that two Washington-based lawyers (Willi and Tom) who represented the Lutheran church in Quedlinburg were flying to Dallas to negotiate with lawyers for the bank and the heirs of Joe Tom Meador in an effort to recover the treasures. I then described the carnival atmosphere in Whitewright, quoting Mayor Tillett and several other townspeople.

Then I went back to the Inn of Sherman and slept for twelve hours.

Friday morning I was on the telephone again, trying to find out which federal or state agencies might be taking an interest in the case. From the moment I had found Jane's sworn statement in the probate court records in Sherman declaring that the accounting of her late brother's property was "a true and complete inventory," I'd felt sure she was in for trouble. I called the Internal Revenue Service, thinking that at the very least Uncle Sam might have sniffed the possibility of an unpaid estate tax. I got the usual federal-agency runaround, but was finally referred to a public-affairs officer named Marlene Gaysek, who told me cryptically, "We cannot confirm or deny that an investigation is under way, but I can say that our office *does* read the newspaper, and we know our job is to assure that the tax laws are being complied with."

My translation: Don't you worry none. We'll get 'em. And, in the long run, I was right.

Mike Krenek, a special agent in charge of the Dallas division of the FBI told me his agency was conducting "a preliminary inquiry" into the matter. The U.S. Attorney for the Eastern District of Texas, the local Attorney for Grayson County, and Whitewright Police Chief Kenealy all told me they had opened files on the case as well, although they would not discuss exactly what they were doing. I could not imagine then—nor could the Meadors or Torigian—how long it would take before law-enforcement officials would bring the case to trial.

Ely Maurer, a U.S. State Department lawyer who specializes in cultural property, gave me some interesting perspective on the case. He said there were two possibilities for criminal prosecution. The first was that someone may have violated the National Stolen Property Act by transporting the treasures across state or international borders. The second was that

Texas law regarding the possession of stolen property may have been violated.

He likened the case to one in 1982 when it was found that two Albrecht Dürer portraits were stolen in Germany by an American soldier at the end of World War II. A United States Court of Appeals ruled that it did not matter that Edward I. Elicofon, a Brooklyn lawyer who bought the paintings from the American soldier for less than $500 in 1946, was unaware that they had been stolen. It was sufficient that the lawyers for East Germany proved that the loss had occurred and, therefore, the artworks had to be returned to their rightful owner. As for Elicofon, he had broken no law; he just made a bad investment.

At about noon, I drove to Whitewright. The people I met seemed a good deal more relaxed than the day before. I saw a few local cars sporting a wry bumper sticker that read "WHITEWRIGHT, TEXAS: GERMANY'S SAFE DEPOSIT BOX." They had been printed in great haste by Chris Jenkinson, the son of a Whitewright policemen. "I just wanted to give the people of Whitewright something they could chuckle at," Jenkinson told me, when I called him in his studio in Dallas.

After lunch at the Cafe Reo, Whitewright's only restaurant, I strolled around town. It was a quiet, languid afternoon. Something possessed me to stop at the town's only public telephone, and, on a whim, I called Klaus Maurice in West Berlin. I hadn't spoken to him since the story broke, and I wondered what his reaction would be. He was at home.

"Have you heard the news?" he exclaimed.

"I'm not sure what you mean."

"I thought that's why you were calling," he said. "Just today, I spoke to a German dealer who has found the second Quedlinburg manuscript! He offered it to me for a very small finder's fee. It's wonderful news!"

I was dumbfounded. I'd been assuming the second manuscript was one of the treasures impounded by the White-wright bank, but now it looked as if Torigian was still able to sneak them out of the country.

Maurice explained that Heribert Tenschert, the Bavarian dealer who had sold the Samuhel Gospel to him for $3 million back in April, had just informed him that he'd acquired the second of the two missing Quedlinburg manuscripts—this one dated 1513—and was willing to sell it for a $500,000 finder's fee. Maurice said he planned to discuss the offer with his trustees in the morning, but felt certain the money would be found.

He added that since the manuscript was then in Switzerland, it was protected by Swiss law and could not be forcibly returned to West or East Germany by legal procedures. "We have no alternative but to pay for it," he said.

I called Tenschert and found him at a hotel in Zurich, where he'd gone on a business trip. He was in high spirits, and told me in an unctuous voice about learning a short while before of the availability of the 1513 Evangelistar, as the second Quedlinburg manuscript is known. He had purchased it immediately, but he refused to give me the name of the seller.

Tenschert said he had offered the manuscript to Maurice for a fraction of what he could get for it on the open market. "I'm receiving only another very modest finder's fee," he insisted.

The whole thing stank to high heaven. I immediately called Marv at the *Times*. "This is for page one," I said. "Another Quedlinburg manuscript just surfaced on the art market in Zurich!"

Chapter 12

UNAWARE OF THE NEWS FROM EUROPE, Willi and Tom believed they were close to striking a deal with Powers and Torigian for the speedy return of the treasures. They had established themselves in the baronial Adolphus Hotel in downtown Dallas; a series of meetings took place in the hotel lobby, during which the wording of an agreement was refined until it seemed acceptable to everyone concerned. Then, Willi, Tom, and Timothy Powers initialed the agreement in preparation for having their clients sign it. Torigian, the Houston lawyer who had sold the Samuhel Gospel in Germany and was now representing the Meador family, gave his O.K. to Powers over the telephone. Buoyantly, Tom summoned an armored car and two photographers.

The armored car was to collect the treasures from the Whitewright bank and then pick up any other medieval knickknacks that might have found their way into the homes of Jack and Jane. The car would deliver the treasures to the warehouse of a moving company called the Fine Arts Express in Fort Worth—Dallas's sister city—where the photographers could take pictures of the treasures for proper identification. The treasures would then be stored in a vault for safe-keeping.

At that point, the settlement was to proceed in two stages. First, Willi and Tom would be permitted to inspect the treasures in a secure room provided by the Fine Arts Express. Apart from that, the objects would not be "moved, transferred, altered, or destroyed during the pendency of any negotiations." Second, as soon as the precise terms of a final settlement were agreed upon, Jack and Jane would release the treasures to Willi, who would return them to Germany. In exchange, the Meadors would be "compensated" by means of a finder's fee or a reward in an amount to be determined on the basis of the number and condition of the items returned.

The agreement on inspection and photographing was made possible because it now seemed in everyone's interest to be sure that the objects in the bank vault were, in fact, the Quedlinburg treasures.

Jack and Jane wanted the treasures authenticated because they hoped to be paid handsomely for surrendering them. Jack, as I had long suspected, was desperate for money. It didn't take a Harvard Business School graduate to figure out why. I'd learned that the Meadors had lost the International Harvester franchise for selling tractors and other mechanized farm equipment back in the 1950s, and I'd seen for myself the ramshackle junk shop that the family's hardware store had become.

I got the lowdown on Jack's financial situation from a director of the bank who was willing to talk on condition of anonymity. Meeting me at a restaurant in Sherman, the director explained that back in January, Jack, whose name still appears with the other bank directors engraved on a marble tablet on the bank's facade, had fallen seriously into debt. As a result, he was asked to resign as a member of the bank's board of directors.

Because of Jack's deepening financial troubles, the director said, the bank asked him in February to provide additional collateral to cover his loan. He offered some of the Quedlinburg treasures and the bank foolishly accepted them.

Powers had a similar reason for wanting the treasures authenticated. It was only by establishing the artworks as what we all hoped them to be that Jack Meador could be paid for returning his share, and thus be able to pay off his loan from Powers's client, the Whitewright bank.

Torigian's motive for going along with the inspection and photographing was pretty obvious, too. By cooperating with Willi and Tom, who he took to be official agents of the West German Government, Torigian thought he might be able to sell more of Joe Tom's treasures directly through them and thus avoid paying a commission to a couple of middlemen, as he had been obliged to do in the sale of the Samuhel Gospel.

With the agreement now as good as signed, the lawyers at the Adolphus broke for dinner. All was in readiness to commence the inspection and photographing, but when they returned to the hotel lobby about an hour later, Powers had a long face. "We can't proceed," he said.

At this precise moment, I walked into the lobby of the Adolphus Hotel. Naturally, I had no idea of what was taking place. All I knew was that Willi and Tom had chosen the best hotel in Dallas and that their negotiations with Powers and Torigian were probably under way. Because I hadn't heard from either Willi or Tom since their arrival in Texas, I'd decided to drop in on them unannounced.

Prowling through the softly glowing antique furnishings, Flemish tapestries, and elegant vases of fragrant, fresh-cut flowers, I spotted Tom seated on a plush settee beside a man I didn't recognize. I didn't see Willi, I later learned, because he was then seated in a chair with his back to the entrance.

When Tom saw me, his boyish face twisted into a look of anguish. He sprang to his feet, walked briskly over to me, and took me firmly by the arm.

"You gotta come with me," he said in an urgent whisper. "The negotiations are at a critical point right now. We promised each other we would absolutely not talk to the press. If the other side realizes I'm talking to the guy from the *Times*, it'll kill the deal. Please understand. You gotta leave." He escorted me to the nearest exit.

When we reached the sidewalk, Tom began backing into the hotel. I was so taken by surprise that I only managed to stammer, "Well—good luck, Tom." Then he was gone. It suddenly came over me that I hadn't mentioned the news that would appear on the front page of the *Times* the next morning. He would certainly be interested to learn that another one of the treasures had found its way to Europe. But what could I do? After what he'd just told me, I couldn't barge into the lobby a second time.

In retrospect, I realize that had I been able to tell Tom that the 1513 Evangelistar had surfaced in Zurich it would have brought the negotiations in the Adolphus to a screeching halt—even faster than if I'd been identified in the lobby as the guy from the *Times*. But we were ships passing in the night. I didn't know what Willi and Tom knew, and they didn't know what I knew.

When Tom returned to the settee where he had been conversing with Powers, I was told later, he explained that I was just an old friend he had to say hello to. Powers shrugged that aside and then gloomily explained that Torigian was now totally opposed to the settlement, and had said he would not abide by it since he had not signed the document. Powers said he felt double-crossed, as Torigian had approved the agreement every step of the way. Powers couldn't understand what had come over him.

It later developed that during the dinner break Torigian had learned from one of his collaborators in Switzerland what I had discovered an hour or two earlier by calling Maurice; namely, that the 1513 Evangelistar—which Torigian had

American soldiers guarding the cave outside Quedlinburg in 1945.
(Courtesy of William Grembowicz)

Bypassed by the railroads, Quedlinburg never lost its medieval character.

Quedlinburg was Heinrich Himmler's Camelot. *Above,* the Nazi chief drops in on the city in 1938.

"We could level a small city in three or four minutes," said a member of the 87th. The teeth of the unit were these 105 mm self-propelled howitzers, *above. Below,* the 87th advances into Germany.

Joe Tom Meador in Paris in 1944. *Below,* Meador is at left in a hastily improvised fire-control center somewhere in Germany. *(U.S. Army Photo)*

Owen Hunsaker, *left,* was both Joe Tom's conscience and lover.

Dede Matthews, *below*, shown here at his wedding reception, advised Meador, *at left,* he was right to keep the treasures. *(Courtesy of Dede Matthews)*

Karl Kulikowski, who witnessed Meador's strange behavior in combat. *(Courtesy of Carole Kulikowski)*

The author at Whitewright, Texas.

Consumed by cancer, Joe Tom, *above*, wore a wig and was openly gay at an Army reunion in 1979. *Right*, Meador at his hideaway in Dallas surrounded by artworks. *(Courtesy of Gordon Young)*

A true esthete, Joe Tom wore a silk shirt while working in his greenhouse. *(The Denison, Texas, Herald)*

American soldiers around the world were vilified after Meador was exposed as the Quedlinburg thief. *Above*, a cartoon by Fiona MacVicar in the London *Economist* in 1990.

Heinrich and Otto being repatriated to Texas by Daniel Honan.

Willi Korte, *right*, having what he called "one of the most intense experiences of my life." (*Barry Shlachter*)

Tom Kline

John Torigian (*Mark Graham*)

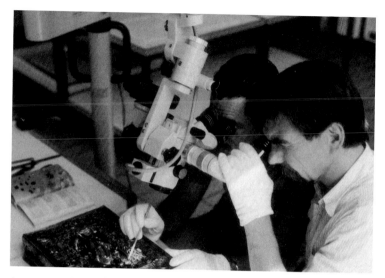

Art experts in Berlin conserving the 9th-century Samuhel Gospel.

The 1513 Evangelistar in a seat by itself flies home after Texas exhibition. *At left*, Gosslau; *right*, Kötzsche.

Klaus Maurice, after paying $3 million for the Samuhel Gospel.

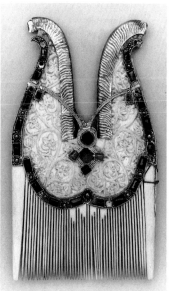

Two reliquaries, a liturgical comb and an illustration from the
Samuhel Gospel. *(Dallas Museum of Art)*

Jane Meador Cook with her attorney leaving Federal court after her arraignment in 1996. Jack Meador, also just arraigned, is behind. *(Mark Graham)*

Today, the cave outside Quedlinburg is largely filled in and forgotten.

placed with a Swiss middleman back in March, at the same time that he'd delivered the Samuhel Gospel—was about to be sold to the German government by Tenschert for $500,000.

For Torigian, the consummation of a second sale changed everything. After four years of lugging the two manuscripts around the United States and Europe, at last they were selling. So why strike a deal with Willi Korte and Tom Kline? he must have asked himself. Maybe now that the market is loosening up, there may be better deals to be had in Europe.

Torigian also had reason to believe that if he backed out of the agreement with Willi and Tom he might be able to move the remaining treasures—the reliquaries, the casket, the ritual comb and so forth—for sale outside of the United States. He knew that after Jack and Jane had given him the two manuscripts to sell, they had divided the remainder of their brother's loot between themselves, and while Jack used his share to secure a loan Jane had put hers into two safe deposit boxes in her bank in Dallas. Now that the market had improved, Torigian thought he might take Jane's share to Europe immediately. Later, he may have thought, he could relieve the Whitewright bank of Jack's share, since the bank might well prefer hard cash to a collection of medieval artworks it did not know how to dispose of.

Willi and Tom, naturally, knew nothing of these arrangements. All they knew was that their deal had fallen out of bed, and that they would have to find some other means of preventing Torigian from taking the remaining treasures out of the country. Glumly, they bid good night to Powers, strolled over to the darkly gleaming, glass-sheathed Thanksgiving Tower, and went up to the offices of Andrews & Kurth on the forty-fourth floor. There they began preparing to file a lawsuit Monday morning.

Paradoxically, Willi was actually relieved that the deal with Torigian had not been consummated. "If we had settled the case right then," he later explained, "Torigian would have asked for money, and that was one of a number of commodities I did not possess."

He was referring to the fact that he had just received some rather devastating news from West Berlin. His German sponsor, the Foundation for Prussian Cultural Heritage, had suddenly withdrawn its support for the effort to recover the treasures. This decision had nothing to do with the way the case was being handled: the Quedlinburg treasures had become caught up in the final convulsions of the cold war.

Quedlinburg was after all in East Germany, whereas Willi's sponsor was based in West Berlin. Although the movement toward reunification of the two Germanys had gained strong popular support after the breaching of the Berlin Wall the previous November, the governments of East and West Germany were still intensely hostile to each other, and bureaucrats in both nations were paralyzed by uncertainty. The directors of the Foundation for Prussian Cultural Heritage were no exception. Not knowing what lay ahead, they backed off from Willi and Tom with the excuse that it would be a violation of their charter to help another nation reclaim its cultural property.

Moreover, a number of higher-ups in Willi's home office refused to believe his excited reports as we closed in on the quarry. After the passage of so many years, they said, the Quedlinburg treasures were certainly gone for good. Willi had doubtless stumbled on the trail of some minor decorations of no more value than a collection of old Christmas tree ornaments, they said. Willi later referred to the skeptics in West Berlin as "the Christmas-tree faction."

Finally, the doubters asked, who is Willi Korte? After five years of investigative work in the United States, his biggest score had been finding several silver place settings bearing the initials of Eva Braun, Hitler's mistress. Crown jewels they were not. In fact, Fräulein Braun's flatware was decidedly unwelcome back in West Germany. The stuff was of no great value, only an embarrassing reminder of a past the Germans were energetically trying to put behind them.

Withdrawal of support from the Foundation for Prussian Cultural Heritage meant that, financially speaking, Willi didn't know where his next meal was coming from. Tom and his distinguished law firm were now engaged in a charitable enterprise, whether they realized it or not. While Willi and Tom did have a letter of authorization from the four-hundred-member church in Quedlinburg (which, of course, had no cash reserves whatever), they had no commitment from any person or governmental agency capable of paying their expenses. Willi was ready to tear his hair out in exasperation, but for the time being kept this news from Tom—and of course from me.

Over breakfast the following morning, they got the next piece of bad news when they read the front-page story in the *Times* reporting that the second manuscript had surfaced in Zurich. They were stunned. Like me, they had mistakenly assumed that the Evangelistar was one of the treasures being held by the bank in Whitewright as collateral for Jack's loan. Its appearance in Europe indicated that somehow Torigian had actually found a way around the impounding action taken by the bank.

"When we read your article," Willi later told me, "we realized that the agreement with Powers and Torigian would have meant nothing even if everyone had signed it. We now had evidence of foul play. We assumed that many if not most of the treasures were already in Europe waiting to be sold, and there was no alternative but to prepare a lawsuit to stop the movement of whatever treasures might still be left in Texas."

He also told me much later that he had felt a terrible emptiness in the pit of his stomach at this time. On the one hand, he explained, he and Tom were attempting to prepare a lawsuit on the basis of extremely slender evidence. "We still had not seen what the bank was holding," he said, "and consequently had no assurance that what we were looking for was actually there."

On the other hand, he went on to say, he was agonized by the fact that he had been less than forthright with Andrews & Kurth about precisely who back in the Fatherland was going to foot the bill for all their high-priced legal service. "When we decided to go for the lawsuit," he told me with a nervous laugh, "I knew that it was a $150,000 decision, and I wondered who in hell was going to pay that bill!"

But that was only the half of it. The church in Quedlinburg had authorized Willi and Tom to represent it in negotiations with the Meador family, but had said nothing about a lawsuit. If Willi and Tom appeared in court the next morning and Torigian learned from one of his contacts in Europe of the unwillingness of the church to become involved in a lawsuit, he could get them thrown out on their ears by arguing that they represented no one but themselves.

Consequently, as Tom Kline, with the help of his colleagues Alan Harris and Steve Rahhal, worked out their argument for a temporary restraining order and the other legal maneuvers they would attempt Monday morning, Willi called the East German Embassy in Washington. There, a sleepy clerk was able to find the telephone number of the Quedlinburg church. It was nearly midnight in Germany, but Willi put through a call and, by a stroke of luck, reached Friedemann Gosslau, the pastor of the church with whom he had corresponded, and who had written the letter of authorization he and Tom were using as their commission. Willi introduced himself and explained that he was in Texas preparing to take legal steps to recover the treasures from a group of Americans who, he believed, had acquired them illegally. "If we don't take these people to court now," he said he told Gosslau, "we will lose the treasures forever. Do I have your permission to file a lawsuit?" The whole case now hung in the balance.

Gosslau is a good-hearted man, but then close to retirement and long ago reduced to penury by the East German Communist regime. He hemmed and hawed. Finally, Willi said, Gosslau declared that Willi should do as he thought best. "Just remember," he cautioned, "the church has no money and cannot pay legal expenses."

Having been shown the door at the Adolphus, I started driving back to my motel in Sherman, wondering what to do next. I'd interviewed just about everyone I could think of. Everybody except . . .

I pulled off the road sharply, parked, and dug into my briefcase for a road map.

I knew that if I tried to telephone Jack or Don Cook again, they would simply hang up as they had when I called them before my story appeared. But now it occurred to me that I might be able to approach them in a different way. It's easier to hang up the telephone on an unwanted caller than to get rid of someone who presents himself on your doorstep. Also, I imagined that if I showed my face to one of the Meadors, some curiosity might—just might—be aroused as to who I was, how I had discovered that Joe Tom Meador was the Quedlinburg thief, and whether I knew any details of the case that hadn't appeared in the newspaper. That could lead to a conversation and—who knows? It was worth a try.

Even if they said nothing to me, or nothing of consequence, I might be able to get a sense of the Meadors as people. Perhaps I could learn something from meeting their spouses, or children, or by seeing the kind of houses they live in, the cars in the driveway, their clothes, manners, or speech.

Sometimes, of course, this trenchcoat bravado, this urge to confront one's subject in the flesh, can be risky. I had, after all, caused these people considerable pain. And this was rural Texas, not Park Avenue. I had not forgotten Jack's welcoming committee in Whitewright and Sherman.

After studying the road map, I drove to Mesquite, just a

few miles outside the Dallas city line. Riggs Circle, where the Cooks live, according to the telephone directory, wasn't hard to find. The house was a modern, one-story yellow brick structure with a well-manicured lawn. A Mexican laborer working on the shrubs greeted me with a toothy grin as I approached the front door. I rang the bell, and a slight blond woman in her late fifties answered the door. This had to be Jane. I pronounced my name carefully and then paused, hoping that it would register with her. Then I said I had come to see her mainly to show that I didn't have horns. Also, I said, I hoped she might be willing to tell me about her late brother. Until now, I said, the people who were willing to talk about him had told me mostly negative things. I was sure, I continued, there was much to be said in his favor. She could help me resurrect that side of her brother.

"We will call you when we have a statement to make," she said coolly, doubtless echoing Torigian's instructions. But she didn't slam the door.

I kept talking. She continued to listen. I said I felt sure she cared about the Meador family name and would like to have it well thought of. I could help her in that way, I said, if she would tell me something positive about the Meadors. I said I had taken particular care to mention her brother's commendable military record in order to present a balanced picture of him, and that I expected to write more about Joe Tom in the future and had come to see her in order to hear the family's side of the story.

At this, Jane opened the screen door between us. She didn't invite me in, but only wanted to get a better look at me. I noticed her focus on my tie, quite an ordinary one, with regimental stripes. I kept talking as fast as I could.

Finally she said, "Well, there's just one thing I will say. I didn't like the picture of Whitewright on the front page of the New York *Times*. It didn't represent the town we know and love."

"Some people don't like their reflection in the mirror," I said, hoping to spark a reply.

"That's *not* our reflection," she shot back. "We don't *like* the way you pictured us."

That was it! Those last words out of her mouth were delivered in a simpering whine that sounded exactly the way John Carroll Collins had imitated her voice when she said, "What if we don't *want* to give the treasures back?"

Just then, a sturdily built young man appeared beside her, casting me a challenging look. "Is this man bothering you, Mom?" he said.

"I can handle this," she replied.

The interview was over. I thanked her for seeing me and returned to my car. I'd learned nothing of substance, of course, but had been given a good chance to size her up. She and her home were the picture of comfortable upper-middle-class American living. She wore an expensive dress and lived in a modern house with a well-tended lawn. There seemed to be plenty of money available. She was hardly a typical thief. Just greedy. Greedy and dumb.

I'd also confirmed my suspicion that the Meadors would be curious about this Yankee journalist. That was all to the good. She had studied me. I would exploit that curiosity again the next day to get a second and much more revealing look at a member of the Meador family.

The next Saturday began in Whitewright with a parade down Grand Street, this time with no TV cameras present. The date was June 19, or "Juneteenth" as it is known to the black people of the region who celebrate the abolition of slavery in Texas on this day. Lincoln signed the Emancipation Proclamation on January 1, 1863, which is the date honored in most states, but here in Texas it is the day a steamer arrived in Galveston, bearing an official copy of the document, that is celebrated.

After the parade, several hundred black residents of Whitewright gathered for a picnic in the local park, as was the custom. Bill Goodson, the lone black member of the Whitewright City Council, told me that Joe Tom Meador was the main topic of conversation at the picnic. "We've got four hundred to five hundred people here today—many more than usual," he said. "A number of people told me they came to our celebration instead of the one in the town where they live because they heard Dan Rather talking about Whitewright on TV."

Goodson then suggested that I might be able to learn something about Meador by visiting Whiterock, a black community a few miles away. When I got there, he said, I should ask around for a man who goes by the name of Skunk. He had worked as a handyman for Meador, Inc., and knew Joe Tom well.

Whiterock, I discovered, is a small village without benefit of paved roads and a good many other of the amenities supposedly enjoyed by all Americans. The small houses were neat and clean, almost toylike, and every yard seemed to contain a vegetable garden. TV antennas sprouted from every roof, of course—poised to snatch Dan Rather out of the ether whether or not he was talking about Whitewright.

Skunk was home watching TV when I drove up to his house. A muscular man wearing a sleeveless undershirt, he cordially invited me in. I told him my name and asked for his. He said his name is Eddie Johnson, "but everybody calls me Skunk."

When I asked about the Meadors, he said that his first wife, now deceased, had worked as a cleaning woman for Mrs. Maybelle Meador at her home on West Bond Street. Mrs. Meador had been a kind mistress, Skunk said, giving his wife cast-off clothing and never forgetting her on Christmas.

As for Joe Tom, Skunk said he first met him when working

part-time in the family's hardware store and grew to know him better when he served as Joe Tom's chauffeur after he became ill. "He was a good man," Skunk said. "He used to call me Babe. He had a nice apartment in Dallas—an apartment with two stories like a house. It had a bedroom, a large livingroom, and a very nice kitchen. I used to carry him there for the weekend. Then, on Sunday or Monday, I'd carry him back to Whitewright. He had a lot of friends in Dallas, cityfolk, not like the people in Whitewright."

"Were they mostly young men?" I asked.

"Yes, suh. Mostly young men."

"Were they gay? You know what I mean? Homosexual?"

"Oh, I couldn't say," he replied.

I asked Skunk if he had ever seen Joe Tom's old books bound in covers of gold, silver, and jewels.

He stared at me and breathed the words, "Maybe so . . . maybe so."

"About this big," I said, indicating that they were much larger than most modern books. "And with real gold covers."

"Was it gold?" he said. "I thought them things was brass."

"No," I said. "They were real gold and real silver."

"Well, suh," he said. "He had something like that always wrapped up in a blanket. When I carried him to Dallas, I used to have to take it up the stairs for him. Sometimes the blanket slipped off and I could see a corner of what was inside."

Skunk shook his head and mumbled under his breath, "I thought it was brass . . . always thought it was brass."

"The black people of Whiterock picked a good spot to build their community," I said as I got up to leave. "It seems cooler here than in Whitewright." Skunk laughed. "Yes, suh!" he said, savoring the victory.

Skunk was the second witness to have observed Joe Tom in possession of the Quedlinburg treasures, or at least what looked like one of them. He also confirmed my suspicion that Meador led an active gay life in Dallas. Evidently he was able to cut loose from his domineering mother at least on weekends. And when he went to Dallas, he took the treasures with him. Why was that? I wondered. What could he do with them in Dallas? Wasn't it risky?

Back in Whitewright, and bolder now, I pulled up in front of 307 West Maple Street, Jack Meador's large but seedy-looking colonial-style house. The wooden steps creaked noisily announcing my arrival. There was a handwritten sign taped to the front door reading "No Reporters." I read that with some relief. The sign seemed a whole lot less menacing than the thought of being greeted at the door by a blast from a shotgun. I rang the bell. In a minute, a tall, slender gray-haired woman in her mid-sixties appeared and regarded me skeptically.

"You a reporter?" she said with an air of hostility.

"Yes."

"Didn't you see the sign on the door—No Reporters?"

I started to reply but she interrupted me, and this time spoke almost warmly. "You should direct any questions you have to our lawyer, John Torigian," she said. "I'll spell out his name and phone number."

She eased open the screen door between us and motioned toward the notebook and ballpoint pen in my hand. Reaching around the screen door, I passed them to her. She spelled out the information and handed the pad and pen back to me. Then she stepped halfway out the door to get a better look at her visitor.

All this was encouraging. She hadn't shut the door in my face. She was actually being cooperative. Could it be that this woman was *glad* to have someone to talk to?

I guess the encounter with Jane had given me an extra measure of self-confidence, because now I surprised even myself with my rapid-fire delivery. I was not just any reporter, I said, but the man from the New York *Times* who had broken the story after six or eight months of investigation.

She seemed interested in that, and asked how I had learned that her brother-in-law took the treasures.

That was the sort of opening I'd been hoping for! In a breezy way, I told her the story of my involvement in the case, and then said that while I felt I knew a good deal about Joe Tom Meador I would be glad to know more.

"Such as?" she asked cautiously.

"Well, for example," I said, "I wonder how he got along with his brother, Jack. You must be Jack's wife."

"I am," she answered. "Jack's not home. He'd kill me if he knew I was talking to you." Her eyes nervously scanned the street behind me. "Now what was it you was asking?" she said.

"I was asking about Jack and Joe Tom."

"Well, it wasn't that they were crosswise like a lot of families I know," she said. "Jack and Joe got along, but they never had much in common. Joe Tom never had much in common with anybody in Whitewright.

"He admired Jack for the mechanical things Jack could do," she continued. "Jack was a pilot in the war, you know. And Jack admired Joe Tom for some of the things he could do."

Then she said the sun was in her eyes so I could come in and sit down, but only for a minute. I surely didn't need to be asked twice, so I followed her into a living room crowded with well-worn furniture and seated myself on a couch. We chatted for a while about the deluge of reporters that had descended on Whitewright, and she spoke of her dislike of feeling "hunted."

She was making an effort to show me what regular folks she and her family were. I let her ramble. "Joe Tom was good with the children, I'll say that," she told me. "Once when we were all watching 'Funny Family Moments' on TV, one of our sons, the dentist, said we should have had a TV camera when we had that birthday party for Uncle Joe Tom. We had so many candles on the cake, the cake caught fire. Uncle Joe was really funny that day!"

I tried to respond genially. But then, realizing that our conversation could be cut short at any moment by the arrival of Jack, I decided to get down to business. I asked if she approved of her brother-in-law's having looted the cave outside Quedlinburg.

Her eyes narrowed. "Everybody was doing it," she said in a husky voice. "Did you ever know a soldier who *didn't* bring home some sort of souvenir?"

I said a multimillion-dollar collection of ancient artworks was not my idea of a souvenir.

"He didn't know how much they were worth," she replied sharply.

"That's not true. He taught art here in Texas before he entered the service."

"Still, he didn't know. I can tell you that."

"Monetary value aside," I said, "these are religious objects, aren't they? What do you think of the morality of his stealing religious objects?"

She parried my question with a couple of questions of her own. "Isn't Quedlinburg in East Germany? And isn't East Germany *Communist?*"

I said yes.

"Well," she said. "You can't have religion in a Communist country, so if Joe Tom *hadn't* taken them someone else *would* have."

"I'm not so sure," I said. "Nobody touched any of the treasures your brother-in-law left in the cave. After four years of Soviet occupation and forty years of Communist government, nothing else disappeared. Nothing. How do you explain that?"

She glared at me, and then muttered vengefully, "I don't like Germans. They started two world wars in this century."

This came out mechanically, and I presumed she was mouthing someone else's words, probably Jack's. It made me wonder how I would be received if Jack strolled through the front door. Even if he didn't have organized crime behind him, I'd been warned that he carried a gun. His wife had just said he would kill her if he found her talking to a reporter, and I guessed she was reliably informed about that. Also, I figured Jack would know that if he found me in his home alone with his wife and shot me dead no Texas jury would convict him of murder. There was a 'No Reporters' sign on the front door. That made me an intruder. I decided it was time to make my exit.

Still, I couldn't resist asking one more question: Had she ever seen the treasures, I asked.

"Joe Tom kept them in his office at the store," she said. "He would unwrap them and show them to certain people. Not to everybody, not to strangers, but to some people."

I asked if he protected them in any way.

"Sometimes he kept them in the safe, always wrapped in a covering, like a blanket," she said. "After he died, it took Jack and Jane a long time to find out what they were worth. We had no idea."

I stood up and said, "When you found out what they were worth, didn't that make you all feel like thieves?"

"We're innocent victims in all this!" she said, raising her voice. "*He* got us into this!"

She quickly collected herself, embarrassed at having revealed her anger.

I wished her well and stepped out into the sun, eager to write down everything she had told me and greatly relieved to have left the house before Jack returned. That was not the place where I hoped to make his acquaintance.

On Monday, June 18, Tom Kline filed suit in federal court in Dallas seeking to repossess the Quedlinburg treasures for the Quedlinburg church. He named as defendants Jack Meador, Jane Meador Cook, and the First National Bank of Whitewright. They were guilty, he charged, of "the unlawful detention of sacred objects and art treasures."

The complaint included an affidavit from Willi, who described himself as a lawyer and historian engaged by the church in Quedlinburg to help recover the treasures. Tom presented a number of exhibits, including seven pages of photographs of the missing treasures, taken from prewar scholarly studies, and three of the U.S. Army documents discovered by Klaus Goldmann. The documents reported the loss of the objects after the American occupation of Quedlinburg.

In the hope that he was not acting too late, Tom asked Sidney A. Fitzwater, the federal district judge hearing the case, to grant a ten-day restraining order prohibiting either the bank or the Meadors from moving the treasures. He also asked for a court order to allow the inspection and photographing of the artworks. The language he used in these latter motions was the same as that in the aborted agreement he had worked out with Powers and Torigian the previous week.

Judge Fitzwater immediately set up a conference call connecting all the lawyers with him by telephone. After listening to what each one had to say, he granted both of Tom's requests. For the time being, at least, no one could take the remaining treasures out of the United States. The inspection and photographing, to be supervised by U.S. marshals, would include Jack Meador's possessions held by the First National Bank of Whitewright, and also those in Jane Meador Cook's safe deposit boxes at her bank, the First Interstate Bank of Dallas.

It was a stunning defeat for Torigian. He had obviously been overconfident; maybe the guy was just lazy. At any rate, Torigian may not yet have realized it but both he and his clients were now being investigated by a number of state and federal agencies. And the civil suit in Judge Fitzwater's court was just the beginning—in time, there would be other charges for them to answer.

The day the lawsuit was filed, I happened to call John Farley, the president of the First National Bank of Whitewright, and evidently caught him off guard. Although gruff on previous occasions, when he had refused to answer my questions, Farley purred like a kitten now. He was "terribly disappointed," he said, that the bank had been named among the defendants in the case, since the bank did not claim ownership of the treasures. "We assured counsel for the church that we informed our customer we could not let the objects be removed pending a satisfactory agreement as to who owned them," he said plaintively. "The objects are safe with us."

I asked if he had ever accepted the treasures as collateral for a loan. "At the present time, and in fact since negotiations began three weeks ago," he said, "the artworks have not been used as collateral but *may have been* in the past." He would not explain or amplify that curious "may have been in the past." That much, at least, he had obviously rehearsed with Powers. Nevertheless, I had a scoop.

I couldn't resist asking one last question. He was the mysterious Texas banker who sent color slides of the manuscripts to Roland Folter at H. P. Kraus, was he not?

"Oh, sure," Farley replied. "That was me. I talked to Kraus on the phone. He wanted to buy both manuscripts, first for $100,000 and then for $150,000. By then we had some idea of what they were worth, so I told him to go fishin'."

I wanted to print that in the newspaper, so I immediately called Folter. He denied the report. I included both sides in my story. When I filed it that afternoon, Marv gave it a five-column banner headline reading, "Bank in Texas Admits It Has Missing German Art Treasures."

Meanwhile, in federal court in Dallas, Judge Fitzwater admonished all parties in the lawsuit not to reveal the time or place of the inspection and photographing of the treasures. He didn't want them lost a second time. Both Willi and Tom cited this injunction when they begged off telling me where the inspection was to take place. Nevertheless, I was determined to get a look at the treasures. Brashly, I thought I could outsmart the judge by arranging a stakeout at the bank with Ben Weaver, the freelance photographer who had been covering the story photographically for the *Times*.

I'd heard scuttlebutt at the courthouse to the effect that Judge Fitzwater was an early riser, and I had a hunch he would tell the U.S. marshal to take the group into the bank well before regular business hours. Consequently, I was up at 5:30 the next morning and met Ben in Whitewright at about 6:20, just as the sun struggled up over a huge rusting cotton gin. We proceeded to sit, or perhaps I should say stew, in Ben's car throughout the entire day, without sighting the procession of lawyers, photographers, and U.S. marshals we had expected to encounter.

Unbeknownst to us, the treasures had been moved to the bank's branch in Denison, about ten miles to the north, and it was there that Willi had what he later described as "one of the most exhilarating experiences of my life."

When I called him at the Adolphus that night, he said he had been overwhelmed by seeing the treasures. I asked if he had found them all. He hesitated. Judge Fitzwater's order that the parties not reveal the time and place of the inspection and photographing might extend to discussing the case in public, he said. Then Willi spoke cryptically. Did I detect a touch of glee in his air of mystery? Yes, of course. He may have felt inhibited by the judge's order, but also I was getting paid back for all those times when I wouldn't reveal Joe Tom Meador's name.

"I can answer your question this way," said Willi coyly. "I would not be surprised if the accountants who review the plaintiff's legal bill will find among today's expenses a case of the very best French champagne."

Pretty funny. We both chuckled, although by now Willi's patience was wearing thin. He was thinking about how crazy it was that, just at the moment he got his first look at the treasures, his government, which stood to gain so much from his efforts, might lose everything because of its unwillingness to pay a legal bill.

BOOK TWO

Chapter 13

BLISSFULLY IGNORANT OF THE FACT that the money had been turned off, Tom Kline shifted into high gear and the lawsuit entered what is known as the discovery phase. Once a complaint has been filed and answered, lawyers for both plaintiff and defendant are granted the legal authority to summon witnesses and compel them to answer reasonable questions under oath in preparation for the trial. This procedure—the taking of depositions—allowed Tom and his colleagues at Andrews & Kurth to begin questioning Jack, Jane, Torigian, and their respective family members and business associates. Willi was permitted to attend the depositions, but kept grimly silent about the withdrawal of his sponsor. And silent, too, about what was coming to light.

Absolutely silent. How I envied both him and Tom! When I asked Tom for even the merest crumb of news, he told me that although Judge Fitzwater had lifted his embargo on discussing the case in public, his lips were sealed for fear of being accused of attempting to try the case in the press. "This is one of the touchiest situations I've ever been in during my whole professional life," said Tom. "These things are irreplaceable treasures of historical importance and, on top of that, we're dealing with some very difficult people. Torigian is constantly threatening to sue the firm. I'm sorry, but I can't tell you anything right now."

I was determined not to be shut out of the story—not after all of these months. There were important questions to be answered. Like what drove Joe Tom Meador to steal in the first place? Why take these particular artworks? Did he work alone? Why make Skunk transport the treasures back and forth between Dallas and Whitewright? And, finally, why keep them for thirty-five years, apparently never attempting to return them or sell them? Before leaving Texas, I wanted every scrap of information it was possible to unearth concerning one of the most successful art crooks in history. And I wanted to understand his brother and sister, too. And their lawyer, John Torigian. And that remote, ghostly town of Whitewright, where the Meadors grew up and still ran a down-at-the-heels farm-equipment and hardware store.

Maybe I lacked the legal power to compel witnesses to answer my questions, but I was not without resources. I had wheels, I had paper and pen. And I had Marv back in New York willing to let me stay in Texas as long as I could keep advancing the story.

Consequently, the morning after my fruitless stakeout in Whitewright with Ben Weaver, I drove to Bonham, a town of barely seven thousand residents some twenty miles northeast of Whitewright. Bonham, I'd been told, was the birthplace of Sam Rayburn, the legendary Speaker of the U.S. House of Representatives, and perhaps for that reason had a public library superior to those in Whitewright or Sherman. Maybe I could learn something there about the background of my thief and his family.

The sun was high and it was another scorcher when I maneuvered into the parking lot behind the public library on

Rayburn Drive. A few minutes later, as I browsed through the local history section, I found myself in luck. I came upon a heavy, two-volume work entitled *The History of Grayson County, Texas.* When I opened the second volume, I was excited to find two articles of about five hundred words apiece concerning the Meadors. The first entry was about Joe Tom's mother and father—Maybelle Meador and her husband, C. J. Meador. The second dealt with their children—Joe Tom, Jack, Jane, and Jim Pat (the latter was a sickly hunchback who died in 1971). The articles were signed by someone who was clearly an authority on the subject, *Jane Meador Cook.*

Well look at that! Let Tom and Willi get what they could out of her in a deposition. I had something better. I had Jane writing about her family in what must have been an unguarded moment.

After taking several pages of notes and catching a quick lunch at a local cafe (where I was the only male patron not wearing cowboy boots) I hurried to Whitewright to keep an appointment with Mary Lou (Douse) Thrasher. She had been the first eyewitness to tell me about seeing Joe Tom in possession of the Quedlinburg treasures, or something like them, but she had insisted on speaking anonymously. Now, she said, she had a change of heart. She said she liked the way I was handling the story and that she was disgusted by the money-grubbing attitude of the Meadors, for whom she had worked for twenty-five years until her retirement. Recently, she said, she had given Jack a dressing-down, insisting that he return the treasures to the Germans immediately.

"Oh, I read his pedigree!" she told me. "What I didn't tell him is what I couldn't think of. I said 'You brought disgrace to your mother. Out there in the cemetery, she'd be so angry she'd kick the dirt off!' "

But Jack ignored her. Consequently, Douse said, she was willing to speak openly about the Meadors and keep everything she said on the record.

Douse had an elderly friend with her when we met. Clara Simmons said she, too, knew the Meadors well and would be glad to contribute whatever she could. I liked them both. They were fair-minded witnesses. When they had something uncomplimentary to say about the Meadors it was spoken in sorrow, not glee. Douse Thrasher was especially convincing. She impressed me as a free-spirited, straight-shooting Annie Oakley type who carries a bumper sticker on the back of her pickup that reads, I LOVE THE SINGLE LIFE. She told me she recently broke her leg when she stumbled into an armadillo's hole, but was on the mend and everything else about her was "just hunky-dory." I spent a couple of hours with the two women—and filled up a steno pad with notes on what they said.

My last stop of the day was at the office of the Sherman *Democrat*, the daily newspaper that has covered Grayson County, including Sherman, Whitewright, Bonham, and the surrounding countryside, since 1879. Once again, I was in luck. The librarian, a shapely woman with a lovely, lilting Southern accent, said she had a manila folder filled with clippings about Whitewright, some dating back to the 1920s and before. When she brought me the envelope, I spread the clippings out on a table and had myself a feast.

When finished, I retreated to my motel room, spread out my notes, and began to scribble. I wanted to set the scene where the Quedlinburg thief grew up. Whitewright, I wrote, became one of the major centers of cotton production in northeastern Texas soon after its founding in 1878. The old Missouri-Kansas-Texas Railroad, known locally as the Katy, had pushed its way south toward Greenville and established a crossing at Whitewright. Gradually, the residents of nearby Kentuckytown, Pilot Grove, and Orangeville knocked down their houses, piled the lumber on carts and moved—lock, stock and barrel, as they used to say—to Whitewright. Still, the town's population remained small, although Whitewright's boosters claimed that they bought and shipped more cotton than nearby Sherman.

So many bales of cotton passed through Whitewright in the great "lint rush" years of the 1880s that at one point the Katy ran short of boxcars and began shipping five-hundred-pound bales of cotton lashed onto flatcars. The practice had to be discontinued because glowing cinders from the steam locomotives then in use would sometimes fall on the exposed bales and start a fire. The flames would leap from one car to the next, soon creating a twenty- or thirty-car conflagration. So spectacular were these infernos that the local Baptist preachers couldn't resist warning their congregations that the fires were a preview of things to come in the next world for drunkards and other sinners.

In its early days, Whitewright had been as wild as any town in the West. On Saturday nights, according to one newspaper article I read, local farmhands would get liquored up at a local saloon and gallop around town whooping like Indians and shooting into the air (and sometimes into houses). No one was seriously hurt, mainly because the townspeople became adept at diving under their beds at the crack of the first shot. But after enduring these assaults for a number of years, the residents voted to go dry, and by the late 1920s, when Joe Tom Meador was a teenager the rough-and-tumble, hard-drinking town had lost some of its rough edges. Residents boasted that Whitewright had three hotels, two variety stores, three banks, two restaurants, two drugstores, four doctors, two dentists, two newspapers, and two public schools—one for blacks and one for whites.

The shopping district was exactly one block long, namely, Grand Street between Bond and Sears. On a warm Saturday morning, it would be bustling with activity. Cotton growers would bring their wives to town and promenade up one side of Grand Street and down the other. They might start at the corner of Bond and Grand, in the shadow of one of the

town's two cotton gins, tin-sheathed factories that housed Eli
Whitney's famous contraptions that combed the seeds, burrs,
and other impurities out of the raw cotton. Given special dis-
pensation by the Baptist clergy, these steam-powered mon-
sters hissed, rumbled, and roared twenty-four hours a day,
even on Sunday.

While the women might compare the price of a bonnet or
pair of shoes at different variety stores before making a purchase, the gents wouldn't miss an opportunity to stop in at
Meador, Inc., to inspect the late model tractors and other
farm implements.

The local banks were closed on Saturday, but at least one
of them added a touch of class to Grand Street even on weekends. The Planters National Bank had its name cast into the
sidewalk in a twelve-foot-long mosaic of bright blue and
white tiles, the remains of which had been duly noted by
Willi Korte. Throughout the week, bank employees cleaned
and polished the mosaic as reverently as if it had been created by the hand of Michelangelo. Passersby got the message
and detoured into the gutter rather than display their ignorance by treading on a Work of Art. Once, it was reported in
one of the newspaper stories I read, a man inadvertently spat
a mouthful of tobacco juice on the mosaic. The instant he
realized what he had done he fell to his knees and wiped the
tiles clean with his shirtail.

Apart from the local restaurants, the main attraction in the
evening in Whitewright was the Palace Theater. Seating two
hundred, the Palace had been among the first small-town
theaters to present talking motion pictures in the 1920s. A
great favorite, of course, were the westerns. By this time,
Whitewright was beginning to lose touch with its Wild-West
past, and the movies, however much they romanticized the
frontier days, helped to keep some traditions alive. "I learned
how to ride and shoot at the Palace Theater," a local resident
was quoted as saying.

In the period between the two world wars, the Meadors were one of the first families of Whitewright. The patriarch, Claude Meador, better known as C.J., was a short, round-shouldered man with narrow, squinting eyes and close-cropped grey hair. Acquaintances said he wore a fixed grin, which some found likeable and others a little spooky.

However one reacted to his countenance, townsfolk were agreed that C.J. was one of the shrewdest traders in the Southwest. Born in Arkadelphia, Arkansas, where his family had been in the livery business selling mules to the U.S. Army, he brought his bride to Whitewright in 1917 and established his business shortly after the United States entered the First World War that April. Almost immediately, C.J. had the presence of mind to acquire the northeast-Texas franchise to sell International Harvester tractors and farm implements. His timing couldn't have been better.

The war created a huge demand for cotton for uniforms, tents, knapsacks, and other military equipment, and at the same time it drew a significant share of the labor force into military service. The result was an almost frenzied demand for all kinds of mechanized, labor-saving farm equipment. In Whitewright, the growers mortgaged their lands at local lending institutions, like the Planters National Bank on one side of Grand Street, and then, clutching a roll of greenbacks, swaggered across the street to Meador, Inc., where they slapped the fenders and kicked the iron wheels of new tractors, plows, harrows, cultivators, and cotton pickers until satisfied enough to make a purchase.

One of C.J.'s best-selling tractors was International Harvester's Titan, a fifteen-to-thirty-horsepower, gasoline-powered workhorse that sold for $1100 in the 1920s. It could do the work of ten horses. Posters displayed in the showroom proclaimed the advent of "the horseless farm." One newspaper advertisement tacked on the wall declared: "We are in a new age. Snail-paced horse farming can no longer keep up with the times. The trend toward power farming is like the gold rush to the Yukon."

As the cash rolled in, C.J. became a pillar of the community. People sought his advice on civic questions. Did the fire station need a new roof? C.J. would lay in a supply of roofing material and then answer the question affirmatively. What should be done about the leaky boiler at the high school? C.J. said he just happened to have a slightly used boiler on hand and would part with it at a bargain price. In time, C.J. became a deacon of the First Baptist Church of Whitewright, an executive of the Grayson County Boy Scout Council, president of the local Rotary Club, a thirty-second-degree Mason and president of the Whitewright school board.

And then suddenly, prosperity came to an end in Whitewright. The decline was brought on in part by the Depression, but there were local forces at work as well. The soil around Whitewright had become depleted by farmers who refused to practice crop rotation. Investors had begun putting their capital in the new synthetic fibers. And meanwhile the giant twenty-thousand-acre farms of the South and West were outproducing and underselling the much smaller farms of northeast Texas. Disenchanted with cotton, some local growers switched to barley, wheat, or oats. A handful survived, but many lost their farms.

Once again, C.J. proved ready to cope with changing business conditions, but this time with methods not likely to be applauded by his fellow deacons and scoutmasters. Douse Thrasher told me she recalled catching him after hours filing the serial numbers off of the engine blocks of shiny, new tractors. The machines had been stolen, and C.J. was preparing them for adoption in west Texas. On another occasion, Douse said, C.J. badgered the staff at the store to put their signatures on fake sales agreements to buy tractors. He then sent the documents to International Harvester headquarters in Chicago to claim a bonus for every six tractors sold. Later, when C.J. actually sold the tractors, he would submit a group of legitimate contracts and collect a second bonus from the manufacturer.

C.J. was involved not only in large-scale thefts and swindles; he was what Texans call a natural-born cheat. Back when he was selling mules to the U.S. Army, Douse remembered, he was observed rubbing black boot polish into the gray whiskers of the mules to take a few years off of their age. Once, when C.J. was caught outright in an act of stealing, he reacted with indignation. Roaring, he said he had a perfect right to take something if he needed it.

As C.J. was crude, practical, and scheming, his wife, Maybelle, was artistic, absentminded, and nutty. A graduate of Baylor Female College in Waco, Texas, she had gone on to study at the Art Institute of Chicago before landing a job as an art teacher at Ouachita College in Arkadelphia, which is where she met C.J.

From her earliest days in Whitewright, Maybelle established a studio in her home where she worked and gave lessons in oil painting and ceramics. Her specialty was china painting, a demanding art because of the necessity of working with speed and precision.

Although admired for her artistic ability, Douse and Mrs. Simmons both remembered that Maybelle's public behavior was odd. She sucked her thumb, talked to herself in strident tones, and made inappropriate remarks. When asked for the time of day, a former neighbor recalled, Maybelle might reply, "You can't swallow a frog that's the size of a man's fist!"

A devout Baptist, she taught Sunday school at the local First Baptist Church for fifty years. Many in the congregation praised her for her devotion to the town's children, but others complained that the Bible stories she told with such conviction were in fact her own inventions. One of those who attended her Sunday school class back then still wonders whether there really was a Babylonian king named Thingamajig.

Aside from art and religion, Maybelle's true love was her first-born. She tolerated her three other children, but doted on Joe Tom, calling him "Honeybunch" and "Baby doll" throughout her life. And Joe Tom, a slightly built, fine-featured youth with lively dark eyes, responded to her attention by taking after her with an interest in art.

In fact, Whitewright was everything Joe Tom wasn't. To him, mechanized farming was about as fascinating as a heap of cow dung. He despised the townfolk, who took pride in calling themselves westerners. That, he said, was only an excuse for their lack of cultivation and refinement. Organized athletics at the high school (where his brother Jack was captain of the football team) was simply loathsome. When asked about his lack of interest in sports, he would say with a grin that he was devoting his mind to "higher things." Like art, for instance. He assisted Maybelle in her art classes and became an accomplished painter himself.

Several other people in Whitewright I spoke to over the next day or two provided additional glimpses of Joe Tom's early years, but the best witness to this period of his life, a man privy to his inmost thoughts, his kleptomania, and even his sexual proclivities, came to me through a tip in the Dallas *Morning News*. A headline splashed across the front page of the newspaper reading "Friend Recalls Art Theft" naturally caught my eye. The news was that a seventy-one-year-old man named Owen Hunsaker, a retired United Airlines executive who had been a lifelong friend of Joe Tom's, had come forward to tell his story.

Hunsaker related how Meador told him he had simply wrapped the treasures in brown paper and mailed them home to Texas through the U.S. Army post office. It was, the *Morning News* declared, the first time anyone associated with the case had explained how Meador moved the artworks to Texas. Even more interesting was Hunsaker's revelation that Joe Tom had "wrestled over the [theft] for years, torn between wanting to return the art to its rightful home and needing it for himself." Hunsaker didn't elaborate on Meador's "need" for the treasures, but this was the first report that the Quedlinburg thief had had second thoughts about what he had done.

Since the newspaper story stated that Hunsaker lived in New York City, it was a simple matter for me to see if his telephone number was available from information, which it was. In less than a minute, 1 was seated at a writing table in my motel room, gabbing with Joe Tom Meador's best friend— and, it would turn out, his former lover.

A courtly, modest man, Hunsaker immediately apologized for having called the *Morning News* before calling me. He said he had been reading my stories about the case in the *Times* but wasn't sure I'd be interested in what he had to say. "I guess I felt more comfortable talking to my old hometown newspaper," he said. Yet now that the *Times* had a human voice he became quite voluble, spinning out the story of his lifelong relationship with a man he obviously had cared for, but whom he did not shrink from judging sternly.

When Meador went off to college at North Texas State Teachers College in Denton, Hunsaker said, he majored in art. He did well in the courses that held his attention, but otherwise was a mediocre student. The two men met in September of Joe Tom's junior year, during a week when upperclassmen hazed the new arrivals.

"Hey, freshman, come here," Hunsaker remembered Meador saying to him jeeringly. Hunsaker obliged, not knowing what to expect.

"Get me two tickets for next week's concert at the Main Auditorium," Meador demanded.

"Yes, sir," said Hunsaker.

When he returned with the tickets, he said, he was pleasantly surprised to learn that one of them was for himself and that he had a "date" with the upperclassman.

"Every time he would see me again," Hunsaker recalled, "it was 'Go up to my room and get my book on such and such and bring it down here to me.' It was all in fun, of course. Before the war, every upperclassman had at least one freshman he could order around."

Joe Tom may have been an unexceptional student, but he had an impressive vocabulary and could salt his conversation with words like "preternatural" and "quotidian." He could be witty, too, making puns and brashly ridiculing certain pontificating professors who intimidated the other students.

Meador also liked to show off the knowledge of the arts he had picked up at the college library. He took particular pleasure, Hunsaker remembered, in explicating whatever sexual subtexts he could discover. For example, when Joe Tom took Hunsaker to a concert at which a Tchaikovsky piece was being performed, he would discuss not just the music but the composer's homosexuality. If the subject turned to literature, he could dazzle Hunsaker by revealing that Proust's lover Albertine was in reality Albert, and by describing André Gide's lust for young Arab boys. Joe Tom was really in his element, Hunsaker said, when he spoke about the visual arts, describing the erotic sculptures adorning the Sun Temple at Konarak, sly Japanese pornographic paintings, and the sexually uninhibited art of the Italian Renaissance.

His passion for erotic art got him into trouble at least once though, Hunsaker recalled. Joe Tom had come across several art books in the university library that included one or two sexually explicit illustrations, and he attempted to steal them. He carried them to an open window, and, after checking to see that he was not being observed, dropped them in the shrubbery at the base of the building. When he went outside to retrieve the books he was arrested. A campus security guard had seen the books fall and waited for someone to try to carry them away. Meador wound up on probation for a semester.

He dismissed the incident as *"une indélicatesse"* (a tactless indiscretion), but Hunsaker thought it was more serious than that. "There had been other incidents like this, all seemingly minor," he recalled, "but the library thing was when I realized Joe Tom wasn't like other people. Something was missing. His credo seemed to be, 'What's mine is mine, and what's yours is also mine if I need it.' "

It would not be long, Hunsaker told me, before he began to sleep over in Joe Tom's room and was subsequently invited to spend a weekend in Whitewright, where he was introduced to C.J., Maybelle, Jack, Jane, and Jim Pat. In time, Hunsaker became a regular visitor to the Meador family's home on Bond Street.

After graduating from North Texas State in 1938, Joe Tom taught art at a high school in New London, a small town in East Texas, and continued to spend weekends with Owen Hunsaker. "We had to be discreet in those days," Hunsaker told me. "The world hadn't accepted the gay lifestyle as it has today." It therefore came as a relief, he said, when Joe Tom proposed that they share a cottage for six weeks at an art colony in Taos, New Mexico. Meador had signed up for classes in life drawing and painting there taught by Alexandre Hogue, a respected regional artist whose murals are in the city hall in Dallas. Many of the participants brought along their spouses, and Joe Tom was permitted to have Hunsaker as his guest. "Living with artists, we could sort of let our hair down," said Hunsaker.

"That was in June 1941," he continued, "I had just finished my master's dissertation at Southern Methodist University. Joe Tom picked up my suitcase from my mother's house in Dallas, then collected me at the university and—pfft!—off to New Mexico we went.

"Joe Tom was the life of the party," Hunsaker recalled. "He was able to be himself in a way that he never could at home in Whitewright, or even at the university. Out there in Taos, where nobody in particular was watching and where artists were expected to be a little eccentric, he was a laughing person, a giggler, a free spirit. He was never pensive, never a withdrawn type person.

"Of course, the study of art also liberated him," Hunsaker continued. "I guess the only thing that Joe Tom ever gave me—it was when I graduated from North Texas State—was a little book on art. I've kept it all these years. It's called *Apollo*; it's a general book on the history of art."

What Hunsaker called "the dark side" of Meador also reappeared in Taos. "Joe Tom stole something," he said. "I don't remember exactly what, but I think it was a supply of oil-paint pigment, which was quite expensive back then. He stole a whole lot of it, more than he could possibly have ever used. And somehow they nailed him, and almost tossed him out on his ear, but Joe Tom—he was so good-looking and likeable— he talked his way out of it."

"Why'd you do that?" Hunsaker said he'd asked his lover.

"I needed it," came the reply.

Chapter 14

BACK IN NEW YORK, there were two messages on my answering machine that seemed almost too good to be true. They were from two former members of the Eighty-seventh Armored Field Artillery Battalion who said they remembered 1st Lt. Joe Tom Meador very well indeed. Better yet, both men said they had served as guards at the cave outside Quedlinburg in April 1945.

I quickly returned their calls. Karl Kulikowski, a retired postman, lived in the Bronx and therefore was easy for me to visit. I rode the subway to the Bronx and met him and his wife, Eleanor, in their small cottage-size house on shady Philip Avenue. Kuli (he said that's what everyone calls him) was a tall, hulking man who walked with dainty steps as if his shoes pinched. He had been boxing champ of the Eighty-seventh, he told me shyly. Then he amazed me by recalling actually having seen Meador remove objects from the cave he was guarding outside Quedlinburg. No sooner had Kuli revealed this to me than he and his wife excused themselves and stepped behind a curtain.

"Eleanor is a diabetic and I give her the shots she needs," Kuli said. When they returned, I switched on my tape recorder and we talked about the cave outside Quedlinburg, and about what he had observed of Meador's comings and goings.

Less than a year later, Eleanor Kulikowski was dead. Kuli had administered the several shots a day she required during the last years of her life. Now he was deeply lonely, and I saw a good deal of him over the next two or three years, frequently dining with him at Sam's, a favorite West 44th Street steak joint. We also took in a Broadway show occasionally, once with all three of my kids—who immediately adopted him as "Uncle Kuli." As an amateur poet and unproduced playwright, he showered me with samples of his writing and sent a long letter almost every week commenting on what I'd written for the newspaper. In 1994, the letters stopped. Kuli's daughter Carole called to say that he had died of a sudden heart attack. I'd lost a good friend.

The other call I returned was from George A. Catton, a retired Michigan State Police captain who lives in Grand Blanc, Michigan. I never got to meet Catton, but we had many long talks on the telephone during which he recalled, among other things, having seen Meador place artworks from the cave in cardboard boxes, in preparation for mailing them home.

Both Kuli and Catton also told about the heavy fighting the Eighty-seventh had been engaged in through France and Germany, and they gave me instructions for getting in touch with other men who had served in the unit. The result was that within a few weeks I talked with more than two dozen veterans of the Eighty-seventh, including Col. George F. Barber, a Princeton graduate who commanded the unit, and Maj. George Aubrey, a West Pointer who assumed command after Barber was wounded near Marienberg, Germany. Drawing on the recollections of all of these men, together with the unofficial history of the Eighty-seventh I'd found in the New York Public Library, and Meador's military records, which I had obtained through a Freedom of Information Act request, I was able to stitch together a detailed picture of Joe Tom's highly unusual adventures during the war.

Two days after the Japanese attack on Pearl Harbor, Joe Tom Meador enlisted in the army as a private. (Hunsaker chose the navy.) Being a college graduate, he was immediately accepted as an officer-candidate and sent to the field artillery school at Fort Sill, Oklahoma. Young officers were being trained there as forward observers (FOs)—one of the most dangerous of military occupations.

As the eyes and ears of the artillery, it was the job of the FO to sneak up to the battlefront, spot enemy troop concentrations or other targets of opportunity and radio coordinates to direct fire from the big guns, which remained a safe distance behind the lines.

Naturally, the enemy would keep a sharp eye out for these agents of death, and do everything possible to neutralize them. Consequently, FOs had a short combat life expectancy. Many would be killed by enemy snipers, some would die at the hands of enemy patrols, and not a few would be killed or captured when they became lost and blundered into an enemy camp. "We were cannon fodder," I was told by Catton, another battalion FO.

Joe Tom appeared to have the makings of a good forward observer. Having grown up in a rural community, he was more at home out of doors than a city boy might be. He knew how to read a map and how to spot and interpret landmarks on the horizon. And as an artist, he understood perspective, a close cousin to the triangulation that an artilleryman must be the master of.

Serving as an FO would prove congenial in another way as well, one that Joe Tom scarcely could have forseen during his training in the United States. Once in combat, working close to the front lines, an FO would be on hand during and immediately after a battle. Although FOs sometimes traveled in scout tanks or armored cars in the company of two or three enlisted men, they were frequently alone, on foot and unobserved. Under such circumstances, there would be little to prevent them from entering, say, an abandoned church and helping themselves to anything portable that might catch their fancy. In short, assignment as an FO could be a license to loot.

Joe Tom qualified as an FO in July 1942. After a series of stateside assignments, in the course of which he was routinely promoted to first lieutenant, he was assigned to the Eighty-seventh Armored Field Artillery Battalion. A relatively small unit, composed of some five hundred men and sixteen officers, the Eighty-seventh was patterned after the German Panzer forces that had swept through Poland and France in 1939 and 1940.

The teeth of this fast-moving, hard-slugging outfit were eighteen self-propelled 105-millimeter howitzers, sardonically dubbed "priests." Mounted on a tank chassis so as to be highly mobile and able to withstand a near miss, the priests could be rapidly shuttled back and forth along the battlefront to hit the enemy where he was not expecting it—and with devastating blows.

"We could level a small city in three or four minutes," Kuli told me. "Our gunners took pride in being able to put three rounds in the air before the first one landed. Not every field artillery unit could do that, but we could, and that's why we were destined to be sent to the front and kept there."

The Eighty-seventh shipped out for England on New Year's Day 1944 and spent the next five months in the picturesque village of Adderbury in Oxfordshire, where the men awaited orders. Joe Tom amused himself by cultivating mushrooms in the basement of his living quarters. In late May, the unit was moved to a staging area, and then, on D-Day Plus One (a day after the first Normandy landings), the Eighty-seventh boarded a convoy of Liberty ships, plunged through heavy seas and landed at Dune de la Madeleine, France, which the Americans had code-named Utah Beach. One of the unit's landing ships was sunk by a mine and another was hit by a German shell.

"We lost some good buddies on the way over," said Kuli.

Four days after the unit scrambled ashore, according to the informal history of the Eighty-seventh, Joe Tom was one of several FOs dispatched to scout enemy positions. As it turned out, it was another FO who spotted a German target and directed fire during the Eighty-seventh's first combat mission, while Meador was crouching in a shell hole not far away. For him, the war had begun in earnest.

Chapter 15

"WELL, I HAD MY FIRST EXPERIENCE at coming face-to-face with a Jerry," Joe Tom wrote in a letter to his parents dated August 2, 1944. "I jumped over a hedgerow and landed beside a Jerry dugout. I shot first, got one, and captured four." This account was in one of two letters by Meador published in the Whitewright Sun shortly after his parents received them. A local historian found the letters and gave them to me.

The letters are nicely detailed and well written, but there's a catch. None of the surviving veterans of the Eighty-seventh recall Lieutenant Meador capturing four prisoners, and there is no mention of it in the unit history. To a man, the veterans doubt that the incident ever took place.

Meador also told his parents that before falling asleep under his tank every night, the questions that raced through his mind were, "Is my gun beside me? Is my knife here?"

More fantasy, according to Catton. "The only time Meador ever drew his knife," he said, "was to slice a painting out of its frame."

Frequently in his letters home, Joe Tom portrayed himself as a two-fisted gladiator single-mindedly determined to rid the world of a hated enemy. Discovering a German anti-tank gun hidden in a haystack, he wrote, he fired an incendiary shell at the haystack: "It burns, out run Jerries, shoot them, move on." Later, he reported spraying a house with gasoline, igniting it, and "we have roasted Jerry in about twenty minutes."

Here again, his letters don't square with the records. In the view of his superior officers, far from effectively destroying the enemy, Meador refused to take his responsibilities seriously. In one of his personal efficiency reports signed by Colonel Barber, which I obtained through a Freedom of Information Act request, Meador is described as "not caring whether a mission was accomplished." Another report, written by Colonel Barber four months later, stated that Meador "tries to do as little as possible and still get by" and "spends too much time and energy on matters of a nonmilitary nature."

It was hardly the first time a commander found fault with a subordinate, nor was Joe Tom the first soldier in history to embellish the truth in his letters home. A lot of craziness takes place in combat, but Joe Tom Meador was something pretty special. Throughout the ten months he was fighting his way across Europe, he acted out his fantasies—often at the risk of his life and those of others.

Kulikowski remembered having once driven his half-track truck near to where Meador was parked in a jeep during a lull in the fighting in France. He heard Joe Tom's voice on the radio giving his call letters to the unit's fire-direction center and shouting excitedly: "Fire Mission! Fire Mission! *Six Jerry tanks!*" Next, he heard Meador give the coordinates to direct fire on a specific position.

Kuli said he and a lieutenant in the half-track checked and rechecked the coordinates.

"The position on which he was calling for fire was plainly

visible to us, but the German tanks were nonexistent," Kuli said. Meanwhile, a few miles back, the howitzers flashed, and Meador began calling, "Shells bracketing the target! Fire for effect!" and finally, "Cease fire. Mission accomplished." The sham was repeated several times that day, Kuli said, resulting in several well-ploughed potato fields but no harm done to the enemy.

Catton, the retired Michigan State Police captain, also recalled instances of Meador's letting his imagination run away with him. "For a while, I was assigned to serve in a small FO detachment under Meador's command," Catton told me. "What I remember best about those patrols is how close he came to getting us all killed. By pretending to know where we were when he had no idea of where we were, he got us lost several times. 'I know *exactly* where we are,' he would say. 'Just follow me and you'll see.' One time he pulled that crap and took us well behind enemy lines without realizing where in hell we were. We came upon a German armored car. Fortunately, we blew the top of it off before it could start firing at us, no thanks to Meador!"

Joe Tom was playing at being a soldier in the midst of the murderous reality of war. His fantasy life also appears to have been at the root of something else the men found strange. When an object attracted his interest, he immediately fantasied a need for it, and then, without further reflection, stole it.

Kuli recalled that only a day or two after landing in Normandy, Joe Tom showed him a set of lace altar pieces that he boasted of having taken from a village church in France. "When I asked him why he took the stuff," said Kuli, "Meador replied, 'It's something I need.' Look, here we were in the middle of the worst war in history with our lives likely to be blotted out any minute and he says he needs a set of lace altar pieces! So help me. That's what the guy said."

And there were other veterans of the Eighty-seventh who

were exposed to Lieutenant Meador's sudden needs. David Olson, a former captain in the Eighty-seventh who now lives in Wheaton, Illinois, told me that somewhere in Europe (he couldn't remember exactly where) he found Meador using a hunting knife to cut an oil painting out of its frame. He watched as Joe Tom rolled up the painting and stuffed it in a duffle bag.

I asked Olson why he hadn't tried to stop Meador. He replied, "You've got to understand, he was a forward observer. Those guys were cannon fodder. I figured he'd be dead in a few days, so why bother?"

Another enlisted man in the unit, Thomas "Whitey" Oldring, now a retired federal guard living in Clearwater, Florida, told me how Joe Tom once tricked him into becoming an accomplice in a looting expedition.

Meador ordered Oldring to take him for a ride in his jeep "to check on some homes," Oldring said. After driving for about a half hour away from their encampment somewhere in France, he said, Joe Tom told him to stop in front of a seemingly deserted country house. Meador entered the building and returned "carrying some things which he had wrapped up," said Oldring.

"I realized he was looting the place," Oldring continued. "I told him never to detail me again to be his bodyguard while he was looting or I'd report him to the commanding officer!"

Later, Oldring said, Meador asked him to take part in another looting expedition, promising to help him "send home anything I wanted." Oldring said he was disgusted and "flatly told him no!" Meador kept his distance after that, he said.

Still another veteran of the Eighty-seventh, James Colamatteo, now an income-tax accountant in Gary, Illinois, recalled that Joe Tom was well known in the unit as a kleptomaniac. Former Sgt. Edwin J. Mehring, a retired carpenter who lives in Clearwater, Florida, was of the same opinion.

"He had the reputation of being a thief," Mehring said.

This is not to say that Joe Tom was the only member of the unit who picked up things that did not belong to him. I gained insight into the widespread acceptance of looting in those days from a photocopy of a letter sent me by one of the veterans of the Eighty-seventh. The letter was by the late Duff Gordon, of Lincoln, Nebraska, who was briefly attached to the Eighty-seventh and then transferred out just before the war's end.

"Lord, what loot I could have had if I'd stayed with those boys," Gordon wrote to his wife on June 21, 1945. "Doc Paull [Capt. Murray M. Paull, the unit's medical officer] has two of the finest movie cameras that money can buy." Gordon, who was so envious of the medical officer, was no ordinary G.I. He was the unit's chaplain!

But the veterans I spoke to made it clear that the looting they indulged in or tolerated was confined to the theft of liquor, an occasional hunting rifle or ceremonial sword, and small items like watches, jewelry, and cameras that, as often as not, had spilled into the street from a bombed-out building. In contrast, they said, Meador was in a class by himself.

By March 1945, after the Eighty-seventh had pounded its way through northern France and the Ardennes, the unit drove into Central Europe. That was where Colonel Barber was wounded by a hand grenade and had to be evacuated. The Eighty-seventh pressed on under the command of Major Aubrey.

In mid-April, the unit was ordered to advance to the Harz Mountains, an area in central Germany of steep, craggy cliffs and densely wooded valleys which had become one of the last pockets of German resistance. Hitler had chosen this redoubt shrewdly. The rugged terrain made the area inaccessible to tanks, thus nullifying an important Allied advantage. Moreover, the Harz Mountains held a mystical significance for many Germans. In Goethe's *Faust*, on Walpurgis Night, hordes of witches in the Harz Mountains smear themselves with sacred ointment and fly on winged horses, cats, goats, and pitchforks to celebrate their sabbath. The Führer had something similar in mind for the last stand of the Wehrmacht, but with his army on the brink of defeat, that was as much a fantasy as the daydreams of Lt. Joe Tom Meador.

The war ended for the Eighty-seventh on April 18, when the unit reached the medieval city of Quedlinburg, a strange and historic part of the Reich.

Chapter 16

As the Americans clambered out of their battle-scarred tanks, half-tracks, and jeeps, they found themselves blinking with amazement. "Quedlinburg wasn't like anything we'd seen during the war," Catton recalled. Virtually unscathed by the fighting, the city's narrow cobblestone streets were crowded with what looked like gingerbread houses—half-timbered dwellings with their structural posts and beams exposed. Painted green, yellow, or red, the houses had steeply pitched tile roofs and two or three upper stories that seemed to lurch forward over the sidewalk.

Bypassed by the railroads in the nineteenth century, Quedlinburg had never lost its medieval character. "You expected to see Hansel and Gretel come prancing down the street," Kuli told me.

And there was perfume in the air, one of the men remembered. The heady scent of golden crowsfoot, blue meadow sage, milky white spiderwort, and other blossoms was intoxicating at this time of year. Since the turn of the century, Quedlinburg had been the flower capital of Germany, and not even the war had dimmed its prosperity. In fact, the war actually stimulated the flower and seed industry. Sentimentality, combined with ruthlessness in the Nazi soul, required that when Hitler's mechanized divisions were on parade they must be draped with banks of flowers whenever possible. Marching soldiers oftentimes carried armfuls of blossoms. And of course funerals—increasingly common as the war turned against Germany—had to be fortified with lavish floral displays. Thus, Quedlinburg thrived during the war years thanks to an industry that never attracted the notice of Allied bombardiers or artillerymen.

Major Aubrey established his headquarters in a hotel facing the marketplace. His orders, he told me in an interview, were to stay put in Quedlinburg, round up deserting German soldiers who were trying to slip through the lines in civilian clothes, and search the city for contraband. Compared to what the men had been through, this was light work indeed, and as it was generally believed that the war was over (Germany's formal surrender would not come for another three weeks), the men relaxed and indulged themselves in sightseeing.

Several of the veterans I spoke to sent me photographs showing themselves and their buddies in groups poking around the city, snapping pictures of each other standing on quaint stone bridges, posing under the city's ornate coat of arms that was chiseled over the entrance to the courthouse, and grinning sheepishly beside a saucy little sixteenth-century cottage built on a stone island in the center of Finkenherd Strasse.

Sgt. Sherwood Bryant, a former stonecutter and carpenter from Depew, New York, and a good friend of Kuli's, explained to the men the principles of half-timber construction in buildings throughout the city. The structural framework was erected like a house of dominoes and joined with wooden pegs; then the spaces in between were filled with plaster or bricks. Sometimes the bricks were set in elaborate herring-bone or checkered patterns. These walls, Bryant explained, were sturdy enough to support a second or third story, and consequently half-timbering gained popularity as medieval cities became densely inhabited.

I didn't need to rely entirely on what the men remembered. After Kuli gave me an account of his visit to Quedlinburg in 1992 (he returned, he said, to apologize to the German people for doing such a poor job of guarding their treasures), I decided to visit the city myself. I had to wait a year before finding the time to go, but in March 1993, I flew to Germany and spent several days hiking around Quedlinburg. I inter-viewed a number of residents and collected a small library of books about the city and its past, both ancient and modern. I had them translated after I returned home. All this helped me to understand the historic importance of Quedlinburg and its treasures, and to learn how its legacy was exploited for politi-cal purposes by Heinrich Himmler, the second-most-powerful official in Hitler's Third Reich and the evil-minded overseer of the death camps.

For years, Quedlinburg had been a national shrine for the German people, because the city was known to have been a favorite haunt of Heinrich I (890–936), the first German king to unify an early configuration of central-European states. Heinrich accomplished this feat in part by ceaselessly travel-ing from one stronghold to another, and in part by keeping his distance from the Pope in Rome, a policy that would later arouse Himmler's interest.

Heinrich refused to be anointed by an emissary of the Pope, because he realized it would be much less humiliating for the Bavarians, Swabians, East Franks, Lotharingians, and others he conquered to accept his rule if he did not insist that they recognize him as both their religious and secular leader. Secular would be good enough.

The Pope naturally resented this display of independence.

Anointing kings and emperors had placed the church, at least symbolically, above the heads of the secular authorities. But Heinrich would rather risk displeasing the far-off Pope than his more immediate and well-armed rivals in central Europe.

"We must assume that Heinrich's early years were marked by a highly un-Christian character," one scholar has written.

Heinrich held his far-flung kingdom together by other means as well. When he visited a city like Quedlinburg, then a capital of power and culture, he did not come empty-handed. He is known to have presented the cathedral with an extraordinary wealth of treasures, including the Samuhel Gospel, a fabulously jeweled reliquary casket, and a magnificent, curvilinear ivory comb. Shortly before his death he arranged for his burial in the crypt of the cathedral of Quedlinburg. His son and successor, Otto I, and his grandson, Otto II, continued to visit Quedlinburg and to bestow extravagant gifts on the cathedral.

Each of the treasures, composed of the rarest and most exotic materials that could be found, and worked by the most gifted artists of the time, had a stunning impact when presented. The closest modern parallel to such splendorous gifts might be the moon rocks and lavish foreign-aid packages that were ceremoniously presented by American presidents to third-world leaders when seeking their allegiance during the cold war.

Down through the centuries, the treasures survived one vicissitude after another. Some were destroyed by fire when the cathedral burned in 1070. Others simply vanished, never to be returned. When a new cathedral was consecrated in 1129, it included a sixteen-foot-square *Schatzkammer*, or treasure chamber, designed to protect the valuables. The stone walls of the chamber were two feet thick. A small window to admit a few rays of sunlight was criss-crossed with heavy iron bars.

In time, the Schatzkammer overflowed. Five altars, dedicated to the memory of more than one hundred different saints, were constructed, and each was decorated with artworks. "The shining of the light and the shimmer of gold contributed to a very beautiful sight," one historian has written of these decorations. Among the relics in the church in its early days was a piece of wood said to be from Noah's Ark, tatters of Christ's swaddling clothes, threads from the Virgin Mary's bedsheets, a vial containing some of Mary's milk, wood from the Cross, and palms from the entrance to Jerusalem. Whatever their authenticity, all have long since disappeared.

At least once, the majestic Samuhel Gospel was stolen. Fortunately, it soon reappeared, together with a note that read: "This book has been returned with shame by the apothecary Hans Walpurger because on January 4, 1602 it had been stolen by this very Walpurger."

When Napoleon defeated Prussia in 1807, his younger brother Jerome took charge at Quedlinburg and promptly auctioned off everything valuable he could find in the cathedral. The Schatzkammer, however, was already bare. Wily Quedlinburgers had spirited the treasures off to a hiding place in Halberstadt, a few miles to the north. They were returned to Quedlinburg in 1813, after Napoleon's defeat at the Battle of Leipzig.

About a century later, in February 1919, thieves broke into the cathedral through a window. They proceeded to the Schatzkammer, which by then was sealed with a massive iron door. They had come equipped with a metal drill, but the instrument broke and the thieves had to content themselves with stripping the altars of objects of relatively small value. Afterward, the church authorities protected the Schatzkammer with a steel door fitted with a modern locking mechanism and an electric alarm.

In the 1930s, Himmler, the so-called Reichsführer-SS, or leader of the elite Nazi troops, saw the legend of King Heinrich and the Quedlinburg treasures as ripe for political exploitation. Like Hitler, he believed that if the Nazi movement were to be completely successful it must replace Christianity, whose doctrines of meekness and charity had led to what Himmler called "the racial decay of the German *Volk*." He concluded there could be no better place to dramatize this revolution than at Quedlinburg, the final resting place of the early monarch—Heinrich I—who had rejected organized Christianity by not submitting his kingship to being sanctioned by the church.

Quedlinburg, then a city of 28,000, also had the appeal of a charming and well-preserved throwback to a bygone time. The cathedral, one of the oldest in Germany, seemed to Himmler a perfect gathering place for the mystical retreats he was fond of hosting.

In 1935, when an aide reminded him that the thousandth anniversary of the death of Heinrich I was coming up the following year, Himmler considered it "a gift from heaven for our propaganda purposes." Over the next few months, he became personally involved in planning the celebration. One of his directives specified precisely how the stairs outside the main entrance to the cathedral should be enlarged so as to accommodate an honor guard.

Another Himmler order called for replacing the tenth-century figure of an eagle surmounting one of the cathedral's twin towers with a modern Nazi-style eagle, a detail I spotted on my visit and that I'm told remains on the church today.

Himmler himself took possession of the key to the Schatzkammer, and arranged for the treasures to go on display at the celebration under heavy guard.

Meanwhile, the Nazi press ballyhooed the coming event. One editorial proclaimed: "Heinrich I unified the German Reich, founded a people's army, and had no inclination whatsoever toward Rome, turning from an ecciesiastical creed to an ethnically pure people's creed."

Himmler was always given to bouts of fantasy, and about this time began to toy with the notion that he was the reincarnation of Heinrich I, and according to one of his biographers, he let it be known that he would not object to being referred to as "King Heinrich." To dramatize his supposed lineage, Himmler ordered the opening of Heinrich's sarcophagus. It was found to be empty. He then called for the opening of the coffin of Heinrich's wife, Queen Mathilda, thinking that after her death the king's remains might have been interred together with those of his wife. But there, too, the remains could not be found. Never at a loss to make political capital from a sudden turn of events, Himmler announced that Heinrich's bones had been stolen by the Communists and proceeded with his plans for the celebration.

He next ordered a tunnel to be excavated from the outside of the south face of the cathedral under the wall and up through the stone floor inside the building, so as to provide a secret entranceway. The day of the ceremony arrived—July 2, 1936—and five hundred top SS and Gestapo chiefs, resplendent and menacing in their brown and black uniforms and gleaming leather belts and boots, marched into the hall, which was lit by torches and draped with huge Nazi banners. Himmler had arranged for a spate of patriotic declamations, interlarded with martial music and the singing of the Nazi anthem. He directed that the anthem be sung at half the usual speed "so as to command greater respect."

At the climax of the spectacle, the Reichsführer-SS conspicuously marched out of the cathedral, crawled back inside through the secret tunnel, and then suddenly rose from the floor, arms outstretched. The performance was said to symbolize King Heinrich's reincarnation in the person of Himmler.

Soon after the event, Himmler appropriated the cathedral and turned it into a "Germanic sanctuary," where SS officers would swear allegiance on a sword he would extend to them. Religious services in the cathedral were forbidden. In 1938, while organizing a King Heinrich Memorial Institution "to revive the spirit and deeds of King Heinrich for our time," as he expressed it, Himmler decided that the architectural style of the cathedral was inappropriate. To bring it into conformity with the ideals of Nazi architecture, he ordered an enormous construction project, which would give the cathedral a new exterior. The steeply pointed, Gothic-style roofs and arches were to be replaced by rounded or square-peaked Romanesque forms.

Himmler had even more elaborate plans for developing Quedlinburg, but he ran into opposition from the city fathers at nearby Magdeburg, who held sway over Quedlinburg. At that moment, he decided not to antagonize the local administration, and consequently postponed his plans for Quedlinburg until after the war.

When World War II broke out in 1939, Himmler had the Quedlinburg treasures moved to a nearby bank vault for safekeeping. In 1943, when Allied bombing of Germany commenced and Himmler was preoccupied with other matters, subordinates moved the treasures to the so-called *Champignonzüchterei*, or mushroom-farm cave, just southeast of Quedlinburg.

There they slept until a new conqueror arrived.

Chapter 17

THE DAY AFTER THE EIGHTY-SEVENTH OCCUPIED QUEDLINBURG, an FO officer named Bob Kubista happened to be in his jeep reconnoitering the area southeast of town, when he was flagged down by a man wearing a green uniform. Kubista, now a retired paint salesman living in Tucson, Arizona, said he thought the man might be a German forest ranger or park guard.

"He had no weapon other than a long cudgel, and he looked older than military age," Kubista recalled. "He spoke no English and I spoke no German, but he made it clear he wanted to show me something off the road. I followed him about a hundred yards across this rolling country until we came to what looked like a tunnel or a cave in the side of a hill."

"The German opened a large wooden door, and we walked in," Kubista continued, "I had a flashlight and shined it around. There were many wooden boxes stacked inside, and from the look of them they were not military cartons. It seemed as though they contained books, vases, and things like that. I also remember there were a lot of narrow crates stacked against a wall. I assumed they contained paintings."

"The German guy used their word *Kunstwerk* which I took to mean artwork," Kubista said, "so I got the idea that the things in the boxes were valuable. He also made the sign of the cross and pointed to certain boxes to indicate that some of the things were religious and belonged to a church. I understood he wanted these things turned over to the American authorities to protect them."

"When we came out of the cave," Kubista recalled, "he closed the heavy door behind us and indicated that he would stay. That was fine with me. When I returned to our headquarters, which was then being set up in Quedlinburg, I reported about the cave to Major Aubrey, and told him I thought it contained valuable things."

Aubrey, who later became the ranking U.S. military attache at the American embassy in Moscow and now lives in Potomac, Maryland, said he recalls receiving Kubista's report.

"I figured it was Nazi loot," he said in an interview, "so I put a guard on it right away. I never got to visit the cave myself. We were too busy rounding up deserting German soldiers."

The guard detail Aubrey dispatched was led by Sgt. Sherwood Bryant, the former stonecutter from New York, and included Catton, Kulikowski, and a few other men whose whereabouts are unknown today. Sherwood Bryant died in 1976.

Catton recently sent me a photograph he had mailed home in 1945, showing himself and a couple of buddies standing at the entrance to the cave. But he could recall few details.

Kuli, on the other hand, said that although he was drunk for most of the twenty days that the Eighty-seventh occupied Quedlinburg, he remembered the experience vividly. After all, he said, the war was over, it was a time of celebration, and the Eighty-seventh had come to rest in Quedlinburg longer than it had been in any one place since leaving Adderbury in England ten months previously.

"I went inside the cave several times to check it out," Kuli recalled. "At the entrance, there was a heavily timbered door on the face of a cliff. There were electric lights inside, but with low-watt bulbs so it was hard to see things clearly. As soon as you got in, there were three Egyptian mummy cases. Then you took a right turn and came to a room filled with antique furniture and wooden boxes. Then you turned left and walked straight back through a corridor. There were hundreds of paintings in crates stacked against either wall. Then you came to the last room, where there were more boxes that seemed to be filled with antique furniture and items of that sort."

"We picked up three girls," he continued. "Bryant and I each got a German girl in uniform. They were dressed something like our WACs—Womens Army Corps personnel. I think another guy picked up a girl from the town, but I don't remember exactly. Anyway, we pitched our pup tents about fifty yards from the mouth of the cave, and we shacked up with the girls every night while we were there. The girls had to disappear in the daytime because we weren't supposed to fraternize with the enemy."

The enlisted men were not the only Americans to violate that order. When I visited Quedlinburg in 1993, Friedemann Gosslau, the pastor of the Quedlinburg church, introduced me to Gunter Schöle, a native of Quedlinburg in late middle age with a ruddy, round face, who told me about his relationship with a certain Lt. Joe Tom Meador. The picture Schöle painted of a lonely young soldier seeking companionship if not congenial sexual relations was recognizably the Joe Tom Meador I was coming to know.

"When the Americans came, I was sixteen and a half and had been working in the ground crew for the Luftwaffe," Schöle told me when I interviewed him in the apartment he lives in with his wife and two children. "The Americans imposed a curfew and searched from house to house for young men like myself who were soldiers wearing civilian clothes to escape captivity. Naturally, they thought I might be in that group, so they took me to a school building where they were detaining about a dozen other young men. An American officer made a joke to the effect that they would turn all of us over to the Russians, and that terrified us.

"One day an American officer came up to me," Schöle said, "He told me his name was Joe. He spoke German very well, and he was very good-looking and charming. He asked me why I was being kept in that building, and I said I didn't know. He said he would arrange for my release; later that day, he led me through a cordon of American soldiers and took me to my home in Quedlinburg, where I had been living with my mother.

"He visited me each day for two weeks," Schöle continued. "I knew he was an officer, of course, but he said I should call him Joe. We used to take long walks together. We talked mostly about the war and how it had changed our lives. Sometimes we talked about nature or animals. Several times he said I should come home to Texas with him. He said I could work as a farmhand and help his mother with chores and that she would be very glad to have me there. But of course I had no intention of leaving Germany."

"Once, when I asked him what his military duties had been," Schöle recalled, "he said, 'I am engaged in special duties like propaganda and can go anywhere and do anything I please.'"

"We took many walks in the park," Schöle went on to say. "There was a canteen there where you could get something to eat and dance, and there were always many American soldiers present. German girls also came to the canteen to meet American soldiers and to dance with them. When we met girls Joe would make jokes with them and talk about music— he knew all the Glenn Miller tunes and titles—but, unlike the other American soldiers, he was never interested in the girls."

When I asked Schöle if he ever had sex with the American lieutenant, he grimaced and rejected the question. "I'm shocked to learn that he was homosexual," he said. "I never knew that about him when he was here."

The park where Meador and Schöle strolled together is directly across the road from the trail leading to the cave where the treasures were hidden, and I asked Schöle if Meador ever mentioned the treasures to him.

"He never expressed any interest in the cave or the treasures," Schöle replied. "I was familiar with the cave because I had played there as a boy, but Lt. Joe Meador never said anything about the treasures there."

"When he learned his unit had to leave Quedlinburg," Schöle continued, "the lieutenant brought a basket of food, wine, and sweets to the flat where my mother and I lived. He was very kind to me, but I never heard from him again."

Another voluble Quedlinburger, Ernst Gille, said he was one of the local inspectors who discovered the theft in the Altenburg cave. He recalled having visited the cave twice in the company of one or two American officers. On their first visit, he said, they had found all of the sixteen crates into which the church treasures had been packed to be undisturbed. On the second visit a day or two later, though, he discovered to his horror that the crates labeled two, three, four, and five had been broken into. Twelve of the most valuable of the treasures were missing.

Grille said it appeared as though the thief had gone about his work in great haste. Packing material from the crates was scattered about, and an important Carolingian manuscript and some outstanding reliquaries had been left in open crates.

A cursory investigation by the United States Army proved fruitless, as I learned from talking to veterans of the Eighty-seventh. Catton said he remembers being questioned about the theft by an army investigator, but can't summon up the details. He and Kulikowski also thought they heard Sherwood Bryant say something about having been interrogated. If records of this investigation were kept, they do not appear to have survived.

Major Aubrey has no recollection of an investigation. "I never knew anything was stolen," he said, adding how pained he felt that the theft took place when he commanded the Eighty-seventh. "We were ordered to move out of Quedlinburg in just a few days, and I was never contacted by any investigators about anything having been stolen," he said.

It was Kuli, it turned out, who actually witnessed the theft of the treasures. "When I was guarding the cave," he explained to me, "I saw Lieutenant Meador enter it at least twice. Our job, you see, was to keep the Germans out, but we let in any American—especially any officer—who wanted to have a look."

Kuli estimated that approximately thirty curious American soldiers entered the cave over the twenty-day period that he was guarding it. He remembered one specific occasion, when he saw Meador "come down from the cave, go to his jeep, and take something out from under his jacket and conceal it under a map or a raincoat in the jeep.

"Then Meador went back to the cave and made another haul," Kuli said. "Stupid me! I didn't even realize he was taking stuff."

Nevertheless, the scene was unforgettable to Kuli. It lingered in his mind as a vague, half-understood impression, until May 1990, when he happened to read my front-page story in the *Times*. There he learned that the West German Government had paid $3 million to recover a long-lost manuscript from Quedlinburg, and that more treasures stolen from the cave where they had been hidden were still unaccounted for. That was when it clicked. Instantly, Kuli knew exactly who had stolen the treasures, and knew that he had witnessed the act with his own eyes.

In an effort to tell the world what he now knew with certainty, Kuli said, he wrote letters telling his story to the New York *Times*, New York *Daily News* columnist Liz Smith, President George Bush and West German Chancellor Helmut Kohl. Only Kohl replied, although with a form letter, which made no mention of Quedlinburg or its treasures.

The difficulty was that Kuli, an inveterate letter-writer, commonly wrote his missives by hand and on odd scraps of paper. As a result, they were often discarded as being unserious. No one at the *Times* who handles mail recalled receiving his letter about the Quedlinburg treasures.

Kuli refused to give up. He wrote to fifteen former members of the Eighty-seventh with whom he had been keeping in touch, enclosing a photocopy of the May 1st story from the *Times* and asking his buddies if they agreed with him that Meador was the culprit. Thirteen out of fifteen responded, either in writing or with a telephone call.

A number, like Colonel Barber, were cautious in what they said or wrote. "No doubt it *could* be Joe Meador," Barber replied to Kuli, "but that's only an assumption. It smells suspiciously like one of our own, but who's to know?"

A clear majority, however, agreed with "Whitey" Oldring, who wrote back, "Boy, you hit that one on the nose! I never trusted that son of a bitch!"

Although no one outside of his circle of fellow veterans took him seriously, Kuli was undaunted. He wrote a play about the disappearance of the treasures in which he identified Meador as the thief. He called his play *The Cave*.

In one of the play's stage directions, Kuli describes himself observing the theft. "Meador comes from the cave and walks to the jeep," it begins. "Kuli looks up as Meador approaches his jeep. He sees Meador take something from under his jacket and put it into the jeep. Meador's back is to Kuli. Then Meador takes a canvas, or a map, and covers the object he put in the jeep."

Kuli told me he sent his play to several theatrical producers in New York and West Germany, but never received a reply. The world, it seems, was unwilling to listen to a retired postman who thought he'd solved one of the greatest thefts of the century.

Chapter 18

In AUGUST 1990, a thick, manila envelope from the Department of the Army arrived in my mailbox. Because of its heft, I knew exactly what it was even before I opened it. And I knew I'd scored.

The contents would tell me more about Joe Tom Meador than I'd ever imagined his Army records could reveal. I would learn how casually and impulsively he stole, how confident he was that if caught the punishment would be no more than a slap on the wrist, and, finally, how close the United States Army had come to catching one of its most wanted thieves.

Back in July, when I received Meador's army records through a Freedom of Information Act request, I'd been intrigued by a cryptic note made by Colonel Barber, the commander of the Eighty-seventh. In his last efficiency report on Joe Tom, the Colonel stated that he had been informed that Meador had been court-martialed during the period covered by the report, but that he could make no comment about it because he had not seen the trial record.

To be sure, the court martial could have been prompted by

some minor breach of Army regulations—being away without leave for a period of time, for example, or becoming involved in a motor-vehicle accident. On the other hand, it could have been something weighty. I made a few telephone calls and found that in cases where records of a court martial proceeding have been preserved—not all of them are—they are in the custody of a federal records center operated by the U.S. Army Judiciary Branch in Falls Church, Virginia.

I had called and, sure enough, they'd found something on file called "*United States* v. *First Lieutenant Joe Tom Meador.*" Immediately, I had asked for a copy.

Several weeks later, when I opened the envelope, I found a trial transcript and documents that ran to eighty-two pages. It told the story of how, scarcely six months after he stole the Quedlinburg treasures, Meador stole again. This time he was caught, tried, fined, and severely reprimanded. By doing some library research and tapping Owen Hunsaker's memory to supplement the trial transcript, I discovered what had happened. It provided fresh insight into Meador's character and formed the basis of my next article for the *Times*.

The summer and fall of 1945, the so-called period of demobilization, was a frustrating time for the millions of American soldiers and sailors scattered around the globe. There were not enough ships to bring them all home at once, and so most would have to find ways to occupy themselves as they waited their turn on the troopships.

In an effort to make garrison life more bearable for them, the War Department improvised an overseas school system, so that troops waiting to be sent home could pass the time by taking high-school or college-credit courses. Among the schools established for this purpose was the American University at Biarritz, located in the idyllic resort community on the French coast, a few miles south of Bayonne.

Meador learned of the formation of the school and applied for the job of art teacher. He was, after all, well qualified. For nearly three years before the war, he had been a high-school art teacher in New London, Texas. And, efficiency reports aside, he had been in combat for nearly ten months. If anyone was qualified for the job, it seemed that he was.

In early September, as the leaves in the thickly wooded Harz Mountains were turning bronze, Joe Tom was given the assignment he had asked for and was transferred to Biarritz. To a war-weary soldier, this was paradise. Built on cliffs overlooking the sparkling Bay of Biscay, Biarritz was known for its charming villas, splendid beach, and mild climate. Before the war, the resort had been a playground for the idle rich. It was at a house party here that the Prince of Wales met Wallis Simpson, the American divorcee for whose love he would later give up the Crown of England.

Joe Tom and four other art instructors were billetted in the Villa Issatsia, one of the lovely cottages in town that had been requisitioned by the U.S. Army. Classes were held in the nearby Villa Banuelos, another charming cottage with a view of the bay. Under the arrangement between the Americans and their French landlords, art classes were held in the rooms on the upper stories of Villa Banuelos, while the owner, the Marquise de Saint Carlos, lived in a room on the ground floor. The Marquise's quarters were kept locked. Only she and her housekeeper, Madame Elise Barbier, had the key.

On October 6, 1945, according to the transcript of a U.S. Army general court martial, Lieutenant Meador observed that the key to the Marquise's room had been left in the door. Instead of giving it to the owner or her housekeeper, he used the key to let himself into the room. Once inside, there cannot have been time for more than a moment's thought. He seized an empty box and loaded it with forty-eight pieces of antique silverware, two dozen antique gold-banded coffee cups, teacups, and saucers, and a similarly decorated coffee pot. Then he carried the loot to his quarters upstairs, where he hid it in a closet.

The total value of the silverware and china was trifling compared to the value of what he had stolen in Quedlinburg—about $200, which might be $2,000 in today's currency. Nevertheless, a complaint was filed by the housekeeper, Madame Barbier, and after the brazenness of the thief came to light the American authorities could not take the matter lightly. An American Army detective and a French police inspector were assigned to the case. It didn't take them long to identify Meador as the thief and charge him with a violation of the Ninety-third Article of War—the wrongful taking and using of property.

Since Meador pleaded not guilty when arraigned, he was placed under house arrest for the next ten days while the judge advocate's staff prepared its case against him. Confinement to quarters for an officer at this time was not strictly observed. The war was over. It was a time for celebration, not condemnation of one's comrades. Joe Tom later told Hunsaker that he attended a party virtually every night he was in Biarritz. Some of these gatherings were self-consciously decadent. At one party, Hunsaker recalled being told, the merry-makers dressed in Chinese attire. At another, there was cross-dressing, with the men wearing women's clothes and vice versa.

Meanwhile, a makeshift courtroom was established in one of the town's municipal buildings, and a four-day court-martial proceeding commenced on November 17.

The first witness for the prosecution was Madame Barbier. Speaking through an interpreter, she explained that on October 6 she had forgetfully left the key in the door to Madame Saint Carlos's room. When she realized what she had done, she said, she returned to the villa and asked Lieutenant Meador—who "seemed to be in charge of all the things in the building"—if he had taken the key. Lieutenant Meador, she testified, insisted he had not.

A short while later, Madame Barbier said, she returned to the villa and surprised Meador in the Marquise's room. This time, when she asked for the key he gave it to her. He then departed and she entered the room. Within a minute or two, Madame Barbier testified, she discovered that the silverware and china were missing. She then reported the theft to the French police.

When asked to identify the man she said she had discovered in the Marquise's room that day, Madame Barbier described him as a "middle-height, dark American officer," and pointed out Joe Tom who was seated nearby in the improvised courtroom.

Next to take the stand was Sgt. Gordon Howard, who explained that, together with a French police inspector, he had been assigned to investigate the case. He said he began by questioning Madame Barbier after she reported the loss, and that she identified Lieutenant Meador as the person she found in the Marquise's room.

Howard said he and the police inspector then questioned Meador, asking if the housekeeper had in fact discovered him in the Marquise's room. At first, the detective said, Meador denied that he had been there. Howard said he then asked Meador if he had ever possessed the key to the room or the key to a locked cupboard upstairs where Madame Barbier said the silverware and china had been hidden. Again, Meador declared he had no knowledge of the key or the missing items.

Howard then spelled out the testimony that was sure to clinch the case. He recalled telling Meador that since Madame Barbier had positively identified him as the person she discovered in the Marquise's room his quarters in the Villa Issatsia would have to be searched. "It was then," Howard declared, "that he admitted taking the silverware and chinaware." Meador promptly gave the key to Howard and shortly brought him the stolen objects as well, the detective said.

If that confession (despite Joe Tom's plea of not guilty) virtually settled the case, what came next added fuel to the fire of the judge's outrage. Detective Howard recalled that at one point during his questioning, the lieutenant remarked casually that stealing the silverware and china had been "worth a chance." It sounded as though, given the opportunity, the defendant was prepared to try his luck again.

After being informed of his rights, Joe Tom elected to remain silent. His court-appointed lawyer put on the stand C.J. Finney, a fellow art instructor at the university. Finney, who was obviously trying to put in a good word for a fellow officer, lamely suggested that Meador had only borrowed the items and had no intention of keeping them.

The military judge, Capt. Thomas R. Clydesdale, brushed aside the defense. If Meador had only borrowed the items, he reasoned, why would he have hidden them in a locked closet? Clydesdale quickly found Meador guilty and imposed a fine of $600. He then proceeded to castigate the defendant.

"You are hereby severely reprimanded," Clydesdale declared. "When a return of the property was requested, you repeatedly denied that you knew its whereabouts, and only after it appeared that search of your quarters was imminent did you produce the silverware from your quarters and the china from a place of concealment to which you alone had access."

With rising indignation, the judge went on to say that Meador's behavior "creates an impression of contempt and disrespect in the minds of the civilian population."

"In view of the serious nature of your offense," he continued, "the sentence imposed upon you by the court is *thoroughly inadequate.* Your actions reflected discredit upon you, were highly reprehensible and a sentence much more severe could properly have been imposed. You are admonished to guard well your conduct in the future, as a repetition of any such offense will not be tolerated."

Clydesdale's decision was reviewed at higher headquarters by Maj. Charles E. Wainwright, the acting staff judge advocate. "All of the facts," Wainwright declared, "indicate fraudulent intent to keep [the silverware and china] permanently, and weigh heavily against the accused."

He therefore upheld Clydesdale's verdict and sentence. Wainwright, too, made a point of declaring that the sentence was "thoroughly inadequate" in view of the fact that a violation of the Articles of War had been committed, but he, too, shrank from imposing a more severe penalty.

If Meador was given a stinging rebuke, no one who heard it delivered—with the exception of Joe Tom Meador himself—understood how thoroughly inadequate it was.

Chapter 19

"COME ON OVER TO MY ROOM and have a look at some stuff," Joe Tom said to his new friend Dede Matthews one day in the winter of 1946.

After their discharge from the service, both Meador and Matthews had enrolled as students at Texas A & M University in College Station, about two hundred miles south of Dallas. I caught up with Matthews while seeking out people who may have remembered Meador. On that day in 1946, Joe Tom was a graduate student in the university's department of architecture; Matthews was an undergraduate majoring in architecture.

Because of the flood of returning servicemen, the dormitories were quickly filled to capacity, and a number of returning veterans like Meador and Matthews were boarded at the local YMCA. That's where the two men met.

Matthews, who became a lifelong friend of Joe Tom's and is today an architect living in Bryan, Texas, told me about becoming captivated by Meador's quick wit and intelligence. The admiration was mutual. Joe Tom took part in Matthews's wedding in 1946 and frequently entertained him and his wife at Whitewright, introducing them to all the members of his family. Throughout Joe Tom's life, Dede Matthews was his only close heterosexual friend.

"Where in the *world* did you get these!" Matthews recalled exclaiming when Meador spread out on his bed his collection of gleaming gold, silver, and bejewelled manuscripts, reliquaries, and other artworks.

Joe Tom explained how his army unit had come to a halt in Quedlinburg after German resistance collapsed. He had happened to be billeted in the center of town near a medieval church.

"I walked into the church and saw this crucifix," Joe Tom told him. "I knew it was from the eighth or ninth century and a real prize, so I couldn't just leave it there. Germany was in chaos. There wasn't any German government I could turn it over to. Also, we were told we'd overrun the position where we were supposed to be, and we'd have to backtrack and let the Russians occupy this part of Germany. Should I leave it for *them?* I didn't think that was right. Or should I tell my commanding officer about it? Well, if I did that, then *he* might take it. Spoils of war, you know! So I decided to take it myself.

"Then I heard there were more things like this in a mineshaft just outside of town where our unit had posted a guard," Matthews remembers his friend saying. "I had a look in there and took some more things, including some oil paintings. I just cut them out of their frames."

Matthews, who has a folksy, rambling style and speaks with a heavily Texas-flavored accent, said he expressed amazement with the artworks, but no word of reproach to his friend for having stolen them. "They's yours," he said he told Meador, "jus' like you made 'em yoself."

Joe Tom was given contradictory advice two years later after he had moved the treasures to his family home in

Whitewright. On this occasion, he was visited by Owen Hunsaker, his former lover from North Texas State Teachers College before the war.

"After dinner one night," Hunsaker told me after we met in New York, "he brought six or seven things out of the closet wrapped in a shawl, and spread them on the dining room table. It was unbelievable. When I picked one of them up I knew I was touching ancient history."

The two men spent several hours together leafing through the manuscripts, examining the reliquaries and marveling over the strangeness and beauty of other items in the collection. When Hunsaker asked Meador how he had come by them, Joe Tom embellished the story he had told Matthews.

"I was in my tank and we suffered a near miss," Hunsaker recalled him saying. "I knew some German gunner had zeroed in on us and his next round would send us to Kingdom Come, so I jumped out and ran for cover. I dove into this cave. Never in my life had I seen so much gold, silver and jewels and such beautiful things. It was like being in Aladdin's Cave!"

Meador said he tore off his field jacket, wrapped it around as many treasures as possible and, as soon as the firing stopped, carried the bundle to his tank, which had survived a brief firefight. Then he began to wonder what to do with his loot. "I finally decided," Hunsaker recalled him saying, "that the best thing would be to wait until we established our next headquarters, then wrap up this stuff and drop it off at the Army post office addressed to myself in Whitewright. If it gets there it gets there, if it doesn't it doesn't."

"But, Joe Tom," Hunsaker recalled saying, "haven't you got something on your conscience?"

Meador repeated the "spoils of war" argument he had given Matthews, and added that he had acted to prevent the artworks from falling into the hands of the advancing Red Army.

"Someday," Hunsaker said to him, "you're going to have to find a way to get these things back where they belong."

Over the years, Matthews and Hunsaker both held to their opinions. In fact, as time went by, both men became increasingly vehement and expressed their quite opposite views repeatedly to Joe Tom. In that way, they gave voice to the mainly silent struggle that tormented Meador for the rest of his life. Paradoxically, for all the slickness and ease with which Joe Tom had stolen, living with his booty was different—and difficult.

What made it impossible for Meador to release the treasures at first was fear, not greed, according to Hunsaker. "During one of my visits to Whitewright shortly after the war," Hunsaker recalled, "he told me that *Life* magazine, *Time*, and probably *Newsweek* had all carried stories about another American officer, also from Texas, who got caught with a collection of jewelry he'd stolen from a castle in Germany. He had received a very stiff jail sentence, and Joe Tom was understandably afraid that if he turned over his treasures to a government official he'd be arrested in a minute and put on trial, just like the other officer. And he said it wouldn't go well for him, because he already had a blot on his record. He wouldn't tell me what that was, but he said it was reason enough to keep the treasures in hiding."

The blot Meador was referring to, of course, was his court-martial in Biarritz; what he had been reading about in the press was doubtless the case of Col. Jack W. Durant, the central figure in a widely publicized criminal trial in 1947. Durant and two accomplices were convicted of stealing $3 million worth of jewelry from Kronberg castle, near the city of Frankfurt, in the closing days of the war in Europe. I learned about the case by checking what Hunsaker had told me against the *Times* index and then reading the relevant back issues on microfilm.

It was no wonder that the case had caught Joe Tom's attention; it had much in common with the Quedlinburg theft. In both instances, the valuables were of historical importance to Germany. Both treasures had been hidden underground for safekeeping, after German cities started being bombed from the air. In both cases, the thieves were American officers, not enlisted men; in both cases the thieves used the U.S. Army postal service to ship at least part of their loot home to the United States.

Hunsaker's memory failed him in one instance. Durant was not a Texan. He was from Virginia. However, there was a Texan who played a prominent role in the case. Cpl. Roy C. Carlton of Kilgore, Texas, was the American soldier who discovered the Kronberg treasures later stolen by Durant and his accomplices.

In October 1944, as Allied bombers began dumping loads of high explosives on Frankfurt, a major German industrial city, several members of the Hohenzollern House of Hesse, a family related to Kaiser Wilhelm II, decided to remove their legendary heirlooms from bank vaults in the city and bury them under the floor of the subcellar of Kronberg castle, a massive fortress fifteen miles outside of Frankfurt (it is now a hotel). Diamonds, emeralds, rubies, and pearls set in rings, necklaces, brooches, and tiaras, and an old family Bible were placed in a specially constructed metal box encased in wood. A pit was dug in the subcellar floor, and, while the Hohenzollerns stood watch, a trusted stone mason lowered the box into the pit and neatly covered it with a flagstone.

A few feet away, a much larger pit was excavated. There the Hohenzollerns instructed the workman to put away no fewer than sixteen hundred bottles of what was described on an inventory as "wines of ancient vintage." The stone mason covered the wine cache as well, but not as artfully as he had concealed the jewelry pit—a mistake that would lead to the discovery of the wine as well as the treasures.

When the Americans arrived they gave the Hohenzollerns four hours to vacate the castle and converted it, still adorned with its oil paintings, tapestries, huge mirrors, and elegant furnishings, into a rest home for wounded and battle-weary American soldiers.

With time on their hands, the new occupants were soon exploring the one hundred forty rooms of the castle; before long they had discovered the wine cache and promptly began helping themselves to some of the world's finest vintages. After a few weeks, Corporal Carlson, the Texas man, happened to be supervising a plumbing repair in the subcellar of the castle when he came upon the treasure chest. Without opening it, he reported his find to Kathleen Nash, a forty-three-year-old captain in the Womens Army Corps who had been installed as the overseer of Kronberg castle.

Nash ordered Carlton to deliver the chest to her quarters. He complied, and that was the last he saw of it. Nash opened the chest in her bedroom and spread out the dazzling contents on the floor. Then she invited her superior officer, Colonel Durant, to come have a look. Durant, a thirty-six-year-old former lawyer, had worked for the Department of the Interior in Washington before the war. He not only had no criminal record, but in fact had won several decorations. Nevertheless, the sight of all that spectacular jewelry was more than either he or Nash could resist. Together, they plotted to steal the treasure. Durant's idea was that the jewels would be easier to dispose of if they were removed from their settings, so he and Nash spent the next several weeks meticulously prying them loose.

Meanwhile, the Hohenzollern clan commenced preparations for the wedding of Princess Sophie of Hanover. When the Princess visited the castle to claim the family heirlooms she planned to wear at the ceremony, she was received by Nash, who told her she would have to wait several days before being given the jewelry. When Sophie returned at the prescribed time, Nash told her the jewelry had been stolen. Horrified, the princess reported the news to her mother, the Hohenzollern matriarch, who in turn registered a complaint with the American military government.

An investigation was launched. Because of Nash's suspicious behavior, she was immediately marked as someone who might have had a hand in the disappearance of the treasure. The investigators became still more interested in her when they learned that she and Durant had married and hastily departed on a honeymoon in the United States. The FBI picked them up for questioning at a hotel in Chicago. When asked about the missing jewelry, Nash at first said she knew nothing about it, but when told that a polygraph test indicated that she was lying she broke down and made a full confession. After being told of Nash's confession, Durant came clean as well, leading to the recovery of most of the gems.

After separate trials, Durant was sentenced to fifteen years at hard labor, as the mastermind behind the theft. Nash got five years, another accomplice three.

Hunsaker recalled Joe Tom showing him newspaper and magazine accounts of the Kronberg castle case, insisting: "You're not gonna see that happening to me!"

At College Station, Meador seemed headed for an academic career. Fellow students like Matthews and J. Frank Peirce considered him brilliant. Peirce, now a retired professor of English, shared a room with Joe Tom at the YMCA. After earning his master's, Meador taught a course in the history of architecture, and Matthews, who was among his students, said Joe Tom was the best teacher he ever had—bright, provocative, and funny.

In 1951, this promising career was cut short when C.J., the Meador family patriarch, suffered a stroke. Maybelle, Joe Tom's mother, summoned him to Whitewright to help his brother Jack run the family store and help take care of both his ailing father and the third Meador brother, Jim Pat, who was misshapen and retarded.

Compared to the free-spirited university town Meador left behind, Whitewright was conservative and loutish. Virtually all of his neighbors were staunch, Bible-thumping Baptists, while Joe Tom called himself a freethinker. Whitewright was also dry, which certainly made life difficult for Meador, who liked to drink. And finally, a small farm town on the rolling prairie was hardly the place where a gay man with the sensibilities of an aesthete was going to feel at home.

Joe Tom made no secret of his disdain for the place. A local farmer told me of one occasion when Meador was seated on a chair behind the counter of Meador, Inc., and refused to get up to assist him until he had finished the page of a book he was reading. "He was arrogant," the farmer said. "My tractor had broke down and I needed a repair part, and he knew it, but he didn't give a damn."

There was no love lost between Joe Tom and Jack. Jack, a glad-hander who looked like his father, C. J. Meador, fit into the community as snugly as Joe Tom stuck out. Eventually, the Meador brothers rearranged the family store in such a way that each had his own private entrance, office, and safe. For weeks, Jack and Joe Tom would work in the store without speaking to each other.

What saved Joe Tom from loneliness and despair, strangely, were his medieval treasures. One day, as a former employee recalls it, he arrived at the store with a quilt bundled under his arm. When asked what was wrapped up inside, he said it was nothing and quickly tucked the bundle under the counter in front of his usual post. But later that morning, when there were no customers in the store, he called out to no one in particular: "Wanna have a look at this stuff I brought home from the war?" Several salespeople ambled over to where Joe Tom was seated. He had placed the bundle on the counter. Carefully, Meador unfolded the covering to reveal the softly glowing Samuhel Gospel.

Everyone present was goggle-eyed. Joe Tom expanded his chest with pride and then, offhandedly, told the cluster of employees more or less the same story he had recited to Owen Hunsaker about how he'd acquired such a remarkable object.

A cowbell attached to the front door clanked as a customer entered the store. Joe Tom quickly wrapped up the manuscript and returned it to a shelf under the counter.

Before he went home that night, he placed the bundle in the large, iron-wheeled safe in his private office. It remained there for several weeks. Then the Samuhel Gospel was replaced by one of the reliquaries, and Joe Tom held another viewing for the employees of Meador, Inc. In time, almost all of his treasures were displayed for the admiration and wonder of the salespeople. "The stuff was interesting," said one of those who saw the treasures at the store, "but it was like Joe Tom was begging for attention."

Eventually, Meador showed his treasures to the mayor of Whitewright—a man he respected and trusted—and to three or four carefully chosen friends as well. It was risky to show them off, he knew, but it was also immensely exciting. He possessed a dangerous secret. Every minute of every day, he knew he harbored something potentially explosive. And what an elixir that was!

There was more. For months, Joe Tom had a crush on a handsome young man I shall call Hank who lived nearby and frequently visited the store to make a purchase. (Hank is a pseudonym the man insisted that I agree to use before he would tell me his story.) Once, Joe Tom had clumsily invited Hank to drop by his home for a game of cards, but Hank had looked at him warily and begged off. It then occurred to Meador that the treasures which had so impressed the staff at the store might serve to start a conversation with Hank.

Joe Tom brought the Samuhel Gospel back to the store and kept it in the safe wrapped in a quilt and ready for the next time Hank stopped by. When he appeared, Meador snatched the manuscript out of the safe and placed it on the counter.

"Howdy, Hank. How's the world treatin' you today?" the young man recalls Meador greeting him. The conversation then proceeded approximately like this.

"Come here. I want to show you something."

"I cain't, Joe Tom. I was supposed to be home an hour ago."

"Bet you never seen anything like this, Hank."

"Tomorrow, maybe."

"Just look at what I got here on the counter."

"My Mama said I cain't stop nowhere, Joe Tom. I gotta take down every screen in the house. Then I gotta. . . . Oh, my sweet Jesus, look at that!"

"Nice, huh?"

"Whared you git it at?"

"See? It opens like a book."

"Yeah. . . ."

"You can turn the pages. Go on, Hank. Turn the page."

"Well, I'll be. . . ."

"That lettering there is written with gold ink!"

"Gol' darn!"

"I got another one like this at home."

"But whared you git it at, Joe Tom? I never seen nuthin' like it."

"Drop by the house tonight and I'll show you a whole bunch of this stuff."

"Yeah?"

"About seven o'clock."

"Seven?"

"I'll be waitin' for you."

That evening, Joe Tom spread out his treasures on the dining room table. Hank, a country boy who had dropped out of school in his early teens, was astounded by what he saw. He recalls Joe Tom explaining that he had taken the objects from German soldiers who had stolen them from museums in conquered countries and carried them into battle in the hope of using them to barter for their lives if captured.

The story didn't make much sense (their captors could despatch them no matter what they had to offer), but Hank said he never thought to question Meador. He and Joe Tom soon became good friends and perhaps lovers. In the process, Meador discovered how to tap the extraordinary power of his stolen artworks. Although created to glorify God, the Quedlinburg treasures also could be used for less exalted purposes.

Joe Tom had another passion, also one in which he used remarkable objects to enhance his self-esteem: his fascination with orchids. After the First World Orchid Conference in St. Louis in 1954, an event that sparked a national craze, he became enchanted by the spell of these exotic flowers. He supervised the construction of first one and eventually three large greenhouses in the vacant lot behind the family home on Bond Street. When fully developed, his artificial jungle contained thousands of orchid plants and a huge cage of twittering, brightly colored tropical birds.

After work at the hardware store, he would saunter home and putter about in the balmy atmosphere of his greenhouses, frequently forgetting the dinner Maybelle had laid out for him on the dining-room table.

When interviewed about his hobby by a reporter for the Denison *Herald*, Joe Tom said the many orchid plants he had under cultivation represented more than one hundred different varieties. Then president of the Southwest Regional Orchid Growers Association, Meador said he knew every orchid hobbyist within a thousand miles of Whitewright.

But Joe Tom's mind was never far from his medieval treasures. When he wrote occasionally to Hunsaker in Paris, Hunsaker told me, he would make teasing remarks, like "I still have all those You-Know-Whats and don't know what to do with them. Any ideas?"

When Meador learned that Dede Matthews was planning a trip to Europe to supervise the installation of a stained-glass window in Cologne, he urged him to extend the trip in order to visit Quedlinburg.

"See what the Russians have done to the town," Matthews recalls Meador asking. "See if the church is still there."

Joe Tom also gave Matthews detailed instructions on how to find the cave outside of town so that he could have a look there, too.

"He had no thought of returning the treasures," Matthews insists. "He was just curious."

It could be that urging Matthews to visit Quedlinburg was nothing more than a case of a thief being drawn—in this case vicariously—to return to the scene of his crime. But maybe Matthews was wrong, and Meador's interest in Quedlinburg was a tentative first step toward exploring the possibility of sending the treasures home.

Whatever the truth, Matthews never made it to Quedlinburg. The division of Germany had aroused such hostility between the two nations that when Matthews reached Cologne, in what was then West Germany, he was told it would be impossible to enter East Germany.

Matthews returned to Texas and explained the situation to Joe Tom, and he still recalls the look of disappointment on his friend's face. For the time being, at least, the treasures were not going anywhere.

Chapter 20

In 1967, WHEN JOE TOM was approaching the age of fifty, he rented a fashionable one-bedroom apartment in Dallas about sixty miles south of Whitewright. It could as well have been six thousand miles from home. Here, on weekends, he would pursue the life of a gay man in blissful anonymity. And here he would wage his final struggle over whether to return the Quedlinburg treasures to Germany.

I learned about Meador's double life in Whitewright and Dallas from half a dozen of his gay friends who called or wrote to me expressing surprise at their friend's posthumous celebrity and offering to share their recollections. Joe Tom, they told me, had been well known in the gay community of Dallas for his elegant dinner parties, caustic wit, and the unusual, museum-quality decorations in his apartment.

Customarily, Meador would drive to Dallas on Thursday evening, strip off his work shirt and baggy overalls and dress himself in elegant, tight-fitting finery. Typically, he would wear an open-necked silk shirt, expensive knit trousers, several gold chains around his neck, and bracelets and rings on his fingers. A tiger's-eye ring was a particular favorite.

The location of his apartment in the Willowick complex in north Dallas had been chosen carefully to suit the life, or lives, Joe Tom was now pursuing. On the one hand, the Willowick was near several of Dallas's gay bars where he could seek out young men with similar sexual interests. On the other, it was just a few blocks from Route 75, on which he could streak home to Whitewright whenever Maybelle demanded his presence. Even for a gay man, Meador had an unusually strong attachment to his mother. His gay friends used to tease him about the fact that the only time he received a speeding ticket was when he was once racing home in obedience to a call from Maybelle.

The Willowick complex, a small village of identical two-story structures, was brand-new when Joe Tom moved in. What especially appealed to him, friends said, was that one of the rooms in the second-story apartments was surrounded by boldly conceived floor-to-ceiling plate-glass windows and jutted out from the building, not unlike the upper stories of the half-timbered houses of Quedlinburg.

He decorated his hideaway with modern furniture and vitrines—glass-faced cabinets where he kept a few of his medieval reliquaries together with bric-a-brac of no particular value. He hung an abstract painting (probably one of those he stole in Europe) on the wall over the living-room couch, and elsewhere an oil painting of himself as a young officer, a photograph of a German soldier wearing a Nazi helmet (probably Gunter Schöle, the young German he befriended in Quedlinburg) and a few modern prints and Balinese and African masks.

The glass-walled room that projected from the building became the dining room. Usually, Joe Tom kept it decorated with a couple of orchids in bloom. He gave the room a medieval sort of name—"the turret."

Like many aging gay men, Meador liked to surround himself with attractive young men who would occasionally become his sexual partners, while he would behave in a fatherly way to them. Apart from Dede Matthews, he almost never sought the companionship of an intellectual peer. For sexual gratification, he looked for fresh-faced physical appeal, not intelligence or even good conversation.

Lee Cadenhead, a tall, dark-eyed young man who was an occasional guest at the Willowick, explained the appeal Joe Tom had for young men like himself. "I guess we're all looking for a father figure," he said, "but Joe Tom had something in addition to that—call it refinement, perhaps. He was devoted to good cognac, good clothes, and good-looking people."

"He had traveled the world, and his apartment was like a revolving museum," Cadenhead continued, "There would be an African fertility goddess on the wall one day and something else exotic there the next time. And Joe Tom could be articulate and he could cook. There weren't many people like that in Dallas back then."

Meador was also noted for his caustic wit. "He had us all falling on the floor one night telling about his experiences in the army," said one friend who spoke on condition of anonymity. "He told us that everyone in his army unit pretended to be super-straight because that's the way the army is supposed to be, but the truth was that one of the top officers had a crush on his sergeant and used to press his clothes for him. The sergeant was drooling over a private who looked like Adonis, and the private, of course, was involved in a steamy affair with the chaplain. I mean, it was terribly, terribly funny, and you wondered how they ever had time to fight the war."

The treasures made frequent appearances at the Willowick. At first, they were simply part of the decor, trophies from the late war in Europe. Soon, however, perhaps remembering how they had excited Hank in Whitewright, Joe Tom found another use for them.

"When I was in Europe in the war I picked up a king's ransom," he would say to a young man who caught his eye in a neighborhood gay bar. "You can hold these things in your hands if you like."

A friend from those days recalled Meador observing wryly that he was only using the treasures in the way in which they were originally intended—"to bedazzle the beholder."

In some cases, this former friend told me, some of the young men invited to the apartment were ignorant of art and unimpressed by the treasures even when handling them. It made no difference. If the treasures failed to excite his visitors, they had the effect of an aphrodisiac on their host.

"You could watch him get charged up over this stuff," the friend recalled. "Whenever he started talking about how he found the treasures or how dangerous it was to have them in his apartment, you could almost see the gooseflesh rising on his ass."

In 1970, Joe Tom was told by his doctor that he had leukemia. He made light of it to Dede Matthews, remarking that he would have to drop by the Anderson Cancer Center in Houston because he had "a touch of cancer." The chemotherapy he received there was apparently successful and the disease went into remission. However, being made to face mortality prompted Meador to ponder anew the fate of the Quedlinburg treasures. What would happen to them, he wondered, if something happened to him?

He brought up the subject over dinner with Hunsaker, who visited him at the Willowick later that year. One possible solution to the problem, Hunsaker recalled him saying, would be to take the treasures across the border to Mexico, bribe an antiques dealer there to write up a phony bill of sale and then use the bill to establish legal ownership of the treasures when he passed through U.S. Customs on his way back to the United States.

"He toyed with the idea that evening but then scrapped it," Hunsaker said. "He was worried that something would go wrong."

But Hunsaker sensed that his old friend might be coming around to the view that the treasures should be returned to where he found them, and consequently delivered "a stiff lecture" on how the treasures were the heritage of all humankind and should be treated as such.

"He wasn't buying it, and I realized it was a mistake to have become a scold. That'll get you nowhere," said Hunsaker. "So I tried another approach. I'm a Catholic, and I said he should give the things to the Bishop of Dallas and let *him* figure out how to get them back to Germany. I offered to take them to the Bishop myself. Well, his eyes lit up when I said that. And you know what? Right then, I could tell he'd been suffering over what to do with those things. It had been costing him something emotionally."

"You really think the Bishop would accept the stuff?" Joe Tom said.

"No harm in asking," Hunsaker replied. "I wouldn't mention your name."

"Give me another day. I've got to check something out," said Meador.

When Hunsaker told me this story, I guessed that Meador's checking out would have been done with Matthews, and when I reported Hunsaker's story to him, sure enough, Matthews said he remembered receiving a call from Joe Tom specifically asking what he thought of an idea to turn over the treasures to the Bishop of Dallas. Matthews, a renegade Roman Catholic who acknowledges that he is not exactly in sympathy with organized religion, said he strongly opposed the plan.

"I told him you do what you want," said Matthews, "but I'll tell you now if you give those things to the Bishop of Dallas they're gonna stay in the *Catholic* Church. It'd be just like you said when you found them—if you give them to your superior officer then *he* gets first choice. Or, if you turn them over to the Russians then *they* keep them. If you give them to that bishop, he'll send them to Rome because that's where he wants to look good. I don't see why you need to give them to *nobody*."

Just before Hunsaker left Dallas a day or two later, he dined with Meador again. "He thanked me for my offer to help," Hunsaker remembered, "but then he got this dreary, transported look on his face and said he didn't want to ask the bishop to serve as an intermediary after all."

What decided Meador at this point in his life was not the fear of a run-in with the law. Hunsaker and a church official could shield him from that. And it was not Matthews's anti-Catholic harangue. The reason Joe Tom could not bring himself to relinquish his stolen art is that over the years the treasures had become part of him. He used them—and had come to depend on them—both as sexual lures and to boost his self-esteem. He could no more give them up than cut off an arm.

Hunsaker understood this dependency better than any of Joe Tom's gay friends. "By then," Hunsaker told me, "he'd kept the treasures for fifteen years and they'd gotten under his skin. You see, the tragedy of Joe Tom was that, clever as he was, he had very little respect for himself. That's why he could stoop to stealing, and that's why he needed the heavy gold chains that he began to wear around his neck, and the rings on his fingers, and all the orchids and, of course, the things from Quedlinburg. Standing naked before God, he was nothing. An empty shell. That's what he felt. But all this stuff he collected somehow made him into a complete person. It's funny. You'd think that possessing stolen things would make him feel guilty and he would shrivel up, but it was the exact opposite. All that stuff made him feel like a king on a throne with a golden scepter. Against a high like that, my arguments had no affect at all."

*   *   *

If Joe Tom was now determined not to part with the Quedlinburg treasures, he may have decided to raise cash at this time by selling other valuables he brought or sent home from war-ravaged Europe. Several of his fellow members of the Eighty-seventh Armored Field Artillery Battalion—most insistently George Catton—said they had seen him cut oil paintings out of their frames. Dede Matthews also recalled Meador telling about having stolen paintings in Germany. Furthermore, a longtime Whitewright resident who spoke on condition of anonymity told me that after the war he helped Joe Tom pick up "a footlocker filled with coins from many countries" that he had shipped to himself and had not received for a year or more. The trunk was so heavy, he said, it could not be mailed and together he and Joe Tom had to drive some distance to pick it up at either a railroad junction or a port such as Galveston. None of these valuables have ever been accounted for, and it is therefore possible that the proceeds from selling these items was used by Meador to finance an increasingly lavish lifestyle at a time when the family business, Meador, Inc., was sliding into debt.

In 1975, when he attended an orchid show in Dallas, Joe Tom met Michael Farner, a handsome blond youth who would become his first live-in lover and open a chapter in his life in which his sexual relationships would become as complicated as the plot of a Restoration comedy.

To begin with, Farner was living with another gay man, and Joe Tom paid court to them both, leaving Farner unaware at first that Meador had any particular interest in him. But Farner found himself drawn to Joe Tom, then more than twice his age. Soon he realized that the attraction was mutual, and before long Farner moved in with Meador at the Willowick.

Farner told me he was not drawn to Meador because of his artworks or orchids, but by his maturity. Despite Farner's boyish good looks and winning personality, he was at that time a ship that had slipped its mooring. He had recently emerged from a mysterious stay in the hospital, and was given to episodes of depression he thought were related to the loss of his father at an early age. He clung to Meador with something near desperation, and told his friends he had entered into a "father-son relationship."

At first, Joe Tom was flattered by the way Farner looked up to him. Feeling flush, he bought matching, light tan Oldsmobiles for Farner and himself. Later, he took pride in presenting Farner at receptions at the gay clubs in Dallas like T.J.'s and the Villa Fontana. One of these events was attended by more than one hundred men and cost Meador several thousand dollars.

Joe Tom may have found a new treasure in Farner, but the old ones continued to obsess him. Farner recalled that once in 1976 when he, Meador, and another couple were driving home to Dallas after having visited the Fabergé gold show at the Witte Museum in San Antonio, Joe Tom announced that his life's ambition would be to have his medieval treasures presented to the public in a similar museum show.

"He said that someday, although he didn't know how, he was going to do this," Farner recalled.

When showing off his treasures at a dinner party at the Willowick, Farner said, Meador would sometimes heighten interest in them by injecting a note of mystery and danger. Dramatically, he would remind his guests that his treasures were "Nazi loot," and that he had "smuggled" them home from Germany. He would warn them that because of the treasures he might be "robbed or murdered or put in prison." Sometimes these announcements were merely titillating; at other times, a little frightening.

Before a year had passed, Farner's clinging dependence had become more than Meador could handle, and he began to retreat from the relationship by bringing home casual acquaintances for nighttime visits.

One day Farner returned to the Willowick after a weekend spent elsewhere at Joe Tom's insistence, and found a drawing of a handsome, seminude man hanging over the bed in the bedroom. It was plain to see that Joe Tom had a new lover. His name, as Farner would soon learn, was Peter Pitsch. Born in Cologne, Germany, Pitsch's mother was German and his father an American G.I., a fact that doubtless intrigued Joe Tom.

As he had with Farner, Meador spent lavishly on Pitsch, buying him clothes and jewelry. Farner became intensely jealous, according to Cadenhead, who knew them both. On one occasion, when Cadenhead and Farner were alone together in the Willowick apartment, Cadenhead asked innocently, *"Who* is Peter?" Farner marched him into the bedroom and pointed to the drawing over the bed. "That! The drawing. *That's* Peter," said Farner, his voice dripping with malice.

Cadenhead also said that Farner, who began to drink heavily, once became so irate about Joe Tom's interest in Pitsch that he threw a cocktail tumbler through one of the plate-glass windows in the turret. "Things were getting to the point where I was worried someone would get hurt," said Cadenhead.

As Pitsch replaced Farner in Joe Tom's affection, it came as a surprise for him to learn that Pitsch—like Farner when he had first met him—was living with another man. Furthermore, Pitsch's companion was not one he was about to cast aside. For the past fifteen years, Pitsch had been living with Gordon Young, a teacher of art at Richland College in Dallas. They were known in the gay world as a "married" couple. Meador soon realized that the only way he could have Pitsch would be to take Young, too.

This arrangement was acceptable to Young, who said he didn't mind Pitsch's occasional flings so long as they were not carried on behind his back. The result was a foursome in which Joe Tom lived with Mike but was infatuated with Peter, while Peter flirted with Joe Tom but was really devoted to Gordon.

After a few months, the deck of sexual cards was shuffled again. Farner drifted south to San Antonio, and Meador, Young, and Pitsch formed a stable menage-à-trois frequently seen at museums and art galleries in Dallas. Young, who is well connected in the local art scene, introduced Joe Tom to a number of art galleries, but recalled that he was not astute in his judgments of contemporary art and really preferred going to antique shops and garage sales.

"Sunday was the day when we always went shopping," Young recalled. "It was Peter, Joe Tom, and me. He loved to pick up junk. Odd objects. He didn't have much aesthetic sense. He just loved old things."

One day in 1976, Joe Tom noticed blood in his semen. His "touch of cancer" had returned, this time to the prostate gland. He underwent surgery and chemotherapy, lost his hair, and developed a gaunt look. Emerging from the hospital aware that his condition was terminal, he became openly gay. He wore a shoulder-length blond wig, powdered his face and heavily decorated himself with jewelry.

At about this time, he attended a reunion of the old Eighty-seventh in Kansas City. His appearance created a stir. According to one of the wives who studied him closely, Meador was wearing a woman's length wig tinted pink and "turned under like a pageboy." He also wore makeup—rouge and powder—an earring, necklaces, and rings.

One morning, a couple of the veterans' wives came upon him in the hotel's breakfast room. He smiled and beckoned for them to join him.

"I never had been around anybody like that!" said one of the wives who lives in a small town in Oklahoma's cattle country. "I was a little bit embarrassed to sit down beside him, but I did and then I was just fascinated with his conversation about his travels."

In October 1978, Maybelle Meador died of a heart attack at the age of eighty-six. Joe Tom was with her when the end came. He was sitting and talking to her when she "keeled over," a member of the family said. He was inconsolable. Against his doctor's orders, he began to drink heavily, and soon became dependent on the painkiller Allodin, a synthetic morphine.

He drank himself to stupefaction at his dinner parties at the Willowick, passed out at gay bars, and once, at an orchid society gathering in Atlanta, collapsed in the men's room of the hotel where he was staying and had to be carried to his room.

Later that year, Hunsaker visited Dallas and saw Joe Tom for the last time. Hunsaker again brought up the subject of returning the treasures to Germany. "By then, what with chemotherapy and all the pain and dreadful side-effects," Hunsaker said, "he had lost the will to struggle with the problem. I think at that point he felt sort of like what Madame de Pompadour said to Louis XV: 'Après nous, le déluge'" (After us, the flood!).

As Joe Tom's physical condition worsened, his need for personal adornment increased. That was why he required Eddie Johnson to deliver the treasures to Dallas every weekend. They reassured him.

At a gay bar one evening, Joe Tom's friends recall, after bragging noisily about his "fabulous treasures," he escorted a young man to the Willowick, and promptly passed out.

The man departed with one of the rock crystal reliquaries. He took it to his home in Houston; later, conscience-stricken, gave it together with Joe Tom's name and address to his Roman Catholic priest. The priest—it would surprise Matthews to learn—had the reliquary delivered to Meador's apartment in Dallas.

By 1979, the cancer had progressed to his spine and

Meador was obliged to wear a neck brace to support his head. If ever a man paid for his sins, Joe Tom Meador was about to do so. He next lost control of one eye, which gave him double vision, requiring him to wear an eyepatch. Gamely, he tried to keep up appearances.

"I remember one occasion when we had lunch together in a restaurant and he just couldn't get the wig straight," Young recalled. "It was terrible to watch him struggle with it."

That summer, the members of the Eighty-seventh decided to hold another reunion, this time in San Antonio. Meador volunteered to help with preparations, but by the time the gathering was to begin he was in the hospital. Paul Garretson, a former private in the unit who now lives in Oklahoma, stopped by to visit Joe Tom on his way to the reunion. The two men had a long talk, Garretson said. Meador began by dramatizing his medical condition, telling Garretson that he had five doctors working on him and they couldn't agree on a diagnosis. After a while, Garretson said, Joe Tom seemed to wilt and dropped his pretense. He spoke slowly and softly, saying: "Garretson, I'm dying."

Two days later, Meador surprised everyone at the San Antonio reunion by appearing at the hotel where the group had assembled. He didn't stay long and spoke to only a few people, one of them being George Barber, the former commander of the unit who had written such scathing reports about him. "He looked like a different person," said Barber. "He was so gaunt, I thought to myself, it must take a lot of guts to show up in this condition. You had to admire that."

Back in Dallas, Joe Tom wrecked his station wagon by running into a hydrant, and it became clear to him as well as to his brother and sister that he could no longer safely handle a car. That was when he hired Eddie Johnson to drive him back and forth between Whitewright and the Willowick.

A short while later, Meador became confused about the various medications he was taking and overdosed. One day

Pitsch and Young found him lying on the floor of his apartment. By the time they got him to a hospital, he was hallucinating.

"The first night," Young recalled, "he jumped out of bed and started racing through the hallway of the hospital. I don't think he was even clothed. The next day they asked if one of us could stay with him at night because he needed watching all the time. We agreed to help out in shifts, but that was when Jack and Jane decided to have him moved to the nursing home in Whitewright. They took away his clothes. They took his checkbook. They had him declared legally incompetent. And they took away the treasures so that I don't think he ever saw them again."

Within a few weeks, Joe Tom Meador was dead at the age of sixty-three.

Chapter 21

I KNEW FROM PREVIOUS INTERVIEWS that Joe Tom's brother and sister had taken possession of the Quedlinburg treasures as he lay dying in the Whitewright Nursing Home, and I also knew that however much Joe Tom had struggled over whether to part with them, Jack and Jane had no such compunction. It never occurred to them that their brother's war loot should be returned to their rightful owner free of charge. For Jack and Jane, it was a matter of finders-keepers.

Yet selling a collection of medieval artworks was no easy matter for a couple of countryfolk who had no knowledge of art and more than a little suspicion of those who did.

All this intrigued me. How, I wondered, had Jack and Jane discovered that the treasures were in fact genuine and worth a great deal of money? I knew about John Torigian's role in the eventual sale of the Samuhel Gospel; was it possible, I wondered, that the Meadors had tried to sell the things through one or more other professionals before they turned to Torigian? Judging from the secretive way they had behaved with Folter, Collins, and Turner, I concluded that

Jack and Jane suspected they might be doing something unlawful, but I wondered if they had any sense of how dangerous the ground they were treading really was. And finally, I wondered, what took them so long? The Meadors spent an entire decade—from February 1980, when Joe Tom died, to April 1990, when Torigian sold the Samuhel Gospel—to dispose of the first of the twelve pieces in the collection. Did it take them all that time to master the art market? Or was it because they were greedy and the offers they received never seemed quite high enough?

I was able to answer a number of these questions when I came across a Whitewright neighbor who told me about the very first effort Jack and Jane made to discover the value of the treasures. The man told me the following rather hilarious yarn on condition that I not mention his name. After hearing the story, I gladly agreed to the condition.

About a year after the death of Joe Tom, Jack Meador heaved a cardboard box into the back of his station wagon and, together with his wife, Genevieve, and my informant, drove south to Houston. Along the way, they picked up Jane and her husband, Don Cook, who lived just outside of Dallas. According to the neighbor, Jack had heard about a man named Bill Simpson, who ran an art-and-antiques auction gallery in Houston. Simpson was a flamboyant Englishman, wore a two-pointed Sherlock Holmes–style cap, and was reputed to possess a vast knowledge of art—including ancient art. Jack and Jane therefore thought he should be just the right person to help them learn the value of the curiosities they'd inherited from their brother.

Already Jack and Jane had divided between themselves most of Joe Tom's assets, including bric-a-brac, a few stocks, and small parcels of real estate in Whitewright. Jane took her brother's jewelry, including the tiger's-eye ring, a gold ring, and several gold chains. Jack held a garage sale in Whitewright to dispose of a few more of his brother's belongings. The hottest

items at the sale were a huge blood-red Nazi banner emblazoned with a swastika, several Nazi uniforms, German cameras, and a pair of binoculars Joe Tom had sent home from the
war. A couple of browsers looked at the manuscripts, but there
were no offers. Afterwards, the manuscripts were placed in Joe
Tom's personal safe in the family store and left there for about
a year, while Jack and Jane pondered what to do with them.
Eventually, they wound up in the cardboard box to be carted
around in hopes of making a sale. Jack rightly assumed that
the two "Bibles," as he called the manuscripts, were the most
marketable of the pieces in the collection. The rest—the casket, the comb and the reliquary flasks—were evenly divided
between Jack and Jane.

Transporting the precious manuscripts in an old cardboard box en route to Houston was a calculated ploy on
Jack's part. "I like to have people take me for a country hick
who don't know the value of things," he explained to his pas-
sengers in the station wagon. "Then I surprise 'em with what
I *do* know!"

The group recognized Simpson's Auction Gallery as soon
as they drove up to it. A large display window was crammed
with oil paintings blackened with age, ornamental vases and
chinaware, a stuffed rhinoceros head, and a pair of giant ele-
phant tusks festooned with chains of jewelry. This *had* to be
the place.

While one member of the party held the door for Jack, he
swaggered in with the cardboard box, trailed by his
entourage. Simpson, who was seated, Buddha-like, behind a
counter, turned out to be a heavily built, bearded man who
must have weighed 275 pounds. As reputed, he was wearing a
jaunty two-pointed Sherlock Holmes–style cap.

Speaking with an English accent, Simpson greeted his visitors, and asked what they had in the box.

"Ole Bibles," said Jack, plunking the box on the counter in
front of Simpson. "What's they wuth?"

Simpson opened the box and peered in. A loud "Hmm!" escaped him. Gingerly, he lifted the Samuhel Gospel from the box. "Hmm!" he exclaimed again. Then he produced a magnifying glass and began examining the cover intently, harumphing at intervals. Finally, Simpson looked up at Jack. "And what were you expecting to get for these?" he asked coyly.

"Make an offer," said Jack.

Simpson removed the second manuscript from the box and began examining it with his magnifying glass. Then he said: "It would be extremely difficult for you to find just the right buyer for something as unusual as these, but I might be able to do so and earn you several thousands of dollars."

"Several thousands?" Jack repeated.

Simpson spoke with a theatrical hush: "Twenty-five thousand!"

"Ain't near enough," Jack shot back, bluffing recklessly. He hadn't the slightest idea of what the manuscripts were worth. At the garage sale, he had told a neighbor he would be happy to part with the two of them for $500. Now, however, the ill-concealed lust the manuscripts had awakened in Simpson convinced Jack that they must be worth six figures and possibly a great deal more.

Simpson rapidly increased his offer to $50,000 and then $75,000. When even the last bid failed to move Jack, Simpson said he would be flying to London in a few days and would like to take the manuscripts with him because the European market for such items is much better than that in the United States. He added that he would take only a modest commission for himself.

Jack winked at Jane and her husband as he returned the manuscripts to the cardboard box. He told Simpson he would think about his proposition and get back to him.

He never did. The Meadors had received what they came for. They had learned that the manuscripts were worth "serious money," as Jack expressed it on the way home.

*   *   *

I learned about the Meadors' subsequent efforts to sell the treasures from Roland Folter, the New York dealer whose late partner may or may not have offered $100,000 and then $150,000 to buy the manuscripts; from John Carroll Collins, the Dallas art and antiques appraiser who annoyed the Meadors by insisting that the manuscripts must have been stolen; and from Decherd Turner, the former director of the Humanities Research Center at Austin who had a fleeting encounter with Jack Meador and his son Jeff in 1986. But what unleashed a flood of information, producing one of the most complete accounts ever of wheeling and dealing in the international art market, were the depositions that Tom, Willi and their colleagues conducted. These were transcripts of the pretrial interrogation of likely witnesses taken under oath that, after some difficulty, I was able to obtain from a confidential source. In all, there were fifteen depositions, more than 2,500 pages of testimony—and they contained some surprises.

For example, a tawdry story came to light as Steve Rahhal, an Andrews & Kurth colleague of Tom's, questioned Leta Harper, Jane's former college roommate and best friend. Rahhal was asking about the contents of one of Jane's safe-deposit boxes to which Mrs. Harper also had access. It was a perfectly legitimate line of questioning. Rahhal was trying to determine whether any treasures were still hidden away, in defiance of Judge Fitzwater's order. Suddenly, a look of alarm crossed Mrs. Harper's face. Randhal Mathis, a Dallas attorney who was present to look after the rights of the Meadors and friendly witnesses such as Mrs. Harper, immediately called a recess.

In the hallway outside the hearing room where their conversation would not be recorded, Mathis urged Rahhal not to press the witness to be more explicit about the contents of the safe deposit box. He explained that Jane suspected Don of philandering, and had hired a private detective to videotape his comings and goings. The tapes, Mathis explained, were stored in the safe deposit box. Rahhal cordially agreed to direct his questions to other matters.

In another deposition it came out that, shortly before his death, Joe Tom had given one of the treasures to Beth Cook, his favorite niece. It was a small silver locket containing wax from sacred candles burned in St. Peter's Church in Rome nearly a thousand years ago. Beth had no idea of the historical significance of the locket. She was attached to it simply because it was a gift from her dying uncle. Since his death, she had been wearing it on a chain around her neck, and she wept bitterly when she was compelled by Judge Fitzwater's order to release it for identification and safekeeping with the other treasures.

It was through still another of these depositions that I first learned of a lawyer named Terry Mitchell, whom the Meadors engaged after their attempts to sell the treasures on their own in dealings with Simpson, Folter, Collins and Turner had failed. The retaining of Mitchell was a milestone in the case because it marked the point at which the Meadors sought the assistance of a professional agent to work in their behalf. At this point, selling their brother's legacy was no longer a game for amateurs; the Meadors were getting serious, and it was clear that they were expecting serious compensation for their trouble.

Mitchell, as it happened, spoke to me quite openly about his involvement. He had conducted himself honorably and had nothing to hide. On the other hand, Christie's, the world-renowned art auction house through which Mitchell attempted to sell the manuscripts in the late 1980s, was closed-mouthed. I was fortunate, however, to find a member of the firm who accepted my argument that Christie's might come off looking better if it were open rather than secretive about its involvement. As a result, I was allowed to read the firm's private file on the case. From these sources, plus depositions by Christie's senior staff, I put together the following account—one that provides an unusual glimpse into the inner workings of a major international art auction house.

In the spring of 1987, Jeff Meador, the son of Jack and Genevieve, introduced his parents to Terry Mitchell, a young lawyer then practicing in Austin. Jeff had come to know Mitchell through his accounting business. Despite the fact that Mitchell was wholly inexperienced in the art market, Jack and Jane were impressed by his energy and enthusiasm ("This is a once-in-a-lifetime thing for me," he told the Meadors after he had been given a look at the treasures). What they did not bargain for, however, were his high ethical standards.

After researching the matter throughout the summer, Mitchell wrote to Stephen Massey, the director of the book and manuscripts department at the New York office of Christie's. He enclosed thirty-five black-and-white photographs of the covers and various pages of the manuscripts, and asked Massey for assistance in appraising and selling them.

Massey later testified in a deposition that he opened Mitchell's letter with a yawn because it was not from a well-known collector or dealer and he had people calling him "twice a week" wanting to sell "a Gutenberg Bible" which invariably turned out to be printed in Old German or Old English instead of fifteenth-century Latin as are authentic Gutenbergs. The photographs, however, took his breath away. Although about to depart on a collecting tour in Europe, Massey rearranged his schedule so that he could inspect Mitchell's manuscripts before he left the country. To cover himself, he engaged as a consultant John H. Plummer, a respected curator of medieval and Renaissance manuscripts at the Pierpont Morgan Library in New York City.

Both Massey and Plummer were on hand on November 27,

according to a memorandum in the Christie's file, when Mitchell and a mysterious "Mr. Cook" arrived with the manuscripts. Massey immediately became suspicious when Mitchell asked him to sign an elaborate five-page agreement pledging never to reveal the name of the seller and serving notice that his clients would sue Christie's for damages if confidentiality were breached. Massey refused to sign the document, agreeing only to execute Christie's standard property receipt stating that the objects had been accepted "for examination." After long discussion, Mitchell and Cook finally agreed to forego their elaborate agreement and accept instead a much less formal assurance that the name of the seller would not be revealed. This assurance came in the form of a letter from Elizabeth J. Kunstadter, then chief of the estates and appraisals department of Christie's.

Another Christie's memorandum shows that when Massey and Plummer examined the manuscripts they knew at once that they had something truly extraordinary in their hands. They identified the Samuhel Gospel as a work of the late ninth or early tenth century and insured it for a whopping $6 million. The second manuscript was recognized as being from the late 15th century and insured for much less—only $100,000.

"The obvious concern of everyone involved," a Christie's memorandum stated, "is that the manuscripts were taken from Europe during or immediately after World War II." If that were the case, the sellers would not possess clear title and Christie's could not lawfully put the manuscripts on the auction block.

Consequently, Plummer hurried back to the Morgan Library and checked the two basic reference works on Central European medieval manuscripts—the Goldschmidt and Bischoff books. From these, he determined that what he had just seen were the long-missing manuscripts from Quedlinburg.

When I interviewed Plummer, he told me that he immediately called Massey and reported that it was almost certain the manuscripts were stolen property. "My conclusion was so obvious it wasn't worth writing a long report," Plummer explained, "I just told Massey what I thought over the telephone."

But Massey, Plummer said, was unwilling to shrug off the matter and send Mitchell and Cook packing—possibly to a competitor. The manuscripts, especially the Samuhel Gospel, were just too rare, too beautiful, too *important*, to be hastily brushed aside. Later, Massey would testify that the Samuhel Gospel is "in the top five of the objects I have ever handled in all the twenty-six years I have been at Christie's." Clearly, he was enthralled, and kept nagging Plummer to see if there weren't some way in which the manuscripts could be seen as legitimate.

Well, said Plummer, yes, there was one way, although it was only "an outside chance."

And what is that? asked Massey with growing excitement.

Plummer explained that one of the two reference works he had consulted, the Bischoff study published in 1974, could be seen as ambiguous about the status of the manuscripts.

"Go on, go on," said Massey.

Plummer continued: Bischoff had written that the Quedlinburg manuscripts were "formerly in the Church Treasury, destroyed" (*früher im Domschatz, vernichtet*). Plummer insisted that the most reasonable interpretation of that statement is the one he made originally; namely, that the manuscripts had been stolen at the war's end. That would explain both how they came into the hands of a couple of Americans like Mitchell and Cook, and also the seller's insistence on the strictest confidentiality. Based on that interpretation, Plummer emphasized, Christie's "shouldn't touch the manuscripts with a ten-foot pole."

On the other hand, he conceded, there was a possibility—

however remote—that Bischoff had meant literally that the manuscripts had been destroyed during the war, which meant that the objects delivered by the two Texans could be something else. Conceivably, these could be a couple of heretofore unknown medieval manuscripts closely resembling those from Quedlinburg that had turned up legitimately.

Massey had what he desperately wanted, a rationale for retaining the manuscripts while he and Plummer investigated the matter more thoroughly. As a result, he did not return the manuscripts to Mitchell, but kept them nearly five months, hoping against hope that a way could be found to sell them—which, of course, would not only earn a huge commission for Christie's but doubtless a juicy bonus and professional stardom for himself.

But Massey was kidding himself. The speculation that the Quedlinburg manuscripts had been destroyed by the fighting in the war while the city itself remained unscathed was far-fetched. I wondered how such an experienced hand in the art world as Massey could refuse to accept the obvious. Another art dealer I spoke to came up with a plausible answer.

"When we connoisseurs see something truly extraordinary," this dealer told me, "we begin to think our whole career has been a preparation for coming upon this precise object, and we can't let it slip through our fingers. That's just the way we're made."

Perhaps so. Yet Massey is no fool. The fact that he was uneasy about the legitimacy of the two manuscripts so long in his keeping is revealed in an interoffice memo he wrote to Elizabeth Kunstadter on December 16.

Before the manuscripts can be put up for sale, Massey began, Christie's must resolve the ambiguity in the Bischoff book. Then, thinking aloud, he speculated that an attempt could be made "through American and German legal sources" to determine the status of the manuscripts in Quedlinburg. But he quickly rejected the idea. Such an investigation, he wrote, "might risk a demand for repatriation of the manuscripts, just as a full-scale international legal inquiry might do so as well." In other words, he appeared to be saying, maybe it's better not to be burdened with knowing the truth.

Mitchell didn't hear from Christie's until December 22, 1987, when Kunstadter called and then wrote to say that Plummer had finally erased all doubt that the two manuscripts were among the stolen treasures of Quedlinburg. In sum, the stuff was hot. Christie's wanted to get rid of it!

In a clandestine meeting at the Los Angeles airport on March 18, 1988, a Christie's agent turned over the manuscripts to an associate of Mitchell's. Yet three weeks later, Massey—still under the spell of the Samuhel Gospel—could not bring himself to abandon all hope of proving the manuscripts marketable. He wrote to Mitchell to surrender a set of color slides that he had made of the manuscripts for sales purposes, and at the same time urged Mitchell to allow Plummer to show the manuscripts to Professor Mütherich, the great authority on Carolingian manuscripts. Mütherich was scheduled to deliver a lecture at the Morgan Library in New York on April 12, Massey said, and she could inspect the manuscripts then.

"If your clients could agree," Massey pleaded, "this could provide an ideal opportunity to show both of the manuscripts to the leading German scholar who would need be approached eventually *if the manuscripts were to be sold*." (Italics added) It seemed that Massey believed in miracles as fully as did Samuhel and his medieval patrons.

Mitchell, meanwhile, wrote to the East German consulate to ask if the manuscripts possessed by his clients could be those from Quedlinburg. Yes, came a stinging reply, they're ours and they were stolen at the war's end by American soldiers. Give them back!

On May 3, Mitchell called Massey to report that after hearing from the East German consulate he was "of the firm opinion" that the manuscripts were stolen property and that he had decided to advise his clients to return them to Germany at once. Hearing this, Massey decided that the best way out for Christie's would be for him also to assist in repatriating the manuscripts. When asked in a deposition exactly how Christie's might participate in this process, Massey regaled the sober-faced lawyers with a wry vision of "a fanfare starring sleuthing Stephen Massey [who] finds [a] hidden hoard in Texas. . . ."

"Stop it!" called out Patricia Hambrecht, the Christie's counsel, fearing that Massey might say something to cast the auction house in a bad light.

Unabashed, Massey went on to say that he was only thinking of "a properly conducted announcement," sharing credit with Plummer and the Morgan Library, which would make the point that the often-maligned commercial art world enterprises like Christie's can be counted on to behave responsibly when presented with stolen art. It was a nice speech, certainly nothing at which Hambrecht (who is now managing director of Christie's) would take umbrage, but it ducked the most serious question raised by Christie's behavior: namely whether, after the auction house had devoted nearly five months of study to determine that the manuscripts were stolen property, it had called the police, as might be expected of a law-abiding citizen. The answer is no. Christie's quietly returned the booty to the agent of the presumptive thief.

If anyone could claim to have acted ethically up to this point it would be Mitchell. As soon as he heard from the Germans, he told the Meadors that there was no longer any doubt but that the manuscripts were stolen and should be returned to Germany without any further ado. He was promptly fired.

"I'd like to be wealthy," he reflected afterward, "but I guess the best I can hope for is that I'll go to my grave as a man with a fairly decent reputation."

In short order, the Meadors found a lawyer more to their liking. Their choice was John S. Torigian, a cocky, bantam-weight Houston attorney who had done well for himself in the dog-eat-dog world of defending building contractors against accident and liability claims. Since Torigian had spoken to me only briefly on the one occasion when he rather than his secretary answered my call, I base the following on interviews with persons who know him, depositions by members of the Meador family, and Torigian's own extremely revealing two-day-long deposition, which was conducted by Alan Harris.

Like his predecessor, Torigian came to Jack and Jane recommended by Jeff Meador. Although mainly a provincial type born and raised in Austin, Texas, Torigian had something special on his résumé that appealed to the Meadors. After graduating from the South Texas College of Law in Houston, he had spent a year at the University of Paris studying European Common Market law. Although he returned to Texas speaking only a few words of French, it was enough to convince the Meadors that he knew his way around the capitals of Europe and was ideally qualified to market their war loot. When Torigian said he would require a five-percent commission on whatever gross sales price he was able to collect for the two manuscripts, Jack and Jane, by now thoroughly frustrated, were only too glad to sign the contract he drew up for them.

In truth, Torigian was far from an expert on art, not to mention medieval art. In his deposition, he acknowledged that when he first tried to sell the manuscripts he thought, like Eddie Johnson, that the covers were made of brass, not gold. But though he was out of his depth in the art world, the Meadors could scarcely have found a more enterprising attorney to represent them than John Torigian.

After making several attempts to drum up interest in the manuscripts in the United States, including a nearly consummated deal with Kren of the Getty Museum, Torigian departed for Europe and began pitching the manuscripts to possible buyers in Paris, Zurich, and Geneva.

At least two prominent dealers, Paul-Louis Couailhac, of Paris, and Jacques T. Quentin, of Geneva, told him that after researching the matter they believed the manuscripts to have been stolen from Quedlinburg and were therefore unsalable. Torigian had his own style of dealing with people who dared to suggest any such thing. He threatened to sue them for slander or libel.

A week or two after his arrival in Europe, Torigian was at the airport outside Geneva waiting for the arrival of the Meadors and their children at the start of a summer vacation trip through Switzerland. Chivalrously, Torigian escorted them to their hotel; over lunch the next day he told his clients that he was close to making a fabulous sale for them. He had received offers for the two manuscripts, he said, ranging from $2.6 million to $10 million. Over the next week, the Meadors went shopping in Geneva, Zurich, and Zermatt with dreams in their heads of opening Swiss bank accounts to contain all their new-found wealth. But something went wrong. The offers Torigian had been so confident of when he met the Meadors in Geneva dried up. Potential buyers, it seemed, were put off by the doubtful provenance of the manuscripts, and Torigian and the Meadors returned to Texas no richer than when they left.

But now Torigian had the itch, and during the next couple of years made no fewer than a dozen trips to Europe lugging the manuscripts with him. In March 1990, he lightened his load and set about hawking only the choice Samuhel Gospel. He would deal with the less valuable 1513 Evangelistar later. Court documents show that Torigian commenced what is known in the trade as riding two horses; that is, simultaneously working out deals with two potential buyers with the object of playing them off against each other. In fact, Torigian was soon riding four horses. First, through Couailhac, the

Parisian dealer, he offered the Samuhel Gospel to Klaus Maurice's organization, the West German Cultural Foundation of the States. The price was $9 million.

Second, through the Swiss dealer Jacques Quentin and the West German dealer Heribert Tenschert, he offered the Samuhel Gospel to Maurice. In this deal, however, the price was only $3 million.

Third, through Quentin he offered the Samuhel Gospel to Thomas Kren, curator of manuscripts at the J. Paul Getty Museum in Malibu, California. The price was $6 million. Since Quentin had served as the go-between in two of these possible deals, Torigian promised him a commission of ten percent of the sale price. (Quentin would shortly receive $50,000 as a downpayment).

And finally, Torigian arranged a deal with Bruce Ferrini, a young dealer based in Akron, Ohio, who worked in partnership with a prominent London dealer named Sam Fogg. Sambruce, as they are jocularly known in the trade, were also interested at $6 million. At first, Sambruce proposed to sell the manuscripts to a client in Norway and then to one in Japan, but when those deals fell through they offered themselves as an alternate conduit to Kren of the Getty.

"I knew the manuscripts had been stolen and there was no way we could legitimately sell them," Ferrini told me. "And yet Torigian kept saying there was a forty-five-year statute of limitations on war loot after the onset of World War II. In my heart, I knew there was no such thing, but we believed it coming from a lawyer. I wanted those manuscripts so badly, I never questioned him seriously. I tell you, it brought out the worst in all of us."

Which deal to grab—$3 million, $6 million, $9 million?

Two of the most attractive deals, from Torigian's standpoint, came with strings attached. One of these was from Kren of the Getty. He wanted Torigian to sign a copy of the Getty's standard warranty affirming that the seller has clear title to the object offered for sale. Torigian signed but only after heavily editing the document. Kren told me that Torigian's changes in the warranty "made it obvious that he did not have clear title." When Kren explained this to Torigian, who was then juggling the other three possible deals, Torigian drafted a second revision of the Getty warranty, signed it and faxed it to Kren. It was still unacceptable.

Kren had told me that when the Samuhel Gospel was first offered to him he began to research its provenance and quickly determined that it had been stolen from Quedlinburg. In that case, I said, why did he keep pressing Torigian to sign what he must have realized would be a false declaration? Kren's answer was evasive.

"When something really terrific like this comes along, we have a responsibility to investigate and see what the legal situation is," he said. "So I investigated. I also asked around in the market. There were a number of stories going around about this piece, and it's my job as curator to find out what the situation is."

At virtually the last minute, Kren withdrew from the bidding. Torigian testified that Kren did so because he was "unable to assemble the funds," and Kren told me it was because Torigian had refused to sign a clean warranty. Kren may well have gotten high on the same aesthetic aphrodisiac that affected Massey's judgment.

Meanwhile, Klaus Maurice, acting as a spokesman for the German foundation, told Tenschert that his agreement to pay $3 million for the manuscript was contingent on Tenschert's submitting proof of his assurance that he was acting altruistically and was not pocketing a commission on the deal. Maurice explained that it would expose his quasiofficial organization to criticism in Germany if it became known that it had enriched a German dealer with German taxpayers' money for recovering works of undisputed German patrimony.

Tenschert acceded to this request, and that cleared the way

for Torigian to accept the relatively low Quentin-Tenschert offer. It is not difficult to guess why he preferred a $3 million deal over one for $6 million or one for $9 million. The Quentin deal offered the advantage of making the sale in Switzerland, whose laws protect such dealings. The Couailhac and Sambruce deals could not approach what lawyers would call the "comfort level" provided by Quentin.

When Torigian and Tenschert met in a hotel suite in Munich for the denouement, Tenschert borrowed an old-fashioned typewriter from the management and wrote not one but two separate agreements. Both were dated March 23, 1990. The first was the sales agreement under which Tenschert purchased the Samuhel Gospel from Torigian for $3 million. This document, signed by both Tenschert and Torigian, was to be presented to Maurice as proof that no money had been diverted to pay Tenschert a commission. However, the second agreement typed in the hotel and signed by both men stated that "with regard to our letter agreement dated March 23" concerning the Samuhel Gospel, Tenschert was to receive "a commission of $500,000."

When Willi told me that Torigian had revealed this double dealing in the course of his deposition, I immediately called Tenschert at his home in Rotthalmünster, a small town in Bavaria where he conducts his business. I spoke to both Tenschert and his wife, Helga, who said she sometimes acts as her husband's spokeswoman. Both insisted that Tenschert had not received a half-million-dollar under-the-table commission on the sale of the Samuhel Gospel. Oh no, they insisted, Tenschert had no intention of exercising the second agreement. It was only "a backup" in case the German government reneged on its commitment to buy the Samuhel Gospel at the agreed-upon price.

It now remained only to physically transfer the Samuhel Gospel from Torigian to Quentin, Quentin to Tenschert, and finally Tenschert to Maurice.

"Did anything else occur at that meeting [in the hotel in Munich] other than the execution of this agreement?" Alan Harris asked Torigian at the close of the deposition.

A smile of triumph crept over Torigian's face. "We drank some champagne," he said.

Chapter 22

WHEN MIKE FARNER TOLD ME THAT JOE TOM once expressed a wish to see his medieval treasures exhibited in a museum like the Fabergé Gold Show they visited in San Antonio, I dismissed it as another instance of Meador's periodic detachment from reality. To be sure, robber barons like John D. Rockefeller and conquerors like Napoleon Bonaparte had been benefactors of great museums, but they at least could *claim* the legitimacy of their collections through military or monetary might. What museum worthy of the name would glorify a common thief like Meador by displaying his loot in the sanctity of its galleries? It would be like inviting a rapist to dance at his victim's wedding. And yet I was rapidly becoming familiar with the rampant venality of the art world, and in fact it would not be long before Meador's outlandish wish would be granted—in full!

The idea for this event was born amid the pretrial maneuvering of the various lawyers in the case. There were, however, a few preliminaries to be taken care of first. To begin with, Tom Kline persuaded Judge Fitzwater to extend the temporary restraining order prohibiting movement of the treasures for ten days. The new restraining order secured them for the duration of the trial, a resounding defeat for the Meadors and John Torigian. Unless they could win their case in court, they had now lost the chance to sneak the remaining treasures off to Switzerland and sell them with impunity.

A day or two later, Torigian asked Judge Fitzwater to excuse him from representing the Meadors. His request was immediately granted; when I called him to ask why he had backed out, he spoke as if through clenched teeth. "We will let our court pleading speak for itself," he said and hung up.

I don't know whether I had helped him make up his mind, but shortly before his withdrawal I'd reported in the *Times* that Torigian "has been identified by a number of art experts as having tried here and in Europe to sell the Quedlinburg treasures since about 1986." By acting as both a sales agent for the Meadors and then their defense attorney, Torigian had blundered into a conflict-of-interest trap and was now trying to extricate himself. For the present he succeeded, but in time he would reappear in the case a great deal more prominently than he might have wished.

The Meadors, now on their third attorney, replaced Torigian with an affable beanpole from Dallas named Randal Mathis. Since it was apparent that a protracted court battle was taking shape, the Meadors pressed Mathis to hold down expenses. In particular, they grumbled about the high cost of storing the treasures in the vault of Fine Arts Express in Fort Worth, the moving-and storage-company Tom had arranged to use when negotiating with Powers and Torigian and that all parties had agreed upon as temporary repository for the treasures. Mathis had agreed to assume half the cost of the storage, but now that his clients were beefing about the size of their bill he had a brainstorm. He called Richard Brettell, the director of the Dallas Museum of Art, and asked if the museum would be willing to store the loot free of charge as a public service.

Brettell, a round-faced, owlish man with a mercenary turn of mind, thought it over and came back with a counter-proposal. He would agree to store the treasures free of charge, he told Mathis, in exchange for the museum's having exclusive right to exhibit them after the case was finally settled. It never seemed to have occurred to Brettell that the reputation of a museum—presumably a guardian of ethical standards—could be tarnished by his striking a bargain with the heirs of a thief. Mathis and Tom Kline, also apparently blind to the implications of the deal, quickly accepted Brettell's proposition.

When I caught wind of the plan, I called the museum. Brettell was not available, so I spoke to Melanie Wright, the institution's official spokesperson. She acknowledged that the lawyers for both parties were "within a hair's breadth of agreement" to give the museum temporary custody of the treasures.

I reported the facts in a brief story for the newspaper. One or two of my colleagues who write for the editorial page of the *Times* must have seen it, because a few days later a blistering editorial appeared at the top of that page, under the headline "T AS IN TREASURE, TEXAS AND THEFT." In it the *Times* excoriated the Dallas Museum of Art, declaring that it had proved itself "kin to Joe T. Meador."

Brettell, I was informed by a museum insider, went a little crazy when he read that editorial. Getting rapped with a negative review on the art page is one thing, but this must really have been a nightmare seeing his institution denounced in a lead editorial in the New York *Times*—a measure of reproach they usually reserved for the rulers of Communist Albania. The Dallas *Morning News* soon followed suit, and Brettell got whacked a second time.

To many, it must have seemed a tempest in a teapot, but

not to Brettell. In his zeal to defend himself, he made things worse. He wrote a letter to the *Times* deploring the editorial that equated him with a thief, and added that the museum had "never announced" that it would exhibit the artworks. The latter remark was true as of that moment because, in fact, no formal announcement had been made even though the agreement had already been endorsed privately by all parties and the museum exhibition *would* be announced sooner or later. Nevertheless, the *Times* took Brettell at his word and published his indignant letter. This was followed only a few days later by my report to the effect that the museum now *had* announced an exhibition of the treasures following the conclusion of the trial. Brettell thus came away from the mess looking even worse than before.

And lest there be any lingering doubts as to why Brettell had been so eager to exhibit the treasures, a reporter for *D*, the Dallas magazine, settled that. In the course of an interview with the reporter, Brettell remarked that if he could only have one sensational show every year like the one he was planning for the highly publicized Quedlinburg treasures, he "wouldn't [ever] have to worry about [a] projected deficit."

Meanwhile, Tom, Willi, and a couple of young lawyers from Andrews & Kurth began conducting depositions, and with that Mathis had his hands full. Apart from protecting the rights of his clients and of the friendly witnesses who took part in the depositions, he had to develop an overall legal strategy for the Meadors. His worries were not limited to Tom Kline's civil lawsuit aimed at forcing Jack and Jane to surrender the treasures. Mathis also had to worry about whatever charges might result from the swirl of investigations by state and federal law-enforcement agencies now under way.

To deal with the civil lawsuit, he came up with a two-part strategy. First, Mathis argued before Judge Fitzwater, since the treasures had been "inappropriately removed" from Germany forty-five years previously, the Texas two-year statute of limitations had long since run its course, and therefore the plaintiff's case had no validity. Second, he declared that Jack and Jane had not stolen the treasures, but had gained legal title to them by "squatters' rights" under Texas adverse-possession law. This statute, normally applied only in real-estate cases, would permit a rancher, say, to gain title to a cow pasture by using it for two years without challenge by its owner. Mathis's contention was that by similar reasoning the Meadors had come into lawful possession of the treasures two years after Joe Tom's death. "Our position," he told me, "is that the Meadors are legitimate owners of the treasures and that they are willing to surrender that claim only for a substantial monetary consideration."

This strategy held Tom Kline at bay for the moment, but a week or two later Mathis—who usually spoke with a youthful, upbeat Texas twang—was sounding all gloom and doom. "We're being investigated by the Internal Revenue Service," he told me. I knew already that the IRS bill could be a whopper, since aside from the estate tax plus interest for all the years since Joe Tom's death, the levy would most likely include penalties for failure to file the estate tax form and to pay the tax when due. Then there was also the capital gains tax on the increase in value of the treasures since Joe Tom's death in 1980. The result could well be a multi-million-dollar bill that Jack and Jane would not be able to pay.

On September 17, Mathis wrote to Tom proposing a ten-point settlement. In a suggested "money package," he attempted to deal with the possible tax levy the Meadors might be faced with. He asked for $1.5 million with a guarantee to pay any estate tax that the Meadors might be assessed, or, alternatively, $2.5 million with no such promise.

At the time Tom received Mathis's letter, he, too, was experiencing difficulties. Willi, almost in tears, had just divulged to him the news that the Foundation for Prussian Cultural Heritage refused to continue supporting the effort to recover the treasures. Tom was stunned. He had not been employed by Andrews & Kurth long enough to feel entirely secure about his position with the firm, and he feared that some of the senior partners might have been uneasy about his taking on the Quedlinburg case. Tom had recently learned that one of the firm's most important clients was the Getty Trust, whose assets are in the neighborhood of $4 billion. The Getty Trust owns and supports the Getty Museum in Malibu, California, which is loaded with antiquities. As with most such museums, some of these objects are of doubtful provenance. Furthermore, Tom knew that the Getty's curator of manuscripts, Thomas Kren, had come close to buying the Samuhel Gospel from Torigian. So Tom's representing a foreign government in an attempt to recover stolen antiquities might—in the eyes of some Andrews & Kurth partners—run counter to the interests of the Getty. And what was bad for the Getty Trust might be equally so for Andrews & Kurth.

But even if the partners did stomach all that, Tom wondered, how would they take it when they learned that the Quedlinburg case, which at first appeared to offer a lucrative contract with the West German Government, was turning out to be a charity case? *That,* for sure, would not sit well with the partners.

Scared and disappointed, Tom spent several days on the phone to Germany. He is a very persuasive talker, and finally found a sympathetic listener in the person of Klaus Maurice, the avuncular chief of the German cultural agency. Sensing Tom's desperation, Maurice prevailed on the West German Foreign Ministry to come across with about $35,000 for Andrews & Kurth (their final bill would run to more than ten times that amount). Willi also received a payment of about $7,000 from the Foreign Ministry, less than he claimed to be owed but enough to keep him in Wienerschnitzl and schnapps for a spell.

Greatly relieved, Tom then began to negotiate the stipulations proposed in Mathis's letter. After a dozen weeks of hard bargaining, he realized that the two sides had now come close enough so that a face-to-face meeting might finally clinch an agreement. There was a certain amount of haggling about when and where the meeting should take place. At first, Maurice suggested Berlin, but the Meadors feared that if they showed up in Germany they could be subject to arrest. Consequently, the Texans proposed New York, but the Germans felt uncomfortable with that. Finally, all agreed to meet on January 7, 1991, in London, that being considered neutral territory.

The adversaries stayed in separate hotels. The Meadors gathered at the Marriott, a flag-bedecked red-brick structure in the Mayfair section of London. The group included Jack, Jane, their spouses, and Randal Mathis. Jane and Don Cook, still in the thick of their marital difficulties, spent the night in separate rooms.

The Germans were housed a few blocks away, at the white stone Park Lane Hotel. They were led by Klaus Maurice, and included Tom Kline and Alan Harris serving as American counsel for the Cultural Foundation, Friedemann Gosslau (pastor of the Quedlinburg church), and enough lawyers and officials to suggest that an international disarmament conference was under way.

Conspicuously absent were John Torigian and Willi Korte, who will reappear in this story before long.

When the parties met in a conference room at the Park Lane, things took a quarrelsome turn. At one point, Jane announced that it was pointless to continue the discussion. While in London, she said, she was going to enjoy herself and go shopping. With that, the Meadors left the conference room.

"It was standard posturing," Tom later told me. "They came right back after lunch."

The negotiations dragged on for a total of eight hours, but by the end of the day a tentative agreement had been reached.

I spoke to both Tom and Randal Mathis by transatlantic telephone and then quickly threw together what turned out to be a front-page story for the next day's paper. The essential part of the tentative agreement, I reported, was that the Germans would pay about $1 million to the Meadors in exchange for the return of the treasures. That would bring their total profit from the treasures up to $2.75 million.

The draft settlement also stipulated that before the artworks could be taken back to Germany they would make their post–World War II debut at the Dallas Museum of Art. Someone "up there" was smiling.

My phone was busy throughout the next day as the reaction set in. "It's not so different from paying ransom to buy back your baby," said Dr. Constance Lowenthal, the executive director of the IFAR, which specializes in tracking stolen art.

I reached Willi in Munich. He was furious about having been left out of the meeting, but even more so about the terms of the tentative settlement. "Paying for the return of stolen property was, is, and always will be a stupid mistake," he snapped.

Robert T. Buck, director of the Brooklyn Museum, was among the more outspoken museum professionals I talked to. He called the agreement "submission to blackmail."

The *Times* also weighed in with an editorial denouncing the ransom payment as "a deplorable precedent," and arguing that the U.S. government must not be swayed by the fact that the Meadors have "wrung a statement from the German government that it has 'no desire' for the U.S. government to take any action against the family." The editorial concluded bitingly: "If the U.S. takes no action [against the Meadors], that will leave the Meadors with their ill-gotten stash—and the rest of America with evidence that honesty is a fool's game."

When I reached Maurice back in Berlin, he was jubilant and recalled that when the Germans flew home together Gosslau reminded the group that the next day was Epiphany. "He told us," Maurice said, "that we three representatives—of the Ministry of the Interior, my foundation, and his church—were like the three kings bringing the treasures to the Christ child."

Unfortunately, this joyfulness did not last long. Only a few days after the London meeting, the IRS made public its ruling that the Meadors were wrong to have filed a tax declaration without mentioning the treasures when Joe Tom's estate was probated. Henry Holmes, a spokesman for the tax agency, told me that the IRS had based its determination on the value of the treasures as of 1980, when Joe Tom died, and would levy a tax accordingly. Mathis told me the bill was in the millions, but would not be more specific. Another reliable source who spoke to me only after being promised anonymity said that the bill, which he claimed to have seen, was for a mind-boggling $30 million. This panicked the Meadors. Mathis immediately challenged the levy with a motion in tax court, but, not surprisingly, Jack and Jane said they could not finalize the London settlement until they had a better understanding of the likely outcome of the contest with the IRS.

The German camp was also seized with indecision. Some officials in the Foreign Ministry feared the consequences of sending a signal that West Germany is willing to buy back thousands of things stolen during the war. Others were concerned that a cash payment might be construed as a lack of faith in the American legal system, a criticism of the United States that the West German government would not feel comfortable making. Still others feared that one or another aspect of the tentative settlement might stir up resentment of Germany.

Despite all such worries, on February 25, 1992, after a year and a half of highly publicized wrangling, the Meadors and the Germans signed a final agreement that included in one form or another all ten of Mathis's original stipulations.

Not overlooked was the provision that the treasures would go on exhibition at the Dallas Museum of Art for six weeks, and that only after that could they be shipped to Berlin, for conservation at the State Museum of Decorative Art, an exhibition, and their final return to Quedlinburg.

Shortly before the museum show opened, I interviewed Brettell. He acknowledged having remarked some months previously that if the museum could have an exhibition like the Quedlinburg show once a year he wouldn't have to worry about a projected deficit. But, he added, he was "sick of being told the museum's role in this was money-grubbing."

"Call it whatever you like," I said, "but isn't it true that you've made a pact with thieves for the purpose of attracting memberships and financial contributions to the museum?"

He was not amused. "Our interest," he said icily, "was to preserve the art in a neutral place during the trial, and we are now pleased to present the treasures because they are important works of art."

I wrote that down. Then I asked about the show's catalogue. I'd been given an advance copy. It was a handsome, parchment-like, thirty-two-page brochure that would go on sale at the museum for $10. Why, I wanted to know, hadn't the catalogue straightforwardly explained how the exhibition had come about? Why were the words "theft" and "stolen" nowhere to be found in it?

Stiffly, Brettell said the catalogue contained all that needed to be said about the background of the show.

"I just don't understand," I continued, "why the only hint in the catalogue of any impropriety is in your introduction, where you say that the name Quedlinburg has provoked 'an intense debate about the ownership of works of art, about war booty, and about cultural patrimony.' You never come out directly and say that these artworks are here because they happen to have been stolen by someone who lived in Texas. Furthermore, there never was 'a debate' about the ownership of the treasures. Randal Mathis acknowledged on almost his first day in court on this case that the objects had been 'inappropriately removed' from their hiding place. It seems to me that by casting a cloud of mystery over the ownership of the treasures you're trying to hide the fact that you struck a deal with people who have been trafficking in stolen property."

I almost had to put my fingers in my ears. "What are you talking about!" he thundered. "Any mention of thievery in the catalogue . . ." He caught himself and lowered his voice . . . "would have been catering to sensational tastes!"

The exhibition—grandly titled "The Quedlinburg Treasury"—opened on March 7, 1992. It was the first public showing of the treasures since 1943, when Heinrich Himmler had directed their removal for safekeeping to a bank vault and later to the cave where Joe Tom Meador found them at the war's end. Art lovers and scholars from throughout Europe and the United States traveled to Dallas to attend the opening. A large contingent from the media was there, including reporters and cameramen representing all of the television networks. I was one of nearly two dozen print reporters covering the event. Tom was also there; Willi, for some reason, had better things to do.

Thinking the occasion would be memorable, I brought along my teenage son, Daniel, who had developed an interest in the case. Also with us were Heinrich and Otto. They were going home.

Naturally, I was eager to set my eyes on the objects that had fascinated me for nearly two years, yet the museum's bargain with thieves made me feel almost voyeuristic. I wasn't so indignant as the *Times'* editorialist (museums *do* have to scramble for money these days), but was disturbed to think that Joe Tom Meador had become a spectral circus master cracking a whip to make the rest of us dance.

Two prominent galleries in the museum's European paintings section had been cleared for the show. At the entrance to the first of these galleries, a lectern and about one hundred chairs had been arranged for the news conference that would open the exhibition. Overhead, a banner thirty feet long proclaimed "The Quedlinburg Treasury." Behind the lectern and to one side, and mounted on a pedestal, stood a showcase draped with a wine-colored cloth. The showcase, I was told by a member of the museum staff, contained the rock-crystal reliquary in the form of two birds featured on the cover of the museum's catalogue. It was to be unveiled by Gosslau, who had flown here from Germany to mark the occasion.

I could feel the tension mounting as the principals arrived and the television lights were switched on. Brettell strode to the lectern and made a brief opening statement. Throughout the long legal struggle, he said, the museum had served as "a sort of neutral Geneva" for the treasures. I shook my head in dismay. Didn't he know that Geneva—the real Geneva—had been the meeting place of Torigian and the Meadors when they commenced their romp across Europe in an effort to sell the manuscripts? Didn't he know that Geneva was the home base of the art dealer Jacques Quentin? Didn't he know that the scandalous laxity of Swiss law has made that country a thief's paradise?

But this was only the beginning. Brettell's callousness would soon be topped by others. I kept waiting for someone to say plainly that the show was being held here in Dallas because this is where the heirs of the local crook who stole them got nabbed. But each of the speakers who took a turn at the lectern assiduously avoided any mention of the circumstances that lay behind the exhibition. It was as if this were just another glitzy international loan show—it was all precisely what Joe Tom Meador had wished for.

Brettell was followed at the lectern by Klaus Aurisch, the German consul general from Houston, who was dressed a little incongruously in a dark business suit and cowboy boots. He was making a fashion statement, I surmised, perhaps indicating that he was in sympathy with the host country yet hadn't quite gone native. Aurisch declared that the occasion was a solemn one, but avoided any explanation of why this might be so. Then, unaccountably, he burst into tears. Hard-bitten Texas ranchers in the audience looked at one another in disbelief. Are Germans really so emotional? they wondered. Aurisch, in his early forties, was hardly a veteran of the war. There had to be some other explanation of this outpouring of emotion, yet he was not about to share it with his audience. He cleared his throat, mopped his face with a handkerchief and quickly concluded his remarks. A man of mystery.

Gosslau came next. A solidly built, square-jawed man in his sixties with an unexpected twinkle in his eye, Gosslau at least hinted at the truth when he remarked, "The objects are comfortable here, but they are getting homesick." I liked him. Having fought the Nazis during the thirties and early forties and then endured Soviet domination for a quarter of a century after that, he had suffered mightily and was not about to lose his dignity in a charade like this.

Someone on the museum staff distributed to the media a statement by the Meadors, and for sheer audacity they could not be matched. It was their first public utterance since the treasures had been traced to their homes and safe-deposit boxes nearly two years before. They declared that their brother had been falsely portrayed in the media as "a high-living thief" but was, in reality, "a quiet man who loved art."

His acquisition of the treasures, they went on to say, was

"fortunate" (italics added) because otherwise they might have "fallen into the hands of the country that occupied East Germany."

I could make no sense of their reluctance to name "the country that occupied East Germany." Did they fear the Soviet Union might sue them for defamation? What was perfectly clear, however, was that the Meadors were pretending ignorance of the well-known facts I had recited to Genevieve Meador the day she invited me into her living room: namely, that the treasures in the cave overlooked by Joe Tom—about forty items—remained untouched throughout the years of Soviet occupation and the rule of Communist East Germany. That fact cannot excuse the Communists for their crimes in Eastern Europe, but it certainly undercuts the argument that Joe Tom Meador's theft had been "fortunate."

Gosslau returned to the lectern to unveil the showcase containing the rock-crystal reliquary, and did so with a theatrical flourish. Then the crowd surged into the galleries.

I had seen photographs of the treasures many times, but they had not prepared me for their splendor. The objects were covered with gold and silver filigree and sparkling gems. Clearly, they were intended to speak to us mortals as if descended from a world where the streets are paved with gold. Almost in a trance, I wandered through the galleries from one showcase to another. Lavish, fabulous, out-of-this-world were the words that kept coming to mind.

The small, toylike crystal reliquaries looked like oversize salt and pepper shakers. About eight inches tall, tilting to one side or the other, they seemed almost comical—although, of course, they were never intended to arouse any such feeling. Medieval craftsmen lacked precision tools and so shrugged their shoulders at aesthetic notions like symmetry and balance that obsess us moderns.

The bodies of these crystal reliquaries looked pretty much like thick glass. One seemed to contain a tatter of red cloth.

Was that supposed to be from Christ's swaddling clothes? Another held a splinter of wood. From Noah's Ark, perhaps? One could be underwhelmed by the supposed contents of the reliquaries yet dazzled by the containers.

King Heinrich's comb, believed to be of Egyptian origin, was also very striking. Large enough to be a fan, it is of carved ivory trimmed with the most finely crafted gold, garnets, and silver pearls. It has balance, elegance, and a wonderful curvilinear shape.

To me, the most impressive of the treasures on display was the reliquary casket. About the size of a shoebox, it is made of wood sheathed with gold, silver, and walrus ivory. The saints' figures on every panel are incredibly delicate, obviously carved by the most highly skilled artists using exceedingly fine tools. Then I noticed something incongruous. On the top of the casket, a bright bluish-violet gem, probably an amethyst, was held in place by two slightly rusted modern-day nails that looked as though they might have come from one of the dusty bins in Meador, Inc. I guessed that the gem had come loose and that Joe Tom, by no means a craftsman, had tried to fasten it in place.

Then I began to count the display cases. Nine! There were only nine treasures in the exhibition! The Samuhel Gospel, I knew, had remained in Berlin since it was considered too precious to risk a second visit to Texas. But there should still be eleven items on display here. It was two short.

I found Tom Kline and took him by the arm. "What gives?" I said. "Two pieces are missing!"

"Oh, you mean nobody told you?"

"Damn right nobody told me! Where the hell are the other two pieces?"

"I wish I knew," he said wearily. "Two of the twelve pieces that Meador stole—a crystal flask in the shape of a bishop's cap and a gold crucifix—are missing. We learned in the depositions that Meador had them at one time. His friends in Dallas recalled seeing them and could even describe them accurately, but when Jack and Jane cleaned out his Dallas apartment they were gone. They must have been stolen."

"Damn!"

"We have the most important pieces right here," Tom continued, "but it would have been nice to be able to return everything."

It took me a minute to recover from the shock. Who could have stolen the missing pieces? I wondered. Maybe it was one of the young men, for whom the treasures were an irresistible temptation. Maybe someday they'll turn up in a pawn shop and nobody will know what they are.

The exhibit that drew the biggest crowd was the 1513 Evangelistar. In the center of its cover, surrounded by a cluster of gold and gems, a three-dimensional figure of Christ in solid gold seemed about to step forward off the book. I almost gasped aloud when I saw that the figure's nose had been slightly flattened by the rough handling that had so appalled John Caroll Collins.

As I studied the Evangelistar, I caught sight of Gosslau nearby. I introduced myself, recalling our several telephone conversations. He greeted me warmly, and remarked that the West German Government had paid for an extra seat on his flight home so that he could travel with the Evangelistar beside him the way prominent soloists fly around the world with their Stradivarius violin or cello in the next seat.

Joe Tom's old lover, Owen Hunsaker, was also present. I introduced the two men to each other, explaining to Gosslau that Hunsaker had been Meador's conscience, urging him for years to return the treasures. Gosslau embraced him.

"I flew in last night," Hunsaker said. "I wouldn't have missed this for anything. For me, it's a kind of closure, if you know what I mean."

Just then I caught Tom's eye. I thought of the two missing treasures still perhaps somewhere here in Texas, and I shook my head. Then, jokingly, I asked Tom if he expected the Meadors to show up for the opening.

"Not likely," he said. "They were here last night."

"WHAT!" I exploded.

"The museum held a pre-opening reception for big shots and important contributors," Tom said. "Brettell invited the Meadors."

"And they *dared* to show their faces?"

Tom smiled faintly and shrugged again.

The day after I filed my story about the exhibition, Daniel and I drove north to Whitewright. I wanted to show him the town. Just before reaching McKinney where I'd hidden out from Jack and his cronies that lonely night two years before, we took the blacktop Route 289—the road I'd traveled on my first trip to Whitewright. Outside a crossroads named Gunter, we came to a stream near where I'd collected Heinrich and Otto. I pulled off the road.

Together, Daniel and I reached into a cardboard box in the back seat. I picked up Heinrich and he took Otto. We had grown fond of these miniature dinosaurs, and I took a picture of Daniel saying good-bye to them. Then we set them down on the soft, waxy loam. Like wind-up toys, both turtles scrambled down an incline and splashed into the cool stream where they hitched a ride on the current. It was hard to give them up, yet we knew it was the right thing to do.

BOOK THREE

Chapter 23

LIFE WAS UNKIND TO THE MEADORS thereafter. In a freak accident in the summer of 1994, Jane's husband, Don Cook—the man who flew to New York City with Terry Mitchell to deliver the manuscripts to Christie's—was struck on the head by a racket while playing racquetball. Even at the age of sixty-two, Cook was an avid player and had recently qualified for the national racquetball championships in his age group. The medical examiner reported that the blow he received caused a massive cerebral aneurysm. "He was dead before he hit the floor," Randal Mathis told me.

The Dallas *Morning News* published a long, laudatory obituary about Cook, with no mention of his involvement in the Quedlinburg case.

In the same year, Jack's wife suffered what some would consider a worse fate. Genevieve Meador—the woman I'd interviewed in her living room back in 1990—developed Alzheimer's disease and required almost constant attention. Douse Thrasher, the former Meador employee who never liked Genevieve (Douse referred to her as "a hoity-toity Mrs.

Astor") was genuinely distressed to tell me of her affliction.

But these blows were only prologue to the drama about to unfold. To be sure, the civil lawsuit against the Meadors had been settled out of court when they agreed, for a healthy consideration, to return the treasures to Quedlinburg, but there was still the prospect of action at the federal level, by the Department of Justice and the Internal Revenue Service against Jack and Jane, and perhaps against John Torigian as well.

In fact, the FBI investigation dawdled indecisively through the early 1990s and might have petered out completely had it not been for an astonishing coincidence in the summer of 1994 when the Meadors were having their run of hard luck.

At that time, Willi Korte happened to visit Whitewright in the company of a photographer from *Stern*, the German newsmagazine. *Stern* was planning an illustrated feature on the case, which had received wide attention in the German media, and Willi had been enlisted to guide the photographer around Texas. When they stopped by the office of the Whitewright *Sun* to photograph the newspaper's 1980 obituary of Joe Tom, they were accosted on the sidewalk by Jack Meador. In the course of a fiery exchange, Jack accused Willi of having stolen a collection of letters written by Joe Tom in 1944 and 1945 describing, among other things, his time in Quedlinburg.

"What letters?" said Willi.

"You know what I'm talkin' 'bout," Jack growled.

Willi responded by saying that when Jack was deposed by Tom Kline in 1990 he had insisted that only one of the letters exchanged between Joe Tom and his parents during the war had survived, and that was from Maybelle to Joe Tom, not the other way around.

Jack replied that Willi had his facts wrong and hunched away, muttering angrily.

Willi mused about Jack's accusation, he later told me. Could it be that somewhere there was a cache of letters which might throw light on the Quedlinburg theft? It seemed too good to be true.

Willi and the photographer were staying at Cedar's Rooming House, a slouching yellow clapboard structure with a wraparound porch. It was the only public accommodation in town, so naturally, word that a couple of Germans checked into Cedar's traveled fast, and on the afternoon of his first day in Whitewright Willi received a visit from a man named Frank Wornhor, who said he lived in the neighboring town of Tom Bean, Texas. Wornhor was curious to meet Willi, he explained, because he, too, was of German ancestry. When it developed that the two men had even more in common—both had been born in the city of Augsburg, not far from the place where the Quedlinburg treasures had remained for a millennium—he invited Willi to come to his home and meet his family.

"With most of the people in the United States who tell me they're German, it just turns out their grandmother came over and they don't speak German, so it all leads to a very boring conversation," said Willi, "but I thought it was pretty weird, meeting somebody from Augsburg here in the middle of Texas, so I agreed to let him drive me to his house."

It was not just a social invitation, Willi discovered as his host poured him a glass of iced tea and began to relate a remarkable story. A couple of years previously, Wornhor said, he had rented a house for his daughter on Route 898 just northeast of Whitewright. His landlords were Don Cook and Jane Meador Cook. This was the house where Don Cook had grown up, and which—for sentimental reasons—he had kept and maintained after moving to Mesquite.

While cleaning out a closet to help his daughter get settled, Wornhor said, he found "three cowboy-boot-sized-shoeboxes" containing numerous letters and photographs. As both a native German and a longtime resident of north Texas, Wornhor said, he had followed the Quedlinburg case with interest, and therefore when he glanced at two or three of the letters in the boxes he suddenly realized that he had come across a collection of nearly one hundred carefully preserved letters and photographs that Joe Tom Meador sent home to his parents during the climactic years of World War II.

In all probability, Wornhor theorized, Jane placed the letters in this closet when cleaning out her brother's apartment in Dallas following his death in 1980. And then, over the years, she must have forgotten about them.

Ever since this discovery, Wornhor told Willi, he and his wife had fretted over what to do with the letters and photographs. They had gone so far as to make a list of people they considered showing them to—a list which included both Willi's name and mine—but when they heard that Willi was in town they decided to give them to him.

Within twenty-four hours, Willi was in New York presenting me with photocopies of what we both recognized as a heretofore unimaginable discovery. Marveling over the letters, we noted such details as the occasional misspellings, the girlish penmanship and occasional odd choice of word that helped to establish their authenticity. It was as though Joe Tom had awakened from the dead to talk to us.

About a dozen of the letters were dated between May and August 1945. They painted a convincing portrait of a restless young soldier consumed with an almost unbearable boredom, which was relieved periodically by flashes of excitement as he described his looting.

"Our principal occupation is boredom and I'm tired of that," he wrote to his parents on May 19, a week after Germany's formal surrender. There were free movies ·almost every night and plenty of free beer to guzzle, he reported, but the days were long and seemingly pointless. In one letter, Meador said he was "going nuts slowly," and in another he went so far as to say he envied his defeated foe. "I'm so fed up with the whole mess, I wish I'd been in the German army—at least the war is over for them and they don't have the 'brass' always breathing down their backs," he wrote.

His tone changed abruptly when he wrote about the glittering objects he was removing from the cave just outside of town.

"Are my packages getting home? I have sent quite a few," he wrote breathlessly on June 17, several weeks after having begun to "liberate" the treasures. "There are two that I want to know about for sure. One is a box that contains a *book*, the cover of the book has a statue of Christ on it. By all means, if it gets home take extra good care of it. I have an idea that the cover is pure gold and the jewels on the cover are *emeralds, jade and pearls*. Don't ask me where I got it! But it could possibly be *very, very valuable*. Don't show it to anyone till I get home and have it appraised by a person who knows their business."

He seems to have harbored no doubt about the morality of what he had done. "No one knew where the book came from so I appropriated it," he wrote, referring to the ornate Samuhel Gospel.

The letters also demonstrate that the thefts from the cave were not isolated acts. He mentioned having sent home a wristwatch, two motion picture projectors, some camera lenses, clothing, and various optical instruments.

In a letter dated July 7, he said the second medieval manuscript he had sent home is bound in gold covers encrusted with nearly eighty jewels. "Please store it most carefully for me as it is very valuable," he wrote.

A week later, he reported that he had sent home "a chest of the same type except the chest has a bunch of ivory inlay in it."

Back in Whitewright, Maybelle Meador was troubled by the arrival of so many extraordinary things. "You will have us haunted by the spirits of the Middle Ages," she cautioned in a letter to her son. In light of the pain and suffering he experienced at the end of his life, and the tragedies visited upon the spouses of Maybelle's other children, she may have had it exactly right.

Joe Tom, however, shrugged off his mother's superstition. On August 2, he stated that he was "most pleased that all my loot is getting home," adding, "I hope it will be worth something to me in a financial way!" But in the same letter, he bemoaned the scarcity of good pickings. The cave outside of Quedlinburg had spoiled him. "Now that the war is over," he grumbled, "it is harder to get things."

I wrote a news story of about 1,500 words reporting this extraordinary find, and Paul Goldberger, who by then had succeeded Marv Siegel as culture editor of the *Times*, gave it a splash illustrating the story with a large picture of the 1513 Evangelistar. As Willi requested, I declared that the newspaper obtained the letters from a source who insisted on anonymity.

Unbeknownst to Willi and myself at the time, the letters provided exactly what federal law-enforcement authorities had been vainly searching for. Here was evidence that the treasures had been stolen, and that Jack and Jane must have known that they were stolen before they set out to cash in on them.

A day or two after my story appeared in the *Times*, I received a call from Carol K. Johnson, a young woman who identified herself as an assistant United States attorney for the Eastern District of Texas based in Sherman. She wanted to know if I could help her find the owner of the letters from which I had quoted. I explained that I couldn't violate a promise of anonymity to an informant and also that the *Times* has long made it a rule in order to protect confidential sources never to share information with law-enforcement agencies. But I gave her Willi's phone number, and told her that he might be more free to talk than I.

A short while later, Willi told me he had been interviewed by Johnson in Sherman, and then had been subpoenaed to testify about the case before a grand jury. Neither of us put much store in that. Grand juries are constantly investigating all sorts of things that don't lead to indictments. And we reasoned that if the Feds were genuinely interested in the Quedlinburg case they would have prosecuted it long before this.

Throughout 1995, I kept hearing reports that federal officials were accelerating the pace of their investigation. At the beginning of the new year Willi, Tom, and I appeared together on a panel discussion of the case in New York, sponsored by the Bard College Graduate Center.

I was glad to be there because it gave me a chance to greet Karl Meyer and Klaus Goldmann, who had flown in for the conference from Germany. They were the two men who had started me on this quest many months before.

Also present was Walter Farmer, a man who until then I had known only through correspondence and occasional telephone conversations. Then eighty-four, Farmer had long intrigued me as being the polar opposite of Joe Tom Meador. Near the war's end, when German art was almost literally spilling onto the streets from bombed-out buildings, Farmer, then a thirty-four-year-old captain in the U.S. Army, had been put in charge of collecting and preserving German art at an improvised station in Wiesbaden. It was a time when some of his fellow soldiers, giddy with victory, might be tempted to loot.

Farmer distinguished himself by safeguarding countless precious artworks—the famous bust of Nefertiti and the Tiepolo ceiling in the Residenz palace in Würzburg among others—but he went a step further.

When some misguided higher-ups ordered him to ship to the United States 200 of the finest German artworks he could put his hands on, he balked. He contacted thirty-five other

American officers in charge of similar art-collection stations set up in Germany, and together with them, drew up a memorandum in which these officers boldly protested their orders.

The so-called Wiesbaden Memorandum proclaimed: "We wish to state, from our own knowledge, no historical grievance will rankle so long or be the cause of so much bitterness as the removal for any reason of a part of the heritage of any nation."

Despite their protest, 202 German masterpieces were sent to the United States and exhibited, but the Wiesbaden Memorandum made its way up to General Eisenhower and then to President Truman who, three years after the end of the war, ordered that the paintings be returned to Germany.

Farmer spoke about his experiences at the conference. I was pleased to be among those who gave him a standing ovation.

After the conference, Willi, Tom, and I were told that, unbeknownst to us, our audience had included Carol Johnson; one of her counterparts in New York; Mike Krenek, the FBI agent who by then had been working on the Quedlinburg case for four years; and a few FBI types from the New York office. They were quietly gathering information.

Several weeks later, Willi called to say that he had been subpoenaed a second time to testify before the grand jury in Sherman. When he returned from Texas, he said he had been forced to reveal Wornhor's name as the source of Joe Tom's letters. He also said Carol Johnson had told him that she and Krenek had recently returned from a three-week trip to Europe in which they interviewed many principals in the case. When they stopped in Quedlinburg, she told Willi, she retrieved the originals of Joe Tom's letters. Someone—it was never made clear who—had given the letters to the Bürgomeister of Quedlinburg, and he, once he realized that they might figure into a trial in the United States, was only too happy to part with them.

All of this sounded promising, but I still wondered what was taking so long. Willi said he had put that question to Johnson, and she explained that the case had faltered until the end of 1994, when excerpts from Joe Tom's wartime letters appeared in the *Times*. Previously, he said she told him, she and Krenek had found quite a number of people who testified about having warned the Meadors and/or Torigian that the treasures were stolen property, but of course the Meadors and Torigian could say they simply didn't believe those warnings. Joe Tom's letters home, however, constituted a confession of theft, and with them in evidence it would be extremely difficult for Jack and Jane to argue that they were unaware of how their brother acquired the treasures. I wondered about that, but was glad to know that the case was still alive and kicking.

At about that time, I began making periodic calls to Johnson in Sherman, asking if an indictment were about to be handed down. I liked her immediately. She was sharp and unpretentious. A former schoolteacher from Greenville, Texas, Johnson frequently spoke of her two daughters and her years in East Texas and southern Oklahoma. Although she was buoyant about her progress on some days, on others she wondered aloud if she was wasting her time. At one point, she hinted that the decision on whether to prosecute was out of her hands. The final determination would be made in Washington.

Hearing that, I made a number of calls to the Department of Justice in Washington, and found out, to my surprise, that the department's Office of International Affairs was helping Johnson to locate witnesses in Europe and that another federal agency, the Executive Office of U.S. Attorneys, was providing her with legal advice. I also learned that at one point Johnson had dispatched to Washington what is known as an "Urgent to the A.G." This meant she had notified Attorney General Janet Reno of her plans, and had obtained the blessing of the nation's top lawyer.

I was told that Attorney General Reno had, moreover, taken a particular interest in the case, perhaps because she had spent one of her formative years living in Germany when her father, a journalist, moved there with his family. The year was 1951—soon after the conclusion of the war in Europe— a time when no visitor could be unaware of either the terrible destruction the war had brought to Germany or the potential harm done to U.S.–German relations by the occasional misbehavior of American soldiers in the Army of Occupation. Reno, it seemed, had been sensitized at an early age to the fact that the German people, horrible as their role in the war had been, had suffered great losses themselves.

And then, on January 4, 1996, I answered my telephone to hear a young woman with a charming Texas drawl (Johnson, of course) telling me that a seventeen-page indictment of Jack, Jane, and John Torigian had just been handed down by a grand jury and was being faxed to me as we spoke.

The story I immediately wrote announced that the brother and sister of the American army lieutenant who had stolen the world-famous Quedlinburg treasures from their hiding place in a German cave in 1945 had finally been indicted in Texas on federal charges of illegally selling two of the treasures they had inherited, nearly three years after the German government had paid them $2.75 million for the entire collection.

Also charged, I reported, was John Torigian, the Houston lawyer who had represented the Meadors in their transactions.

I'd been waiting six years to write that.

I was pleased as I read the indictment. Johnson and Krenek had discovered several aspects of the case that were new to me—the precise numbers of the Swiss bank accounts opened by Torigian, for example—but basically the indictment followed my procession of witnesses, from Roland Folter and Decherd Turner to John Carroll Collins, Heribert Tenschert, and Klaus Maurice. All those long-familiar names were there.

The indictment accused the three defendants of conspiring to sell the treasures after knowing they had been stolen. Only the two manuscripts were mentioned, evidently because the paper trail the Meadors and Torigian had left in their efforts to sell these items was the most complete.

If convicted, the indictment specified, each of the defendants could be imprisoned for up to ten years and fined as much as $250,000.

Jack, Jane, and Torigian did not return my calls, but Jane just about fell apart when she spoke to a reporter for the Sherman *Democrat*. "I can't believe this is happening to me," she wailed. "I don't know where to start trying to explain how this all happened. This is so *ludicrous!*"

I reached Mathis in the office of Jim Burnham, a specialist in criminal law whom Mathis had enlisted to serve as co-counsel for the Meadors. "It's a tragedy and an outrage that these two elderly people have been charged," Burnham said. "Jack is seventy-seven and Jane is sixty-three. They're going to plead not guilty, and we're going to demand a jury trial."

When my story was done, the news desk gave it pride of place as the lead story the next day on the national page, illustrated with pictures of Heinrich I's ceremonial comb and the cover of the 1513 Evangelistar.

I called Tom Kline. He was delighted with the news. When I reached Willi, who happened to be in New York, he was jubilant and decided to stay up until he could get a copy of the next day's paper with the story of the indictments.

It was by then about 10:30 in the evening, so I told him to meet me at Grand Central Station, where I'd be able to hand him a copy of tomorrow's newspaper just before boarding a late train home.

Willi hadn't changed a bit when I met him—the same scruffy beard, prominent beaver teeth, and that wild glint in his eye. "We got a page-one reference box and two illustrations on page ten," I crowed, handing him the paper.

Willi scrutinized the story as we walked briskly through the station to the track my train would be on. "I thought you told me they indicted Jack, Jane, *and* Torigian," he said.

"That's right."

"But the headline here says '*Two* Charged with Selling War Booty,' "

"Omigosh!" I exclaimed, looking at my copy of the paper. Willi was right. Quickly trotting to a pay phone, I called the copy desk and asked that the headline for the second edition be corrected.

"They'll catch most of the press run," I told Willi.

"In that case," he replied with a look of glee, "this copy you've given me is a collector's item—a real treasure!"

The federal courthouse in Sherman is a three-story square limestone box only a couple of blocks from the state courthouse where I'd found important records relating to Joe Tom Meador six years before, and it was in federal court that Jack, Jane, and John Torigian would be asked to state their plea, guilty or not guilty. A date would also then be set for the beginning of the trial. Equally important, from my point of view, was that the occasion would give me my first look at both Jack Meador and John Torigian.

I arrived early to reconnoiter the scene. A guard told me that the only public entrance to the courthouse was on Travis Street. Ever since the bombing of the federal building in Oklahoma City, the side entrance on Pecan Street had been kept locked. That limitation of access was good news to me, as I would be able to tell our photographer, Mark Graham, that the defendants would have no back door enabling them to elude him. Over the years, the *Times* had published many pictures of the treasures and of Joe Tom Meador, but we had never been able to get photographs of Jack or Jane or of John Torigian. The arraignment would provide an opportunity to make up for that lack.

As I was jotting down a few notes about the courthouse, a classic example of Romanesque style built in 1905, a car pulled into the parking lot beside the building. Out stepped a dapper, dark-haired man who greeted me saying he recognized me from my picture, which had been carried in the Sherman *Democrat*. He introduced himself as Robert Faulkner, the magistrate judge who would be presiding over the arraignment.

"I been readin' your stuff," he said cheerfully, "And I can tell you I've heard lots of talk on both sides of the case. Did you come down here jus' for this?"

I said I had, and that the case had attracted international attention. "I expect there will be more than one language spoken on the press bench this morning, Judge," I said.

"Well, then I better get a move on," he replied, and with a courteous "Nice to meet ya" scurried into the courthouse.

What delightful informality, I thought. Everybody knows everybody in these parts.

I had to wait a few minutes before the courthouse was opened to the public, and I then entered, along with a slim young man from the Deutsche Presse Agentur, the German press agency, someone from the Sunday *Mail* of London, a woman from an Australian newspaper, and a cluster of reporters from various American news media.

When the defendants and their lawyers seated themselves at the defense tables, Jack was easy to spot. That was partly because of his age—although he certainly seemed in vigorous good health—but also because of his cocky manner. None of the other defendants would ever strut like that in a courtroom. Clearly, Jack Meador thought of himself as a rough and tough hombre—and he wanted the world to share that opinion.

Given my first sight of the man I'd been tracking for so many years, I studied him closely. Lean and erect, Jack was bald, with a fringe of gray hair and conspicuous dark eyebrows. He had an oddly shaped, bulbous head, large ears, a slightly flattened nose and dark, shifty eyes. Now and then, my stomach muscles tightened as I became aware of the anger coiled inside him. Yet, the fact was he had been defanged. He was not Richard III; he was the Wizard of Oz— a man who had frightened me on the streets of Whitewright and Sherman, and whose wife had told me that she, too, feared him, yet who was now revealed as merely a lame old man.

Jane was something else. Although I hadn't seen her for six years, she was also quite conspicuous—as much for being overdressed as for being the only woman to take a seat at the defense table. Her hair, which I recalled as having been sandy blond, was now dyed gold and shaped into a large beehive, which bounced as she walked. Maybe it was a wig. She also wore an expensive-looking black dress that flared around her just over the knee and had big gold buttons down the middle, gold earrings, and a gold bracelet. Her outfit would have been more appropriate in a ballroom than a courthouse.

Judge Faulkner opened the proceedings in a down-home style. "I trust ya'll have had an opportunity to review th' indictment," he inquired. The lawyers acknowledged that they had.

Then Jack was called to the dock and asked to state his plea. He spoke in a loud, almost sneering voice, "Well, ah, not guilty!"

Jane came next, and she, too, seemed defiant, tossing her head as she proclaimed her innocence.

Then it was Torigian's turn. Short but broad-shouldered, with dark, darting eyes, a sallow complexion, and an almost sinister-looking dark mustache, he would be well cast as a villain in a Victorian melodrama. I noted that he had not spoken a word of greeting to either of his former clients. Instead of a plea, Torigian filed a motion to bar the prosecution from taking action against him because the statute of limitations had run out. It seemed a desperate, sure-to-fail gambit yet one that would have explosive consequences later in the year.

Judge Faulkner said he would rule on Torigian's motion at a later time and set April 1 as the date for the commencement of the trial. With that, everyone filed out of the courtroom. It was like the conclusion of a funeral. The elders—the defendants in this case—strode out first, followed by their lawyers and family members and then the press.

As Jane passed me, she gave me a cold stare and a smile of contempt. I couldn't help feeling sorry for her.

Jack looked at me quizzically as he filed out. I think he suspected who I was, yet couldn't be sure.

I followed the group of defendants, with their lawyers and well-wishers, to the exit. Jack was just ahead of me in the crowded hallway, and I overheard him remark with a chuckle, "You'd a-think we robbed a bank!" There was a murmur of laughter from his entourage.

I felt that I shouldn't hide from Jack. He, after all, had been compelled to identify himself: why shouldn't I do the same? I caught up with him, and called out his name, touching him on the shoulder. Jack was chuckling again, over some jest with a family member. He looked around. That brought us face-to-face. I studied him for an instant. The fear in his eyes was now gone. I gave him my name and said: "I just want you to know who I am, and, I guess, wish you luck, Jack."

His eyes opened wide and he half lunged at me, roaring: "It's a hell of a time for you to say that!"

A young man—probably his son Jeff—pulled him away.

"Come on, Dad," he said.

A couple of weeks after I returned to New York, I received a call from Alan Cowell, my New York *Times* colleague stationed in Bonn, Germany. He knew that I'd become the house expert on the Quedlinburg theft, and since he was preparing a story that might touch on Joe Tom Meador, he wanted to check a few details with me.

I helped him as best as I could, and then asked what he was writing.

"I'm just using Meador as counterpoint," he said. "The story is really about a man named Walter Farmer. Do you know him?"

"Sure I do!" I said, recalling our meeting at the Bard College conference the previous year.

"Well," said Cowell, "the German government has decided to present Farmer with the crimson Commander's Cross of the Federal Order of Merit, its highest civilian medal. It's in gratitude for what he did to preserve German art. They haven't forgotten."

Cowell wrote a beautiful story about Farmer, using Meador, as he said, for counterpoint.

Chapter 24

THE TRIAL—TWICE POSTPONED to give the defense time to question witnesses overseas—was finally scheduled to take place on November 4, 1996. By this time, the three defendants were represented by a new team of lawyers. The Meadors had lost confidence in Randal Mathis after years of being assured by him that the U.S. Department of Justice would never dream of prosecuting them. The indictments in February cured them of all such optimism.

The new defense team was worthy of a Hollywood celebrity trial. As in all criminal cases, each defendant had to be represented by a different lawyer since their personal interests might at some point differ from those of their fellow defendants.

Torigian chose Dick DeGuerin, the best-known criminal defense attorney in Texas whose well-known clients included David Koresh, the leader of the ill-starred Branch Davidians; Texas Senator Kay Bailey Hutchison when brought up on charges that she misused her position as state treasurer; and three New York Mets baseball players who got mixed up in a barroom brawl with a few Houston police officers. Flamboyant, imaginative, and shrewd, DeGuerin's presence promised fireworks.

Jane was represented by Mike Gibson, a scholarly, low-key former professor at the Southern Methodist University School of Law. Jack picked Jack Kennedy, a good old boy like himself who had served as mayor of Sherman in the 1980s and who addressed me, whenever I called, as "partner."

DeGuerin, Gibson, and Kennedy. A powerhouse, a professor, and a provincial. It sounded like a law firm and was as strategically well balanced as the best of them. I made it my business to cultivate each of these lawyers, swapping information and picking up tips in a series of telephone conversations throughout the summer and fall.

If Carol Johnson was intimidated by such adversaries, she never showed it. At forty-four, she was at the top of her game. She had spent six years as an assistant U.S. attorney handling relatively minor cases involving bank fraud, extortion, and drug and firearms violations, and now she was eager for a greater challenge. In Sherman, they called her the Marcia Clark of Texas.

Johnson told me she realized the stakes were high for her professionally, and I understood that to mean that if she handled this case well she might be in line for a judgeship or possibly a nomination for elective office.

Over the summer, the defense got busy churning out a flurry of pretrial motions. In one of these, DeGuerin argued that the charges should be dismissed because the prosecution had exceeded the United States statute of limitations—by *one day*, according to his calculations.

DeGuerin had another card up his sleeve, too. "We've had a couple of researchers working in Germany," he told me. "And now we have plenty of good authority that the treasures didn't belong to the church after 1936. That was when Himmler and the SS nationalized the cathedral and its treasures. We will argue that no crime had been committed because the treasures did not belong to the Quedlinburg cathedral but to the SS. Does the United States government want to punish its own citizens for stealing from the SS?"

DeGuerin may be very effective when on his feet in a courtroom, I thought, and maybe he can use the SS as a fright wig to stampede the jury, but his argument seemed plainly absurd to me. Stealing is a crime, no matter whether you steal from friend or foe. It looked to me as though DeGuerin & Company were desperate.

The serious business would begin, I surmised, when the trial got started and Johnson introduced Joe Tom's letters in evidence. They were sure to be hotly contested. And in that contest, the testimony of Frank Wornhor, the German-born resident of Tom Bean, Texas, who had discovered the letters in Don Cook's home, would be critical. Wornhor would have to tell the jury convincingly where and how he found the letters and what he did with them.

I happened to mention Wornhor's name one day in a phone conversation with Jack Kennedy, and was given some grim news. Since Wornhor's name had been brought to light in one of my stories, Wornhor had suffered from stress and inner turmoil, Kennedy related. Wornhor had expected—naively, to be sure—that he could tell his story to the prosecutor and the grand jury anonymously and would not have his name made public during the trial. But that was not to be. Following his exposure, the Texas media picked up the story and suddenly Frank Wornhor's name was on the lips of virtually everyone in Grayson County. The fact that he had been born in Germany, which he had tried to forget while living in Texas, was now common knowledge, and many who knew him, Wornhor came to believe, thought he had betrayed a neighbor by giving the letters to someone who showed them to the New York *Times*. Local residents, Wornhor believed, began to avoid eye contact with him. He had become a pariah.

"And then," Kennedy told me, "he developed cancer. I've always believed that stress does it. It weakens the immune system. And now, Wornhor may not be able to appear at the trial."

I was shocked. I had long regarded Wornhor as one of the few people of integrity involved in the case.

The real wild card in all of this would be the jury. Would the jurors sympathize with Jack and Jane because of their age? Or would they side with the Meadors as down-home folks who spoke their language? And what of Torigian? Would his swarthy complexion and Armenian name arouse their hostility?

Local juries, especially local Texas juries, have a reputation for siding with local defendants against outsiders no matter what the evidence against them. The most famous such case was when a Texas jury stunned the financial world a few years ago by ordering Texaco, Inc., the oil giant based in White Plains, New York, to pay Pennzoil, whose headquarters is in Houston, $10.5 billion in damages for having improperly acquired Getty Oil. It was by far the largest such award ever, and the judgment drove Texaco into bankruptcy. That case, and others like it, made me wonder whether a bunch of independent-minded folk, recruited from farms and ranches in northeast Texas, might feel hostile to a case brought before them by a federal prosecutor.

Two weeks before the trial was to begin, I was chatting on the phone again with Jack's lawyer, Jack Kennedy, when he remarked that Judge Paul N. Brown, the trial judge, had seemed impressed by the pretrial motion calling on him to dismiss the charges and cancel the trial. "I think he agrees with us, partner," said Kennedy.

When I arrived at the office on Wednesday morning, October 23, my phone was lit up. Just one message. It was from Mike Gibson, Jane's lawyer. He said he was returning my call, and then added: "You might want to check with the court, but I believe this case is over."

I stared into space blankly. Over? The case is *over?*

I called Gibson.

"We received a call from Judge Brown's clerk late yesterday afternoon," he said. "He informed us that the judge was granting the motion to dismiss. He said we would receive the written ruling in a day or two, but the judge wanted to give us advance notice so we wouldn't continue to prepare for an elaborate international trial that would not take place."

Numbly, I thanked him and called Johnson.

"Is this the end?"

"It could be."

"That's crazy!"

"Well, I haven't yet received the ruling."

Her tone was funereal. "We're going to take a look at this, see what our options are, and then decide how we proceed from here."

I called Willi. No answer.

Then I tried Tom Kline. He was stunned by the news.

I asked if he knew where Willi was. Tom said he was somewhere making a documentary film about lost treasures. "What *else* would you expect Willi to be doing?" he said wryly.

Kennedy's office faxed me Judge Brown's fifteen-page ruling later in the day. The dismissal turned on the provision in criminal law that permits an American prosecutor to gain a suspension of the statute of limitations if evidence must be obtained from another country. In this instance, Johnson had been granted such an extension in order to interview witnesses in Europe the previous June, but then, according to Judge Brown, she continued to gather evidence after the extension had run out.

"The prosecutor screwed up," DeGuerin told me.

I went to see Alex Ward, the editor with whom I'd been making plans to cover the trial. "The wild card wasn't a Texas jury," I said. "It was a Texas *judge!*"

"You better get busy," Alex said, and began clearing space

in the paper for what might be my last story about the case. I wrote about a thousand words, explaining the development.

Jack Kennedy told me this was the first time in Brown's twelve years on the federal bench that he had dismissed charges like this. Did Brown think it would be too divisive for the community? I wondered. Was it that he felt the Meadors and Torigian had suffered enough? Did he consider the fact that the treasures were back where they belonged? Was there some such underlying thought in his mind? Or was it simply that Johnson had indeed screwed up, as DeGuerin said? Judges are not required to explain their decisions, so there was no point in my asking this one.

Johnson was out of her office for the next couple of days and couldn't be reached. There were rumors that she had resigned, and rumors that she had flown to Washington to seek advice from the Department of Justice. She had devoted nearly her whole career as a prosecutor to this case. After all that time and money—the latter could come to half a million dollars—the dismissal of charges wouldn't look too good on her résumé, to put it mildly.

When she returned to her office, Johnson filed a motion for reconsideration, the defense responded, and a couple of days before Thanksgiving 1996 Judge Brown denied Johnson's motion. But then, her superiors in Washington decided to appeal. Consequently, the case is likely to be jerked around by the courts for months.

If Torigian and the Meadors had escaped the immediate possibility of a jail sentence or a heavy fine, the Meadors still faced an estate tax liability which by 1997 had risen to nearly $50 million, including penalties and interest. They will have to fight that out in tax court when the government issues a notice of deficiency.

Early in 1997, while writing the final words of this book, I hiked up Sixth Avenue, hands in my pockets and my tie flapping over my shoulder in the breeze. Memories raced through my mind. I thought of Willi, whose enthusiasm had been so infectious. I thought of Kuli and Owen Hunsaker, both now gone. It angered me to think that the apparent wrongdoers were still unpunished while a true hero like Frank Wornhor lay on a bed of pain.

I also thought of Christie's, the art dealers, and the museum curators who, after learning that the treasures were stolen property, neglected to share that knowledge with the rightful owner or, indeed, law enforcement authorities. There is a conspiracy of silence in the art world that fosters such misconduct. Oh, what an unwholesome stew the art world is! Humankind, I began to think, isn't ready for the gift of great art. It mainly arouses our greed!

Then I remembered Walter Farmer, the U.S. Army officer who had commanded the Wiesbaden collection station to preserve German art and had risked the wrath of his superiors by organizing the protest against shipping many of these prizes to the United States.

Back in my office, I called Farmer at his home in Cincinnati. Now eighty-six, he sounded as full of beans as a teenager. Had he heard about the dismissal of the case in Texas? I asked.

"I turned absolutely red when I heard about it," he said. "It's outrageous. The dignity of our country is at stake.

"But you know what?" he continued. "The Germans are giving me *another* medal." He roared with laughter. "Why should they give me a medal just for doing the obvious? Well, I told them I'd accept it on behalf of all the other American officers who ran the art collection stations in Germany who are no longer living. I'm the last of them. In all the clamor about Meador, these people deserve to be remembered, too."

I liked what he said, and thought it made as good an ending as was possible under the circumstances.

Postscript

WHEN MY EDITOR AND PUBLISHER, Fred Jordan, proposed that I make a seven-state tour of the country to announce the publication of *Treasure Hunt*, I leapt at the chance. Naturally, I'd be glad to help sell books, but also I had something else in mind.

As for the Meadors and John Torigian, there was nothing more I could do. They were entangled in the courts, and, one way or another, the courts would decide their fates. What I realized I could do on this tour would be to shine a spotlight on those art dealers I had come to see as among the principal wrongdoers in the case, and who seemed about to walk away from it scot-free.

The conduct of Christie's, it seemed to me, had been especially reprehensible. As the world's biggest art auction house, and whose sales volume came to $1.6 billion last year, Christie's possessed vastly greater resources than any of the dealers for determining whether the Quedlinburg treasures were stolen property. Nevertheless, Christie's kept the two manuscripts for nearly five months. And then, once it could no longer be denied that the objects had been stolen and could not be sold legally, officials at the auction house set up the clandestine meeting at the Los Angeles airport at which their agent turned over the treasures to the attorney for the presumptive thief.

I think that was very wrong. If we wish to call ourselves a civilized society, it seems to me we can't allow such practices to continue. We must take steps to regulate the art trade—which is the biggest unregulated industry in the world.

It's an open question whether under present law Christie's and some of the other dealers acted illegally in their failure to notify the authorities once they realized what they had in hand. In the December 9, 1997, issue of *The New York Law Journal*, Harlan Levy, a former prosecutor, and Constance Lowenthal, who is now director of the newly formed World Jewish Congress's Commission for Art Recovery, argued that both the National Stolen Property Act and various state laws that make it a crime to knowingly possess stolen property would appear on their faces to apply to an auction house or art dealer who knowingly returns stolen art to a party other than its true owner. I earnestly hope they are proved right.

But since the outcome of any such prosecution cannot be guaranteed, I am led to the conclusion that although Christie's conduct in this case was morally indefensible, it was not in clear violation of the law—and therefore the law must be changed. I propose new federal legislation to require art dealers, art auctioneers, and museum officials to report to law enforcement authorities any sale or purchase of $50,000 or more, and also—importantly—to report any information they may obtain that might reasonably suggest that an object submitted to them for sale or appraisal is stolen property.

That's not asking too much. Under the Federal Banking Secrecy Act, financial transactions greater than $10,000 must be reported to the government. Treasury Department officials say the practice has been extraordinarily effective in disrupting money-laundering schemes and drug dealing between the United States and Colombia. And what's fair for banks should be fair for the much-less-principled art market.

Still, the rights of citizens must be protected. Under the American system of law, ordinary citizens have no duty to report a crime. That's as it should be. We don't want to become a nation of informers peering over one another's shoulders. Nevertheless, museums, art auction houses, and dealers who trade in national treasures have a public trust and must meet a higher standard of behavior. Consequently, any new federal law imposing special obligations on those who deal in art should be limited in its application to professional traders and should be part of a licensing procedure.

That is the message I wanted to carry on my tour throughout the country.

Naturally, I gave Christie's officials ample opportunity to explain their action before I said anything against them. Patricia Hambrecht, the managing director, was never available to return my calls, but I spoke at length about the case with Taggarty Patrick, Christie's spokesperson. Why, I asked, had Christie's not turned over the treasures to the police or at least notified the Germans that their patrimony was being hawked on the street?

Ms. Patrick answered that Christie's had signed a confidentiality agreement with the owners of the treasures and was therefore bound to secrecy. Baloney, I said. I read that agreement when I examined Christie's files on the case and although there was boilerplate language about confidentiality, there was not a word in it to indicate what the parties might do if the treasures should turn out to be stolen property. And even if there had been some such agreement, it would have been unenforceable.

I decided to begin my tour with a news conference at the Adolphus Hotel in Dallas, where one of the climactic scenes in the story had taken place. Our publicist, Susannah Greenberg, worked out the details and then booked me for a series of newspaper, radio, and television interviews in the seven cities I would visit.

It was a hectic schedule. I started out with an appearance on *Good Morning, Texas*, a TV show broadcast from Dallas throughout the Southwest, then leapt into a waiting limousine and made it to the Adolphus just in time for the news conference. A good crowd had assembled at the hotel, but there was a surprise in store for me. After I'd made my opening remarks and answered a few questions, a woman in the audience stood up and asked whether I had exaggerated the danger I placed myself in when I first came to Texas to search for the thief. "Weren't you just trying to cook up a good story?" she said.

I replied that I had exaggerated nothing. Just then I spotted John Farley in the audience. Farley is the president of the First National Bank of Whitewright, and he was the one who had accepted Jack Meador's share of the treasures as collateral for a loan. Shortly after the treasures had been safely returned to Germany, Farley and I had lunch together and we spoke frankly about the case. Among other things, he told me how frightened he had been when he first learned that I was prowling about the state in search of the treasures. Remembering what he told me, I introduced him at the news conference and asked him to step up to the podium and explain how he had reacted to the situation back then.

"The truth is," he told the audience, "when I learned that a stranger in town was looking for the treasures, I was scared to death. I knew that foreign governments were involved in this, and that huge sums of money were at stake, but I didn't know who the players were. Those were scary days. I didn't want to make myself or my family targets, so I moved them for several weeks to a motel outside of town."

There were no more questions about my having exaggerated things.

At about this time, reviews of the book began popping up in

newspapers and magazines across the country. Suffice it to say, they were the kind that an author dreams of, but I will quote only one. Writing for the Sunday book review of *The New York Times*, Lynn Nicholas expressed admiration for the book and then declared that "one of the greatest accomplishments in *Treasure Hunt* is the author's revelation of the virtually total absence of conscience in the art world . . . Here the art trade is revealed in all of its elegant corruption."

As I raced on through Houston, Los Angeles, and San Francisco, I kept hammering away at that elegant corruption and the need for new legislation. Later, I heard from friends that I'd been seen as far away as Hong Kong and Amsterdam, thanks to CNN interviews with Ralph Begleiter and Judy Woodruff. I also made appearances in Washington and New York City, including NBC-TV's nationally broadcast *Weekend Today* show. The feedback suggested that my message was getting across.

The climax of the tour did not take place before the biggest audience; it came when I was invited to address the National Arts Club in the beautiful old Tilden mansion in New York City. Jill Seiden, the publicist for the club, had read this book, and—sharing my sense of indignation—dispatched a news release in which she said my talk would focus on "the role of Christie's in concealing what it learned about the theft of the Quedlinburg hoard." She also quoted me as saying that while Christie's may not have crossed the line into criminal conduct, it "encourages greed and unethical behavior." She then mailed invitations to my talk to all the brass at Christie's, from Hambrecht down to Patrick.

A couple of days later, Jill called to say that Ms. Patrick had screamed at her over the telephone, calling her "unprofessional" for having sent out invitations that gave Christie's officials only three days' notice. Talk about lame excuses! The next day, I received a similar upbraiding. I couldn't have been more pleased by Ms. Patrick's performance. Christie's wouldn't have reacted nearly so violently, I figured, if they hadn't been worried about the public sentiment mounting against them. Sotheby's, their chief competitor, had just come under criticism as well. Peter Watson, a British journalist, had just published a book called *Sotheby's: The Inside Story*, contending that Sotheby's London had sold antiquities it knew to be smuggled out of Italy in violation of export laws designed to protect that nation's patrimony.

Despite a freezing rain on the night of November 14, 1997, almost every seat in the assembly hall at the National Arts Club was filled when I arrived. The best thing about the event came when I was autographing copies of *Treasure Hunt* after the talk and a young man introduced himself to me. He said his name was Victor Wiener, and he presented a business card that identified him as the executive director of the Appraisers Association of America. He said that after hearing what I had to say about Christie's, he had decided to propose to his membership that they adopt a resolution that would commit members to notify law-enforcement officials whenever asked to appraise an artwork they have reason to suspect is stolen property.

Now I was getting somewhere! Subsequently, I learned that the Boston Museum of Fine Arts had become the first major American museum to adopt a similarly tough policy. Malcolm Rogers, the director of the museum, announced to his staff that any "suspicious works of art" shown to them for appraisal or possible sale must be "reported to the proper authorities."

In addition to these signs of rising concern, a number of currently available books are calling for reform of the art trade, and are also helping to reawaken interest in an even greater issue dealt with in *Treasure Hunt;* namely, the recovery of art looted during World War II.

The book list begins with Lynn H. Nicholas's *The Rape of Europa: The Fate of Europe's Treasures in the Third Reich and*

the Second World War. Hector Feliciano, a Paris-based journalist, has tracked down and identified missing French masterpieces in his current book *The Lost Museum: The Nazi
Conspiracy to Steal the World's Greatest Works of Art.* A good li-
brary on this subject must also include *Beautiful Loot: The So-
viet Plunder of Europe's Art Treasures* by Konstantine Akinsha,
Grigorii Kozlov, and Sylvia Hochfield; *Art As Politics in the
Third Reich* by Jonathan Petropoulos (University of North Car-
olina Press); *Spoils of World War II: The American Military's
Role in the Stealing of Europe's Treasures* by Kenneth D. Alford
(Birch Lane); and *The Spoils of War* compiled and edited by
Elizabeth Simpson.

Thanks to this ferment, I feel more hopeful now than at any
time since I started on the trail of the Quedlinburg treasures
back in 1989 that we can do much to reform the art market
and recover lost art in what I call the unfinished business of
the twentieth century.